LIGHTNING STRIKES:

The 475th Fighter Group
in the Pacific War, 1943-1945

To the students of R.C.C.,
thank you for the inspiration
you provided, and the time taken
to view this small work.

My best regards.
Ron Yoshino
RCC
18 May 1989

LIGHTNING STRIKES:
The 475th Fighter Group in the Pacific War, 1943-1945

Ronald W. Yoshino

Sunflower University Press ®

1531 Yuma (Box 1009), Manhattan, Kansas 66502-4228

ISBN 0-89745-104-X

Copyright 1988 by Sunflower University Press

Design by Lori Daniel

*Use of cover art donated by Stan Stokes. Cover
separations donated by Madison/Graham Color
Graphics, Los Angeles, CA.*

Dedicated to
The Officers and Men of the 475th Fighter Group
Who Fought for America's Freedom

and

To My Parents
Reiko and Bill Yoshino
Who Made That Freedom Work

Acknowledgments

This book depended on a number of people for its completion. The former members of the 475th Fighter Group were very helpful in a number of ways. Many provided useful information through a survey sent to all members; others went "above and beyond the call of duty" in seeing this work to its end. The following men provided extensive documentation, comments, interviews, photographic aid, and in some cases, read and commented on the manuscript: John S. Babel; Carl E. Begh, Jr.; Dennis G. Cooper; Perry J. Dahl; Louis D. DuMontier; Raymond M. Giles; Robert A. Hall; Teddy W. Hanks; Ferdinand C. Hanson; William L. Hasty; John L. Hood; Leland F. Howerton; Bascom S. Jones; Marion F. Kirby; John S. Loisel; Charles H. MacDonald; Joseph O'Neil, Jr.; John E. Purdy; Vincent F. Straus; Douglas S. Thropp, Jr.; John A. Tilley; Henry C. Toll; Robert M. Tomberg.

Former Hades Squadron pilot, H. N. "Pete" Madison provided valuable information and contacts. He also generously supported this project with technical aid on the graphics. Louis E. Lynch was the group's wartime historian and this work owes much to his meticulous and far-ranging history. The late Carroll R. Anderson, ex-433rd Squadron member and unofficial group historian, did so well in preserving the spirit of the 475th in words and documents, which his wife Virginia graciously allowed me to use. And a special word of thanks to the 475th Group's Robert K. Weary who made this book possible through his generosity.

This book would not have seen publication without the invaluable aid of Tammy L. Monohan and John R. Neff, two better assistants one could not hope to find. Diana L. Zeilenga typed and edited with skill and verve. Dr. Robin Higham of Sunflower University Press has twice come to my rescue, as a dissertation reader and then as this book's editor, never failing in either of those endeavors. Thanks are due to Sue Barton and Carol Williams of the Press.

Others helped in significant ways. Ed Maloney and the staff at Chino Airport's Planes of Fame Museum, Chino, California, always responded to my research needs in a friendly manner. Ex-WAAF ferry pilot Iris C. Critchell patiently answered this groundling's questions on flying the Lightning and its idiosyncrasies.

Riverside Community College's President, Dr. Charles Kane, supported this effort from start to finish, as did my Social Sciences and Humanities Dean, Joyce Black. Maureen "Mo" Estes and her staff at the college's Communications Center greatly lessened burdens through their technical expertise. Professor Al Parker unraveled the History Department's computer maze for me. Fellow historian John Bradshaw contributed periodical evidence. Colleagues who took time from their busy schedules to read and comment helpfully on portions of the manuscript were Kristina Cline, Jim Hill, Linda Sherman, and Bill Wiley.

I am indebted to Dr. Sidney H. H. Chang, California State University-Fresno, who treated this student better than he deserved. Professors Leonard Levy, Robert Dawidoff, Sue Mansfield, and John Niven of the Claremont Colleges, California, found time to move me towards a life of the mind.

Thanks also belong to Carlos Razo who has been through it all before, my alter parents, George and Aiko Fukagawa, and my brothers and sisters, both blood and by marriage, who never lost faith. Lastly, my gratitude to daughters Brooke and Erin who wisely understood laughter cures all and especially to Karen, ace wife to whom I fly a poor wingman.

Contents

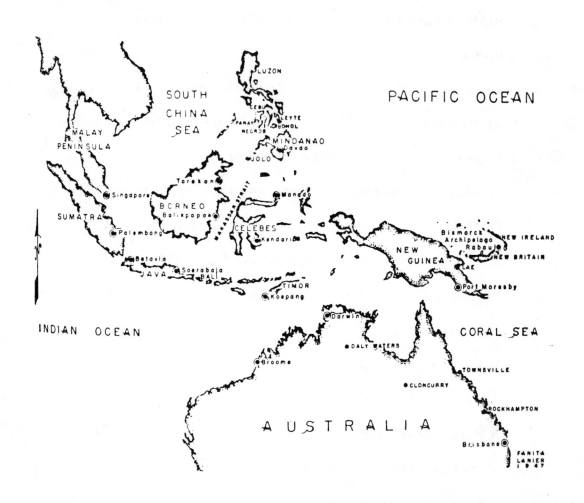

*The Southwest Pacific Area. From Wesley Frank Craven and James Lea Cate, **The Army Air Forces in World War II**, vol. I (Chicago, IL: University of Chicago Press, 1950), p. 389. Copyrighted 1950 by the University of Chicago. All rights reserved.*

Prologue

A day after Christmas 1943 sixteen twin-engined fighter aircraft ranged the eastern end of New Britain. They were well used after months of combat and were flown with a purposefulness that marked veteran pilots. At 1425 hours, shipborne radar plotted bogies and vectored them towards an interception point. Ten minutes later the big fighters encountered thirty to forty Japanese Navy Zeroes and Army Oscars, a melee breaking out.

A young Army Air Forces captain led his flight of four into a head-on pass at the enemy but more than a dozen hostile fighters dove from the flank. Breaking off, he pushed over and escaped by slicing beneath the onrushing aircraft. The captain's flight then spotted twenty-five to thirty Aichi Val divebombers. Calling out their position to the rest of the squadron, he dove his airplane into a string of the bombers at 10,000 feet.

Chasing one hostile down 2,000 feet, the Army pilot fired a short burst that drew smoke, the fixed-gear airplane plunging into the sea. Surviving Vals dropped to wave-top levels as the flight of fighters pursued them with deadly intent. The captain attacked another Val from astern, gunfire holing tanks until the aircraft flared and then exploded in mid-air. He then dove on yet another Aichi as it twisted from thirty degrees deflection to a position directly ahead of him. The twin-tailed fighter shook as .50 caliber and 20 millimeter rounds arched out, enveloping the Japanese craft an instant before it broke up on the ocean's surface.

The combat had carried the American along Borgen Bay's shore. Alone, he made a diving pass at a fourth divebomber that started it smoking, dark plumes trailing over sea, beach, and jungle as the wounded ship dove inland. Suddenly a Republic P-47 Thunderbolt joined the hunt, the two Americans trading firing passes on the Val as it skimmed the green canopy below. The Army captain lined his fighter up and triggered a long burst that blew chunks off of the staggering Aichi. It tore into a tree, exploding just as the captain flashed past, fragments ripping his fighter's horizontal tail fin. Climbing for altitude the fighter and the man flew for home.

The man was Captain Thomas Buchanan McGuire, Jr., on his way to becoming the United States' second highest scoring fighter pilot in World War II. His weapon of assignment — and preference — was Lockheed's twin-engined thoroughbred, the P-38 Lightning.

Earlier they had joined the new 475th Fighter Group formed at Amberly Field, Australia, in mid-1943. The man,

the fighter, and the group — all existed to stop an implacable foe that had turned the Pacific into an inferno two years and nineteen days before. At that time the enemy was at the gate; and time was running out.

* * *

Blows fell swiftly, each on a vital spot, each with finality. The Japanese had two dominant goals in 1941: to secure a "Southern Resource Area" centered on the Netherlands East Indies, rich in petroleum and bauxite, and to protect the Home Islands from Allied retribution. To those ends all actions were directed.

The surprise strikes against Pearl Harbor and the Philippines on 7 December 1941 neutralized American military power in the Pacific basin. The U.S. Navy took a body blow at Pearl Harbor, while the Army in the Philippines began a steady retreat that would end in its final surrender at Corregidor. Enemy forces captured American Wake and Guam Islands closing eastern routes to Japan. The U.S. Army Air Forces (USAAF) also fought lost battles.

The Far Eastern Air Force stood lone sentinel duty over the Philippines on 8 December 1941. Commanded by Annapolis graduate Major General Lewis Hyde Brereton, the V Interceptor Command (Provisional) depended on its 24th Pursuit Group to defend the islands. The recently-formed 24th was decimated over the Philippines with outnumbered green pilots flying obsolete craft. Their gallant efforts slowed but did not staunch the Japanese flow. The last survivors had retreated south long before the American surrender on the "Rock," Corregidor.

The Japanese earlier sealed southwesterly approaches by capturing British Hong Kong on Christmas Day 1941, followed by the Malayan bastion of Singapore in February of the new year, nailing shut avenues for British reinforcements from Imperial India. They had also thrust a blade between the United States and its southern Allied anchor, Australia, by capturing the magnificent harbor of Rabaul, New Britain, in January 1942.

Barricades arose next over Java, heart of the Southern Resource Area. Tired veterans of the Philippine debacle were mingled with hastily forwarded American replacements from Brisbane, Australia. Once assembled, most of the surviving pilots from the 24th Pursuit Group led five provisional squadrons in the defense of Java — the 3rd, 13th, 17th, 20th, and 33rd. By February 1942, they engaged the Japanese regularly, flying air defense, escort cover, and just before the island's fall, surface attack missions. Early in March stragglers boarded Consolidated LB-30s, Boeing B-17s, and assorted transport airplanes, and again escaped, this time to Australia.

In the minds of Allied leaders Australia's fall was inconceivable. Its survival insured a base of operations in the South Pacific, a grounded aircraft-carrier capable of supporting offensives back up the Japanese-held island chains. But enemy conquests of the Netherlands East Indies to the northwest, plus his easterly investment of Rabaul Harbor, threw a net that rimmed approaches to that island continent. This left Australia open to air attack and invasion. A huge island off the north coast — New Guinea — held possibilities of being either an Allied base or a launching point for enemy attacks. By March New Guinea was compromised.

On 7-8 March Japanese occupying forces crossed the Solomon Sea snatching up Lae and Salamau just two hundred miles north of Port Moresby, the major Allied base located on the southeastern littoral. From crude airfields, they began to launch air raids against that port.

The USAAF was called upon to defend both areas. In that same month three groups, the newly-arrived 8th, the 35th, reconstituted after losing its 21st and 34th Squadrons in the Philippines, and the 49th, were assigned defensive duties. From March to April 1942, the 49th Fighter Group defended Darwin from Japanese air raids emanating out of the Netherlands East Indies. In October they moved to Port Moresby, joining squadrons of the 8th and 35th Fighter Groups which had fought the Japanese since their arrival on 1 May when they had joined the Royal Australian Air Force's (RAAF) 75 and 76 Squadrons. Inadequate numbers of aircraft, faulty tactics, and minimum warning times hampered operations in Australia and later at Moresby.

By mid-year the situation had stabilized briefly because other spots boiled over in the Pacific. On 18 April Colonel Jimmy Doolittle's raiding North American B-25 Mitchells struck Japan on a single, morale-building mission and their wake exposed cracks in that island's armor. The Japanese decided to seal their empire once and for all with two last offensives: a combined Army-Navy assault on the Allied stronghold of Port Moresby, followed by a Navy invasion aimed at the capture of Midway. The first objective, which would decide the fate of New Guinea and Australia, was implemented one month later in May.

Before the first offensive could be launched the Fourteenth Naval District's Office of Naval Intelligence, located at Pearl Harbor, had broken the Japanese Navy's top secret code JN-25 and alerted commanding Admiral Chester W. Nimitz of the impending attack against Port Moresby.

The resultant battle of the Coral Sea was history's first pure carrier-to-carrier conflict. Rear Admiral Frank Jack Fletcher's force, in a series of wildly swinging air raids, fought the Japanese invasion fleet to a standstill. Though losing the carrier "Lady Lex," the USS Lexington, the Navy forced cancellation of the Moresby invasion. The Japanese

planned to restart the aborted mission in the future but the American Navy's tenacity soon altered that assault in fundamental ways.

In June Japanese strategist Admiral Isoroku Yamamoto, executing the second offensive, plunged south to capture Midway as a prelude to an invasion of Hawaii. He hoped to force the U.S. Navy back to the West Coast. Through good intelligence, luck, and hard fighting, the American Navy completely crushed the Midway invasion fleet changing the Pacific War forever. Stymied to the west and south, the Japanese settled in for a long, tough war.

With the enemy checked the Americans now began to probe the Japanese perimeter. Both the Navy and the American commander of Allied forces in Australia, General Douglas MacArthur, sought first to insure their southern Allies' survival by recapturing Rabaul in New Britain. Though like-minded in goals, they parted over methods with MacArthur proposing a lightning, three-week campaign striking directly at the target through a seaborne invasion.

The Navy, husbanding its limited resources, even thinner after the Coral Sea and Midway fights, proposed a more conservative island-by-island approach. Eventually both parties agreed on three "tasks": (1) a Navy-Marine invasion of Tulagi in the Solomon Islands; (2) an Army offensive to clear the east coast of New Guinea; (3) a final combined pincer attack that came at Rabaul from both eastern New Guinea and up from the Solomon chain. Plans were drawn up to trigger the first task in August.

A month prior to that first U.S. offensive the Japanese again moved on Port Moresby, opening gambits that would soon split the South Pacific into two warring arenas. The Japanese Army still viewed the big island as a major goal in spite of the defeat of their original plan to invade Port Moresby with nine divisions of the Seventeenth Army transported and supported by the Navy. But in the month following the Battle of the Coral Sea both branches vacillated, the Navy because of losses at the Coral Sea and Midway, the Army because of divided opinions among its officers, some of whom desired western-bound offenses seeking to link-up with the Nazis at Suez.

By the 11 July start-time the Moresby thrust had been diminished in scale, if not ambition. It remained the target but fewer Japanese Army units were committed and, critically, the Imperial Navy's reticence forced generals to transform a direct water invasion into a conventional land attack over the Owen Stanley Mountain range, some of the roughest terrain in the Pacific. Worse, Douglas MacArthur had already beaten them to the punch.

Four days before the projected Japanese invasion, Mac-Arthur ordered the Australian 39th Battalion (militia) and a battalion of constabulary troops to reconnoiter north over the Kokoda Road, somewhat more accurately described by the locals as the Kokoda Track. Eight days later and one hundred miles further, the Australian force began to create a base at the waystation of Kokoda, approximately half-way to the Track's north coast terminus at the government station of Buna. From Kokoda MacArthur planned to take Buna and with its fall, invest the Japanese bases of Salamau and Lae up the coast. Like a spark near gasoline, Japanese reactions were instantaneous and violent.

Within hours after the Australians arrived at Kokoda, Japanese Lieutenant General Haruyoshi Hyakutake sensed MacArthur's intentions and countered with a 2,000-man vanguard of the *Nankai Shitai*, the veteran South Seas Detachment, fresh from its victory at Guam. Ordered to break trail for the rest of their unit, the spearhead group landed north of Buna intent on taking the Australian base, the Kokoda Trail, and ultimately, Port Moresby. Badly outgunned, the Aussies fell back along the dreadful length of the Kokoda, fighting as they retreated. By 21 July, MacArthur realized that the New Guinea struggle had begun.

The rest of 1942 saw continuous combat between Japan and the Allies on New Guinea and another jungle island, for in August the Marine Corps had launched America's first land offensive amidst the swamps and copra groves of Guadalcanal and neighboring Tulagi. It stirred up a hornet's nest. The desperate campaign created a vortex that sucked in all available supplies in the face of determined Japanese attempts to recapture Guadalcanal, especially its single airfield named Henderson by the Marines.

By 13 August 1942, after a gallant Australian defense, the Kokoda waystation fell, the Japanese pushing the Westerners before them. Thirteen days later the enemy main force came ashore beginning their sweep south along the Kokoda Trail towards Moresby. The Aussies gave ground begrudgingly, stiffened by Allied air interdiction and most importantly a precipitous terrain made for defense. By 7 September the South Seas Detachment had forced the Gap, the single mountain passage leading down to Port Moresby but three weeks later Australian counterattacks against the breach and American flanking movements dislodged the *Nankai Shitai*, forcing its retreat to eventual defeat and destruction.

The Solomons struggle ended by February 1943 with the Japanese destroyed, but not without a high tariff paid by the United States. "Iron Bottom Bay" lay strewn with shattered American and Japanese ships. Major General A.A. "Archie" Vandegrift's First Marine Division was shattered and would take months to recover. The strange melange of American air units which fought over Guadalcanal — Marine, Army, and Navy — reached so desperate a plight that even MacArthur dug deep and handed over eight of the Pacific's premier fighters, Lockheed P-38 Lightnings, from his pitiful stocks in November 1942. Whatever the cost, however, the Joint Chiefs of Staff's "task one" had been completed leaving General MacArthur to complete "task two" — the capture of Eastern New Guinea.[1]

Like Guadalcanal, Allied encounters with the Japanese in New Guinea were prolonged and bitter. They must also be viewed within the context of the Guadalcanal campaign which began two and one-half weeks after the enemy waded ashore at Buna, New Guinea. The "Canal" was America's

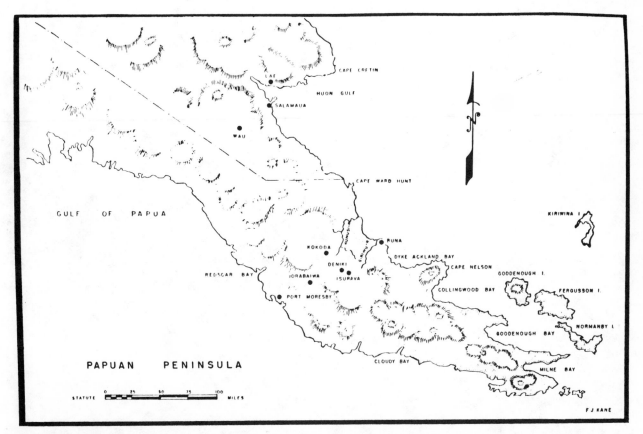

*The Papuan Peninsula of New Guinea. From Wesley Frank Craven and James Lea Cate, **The Army Air Forces in World War II**, vol. IV (Chicago, IL: University of Chicago Press, 1950), p. 95. Copyrighted 1950 by the University of Chicago. All rights reserved.*

first offensive and fierce Japanese reactions gave that campaign top priority in an already resource-poor theater. MacArthur faced a full blown Japanese attack with virtually no aid save the men and equipment on hand.

Again paralleling events on Guadalcanal, the remainder of 1942 and early 1943 were spent reducing Japanese strongholds on New Guinea. The enemy eventually dug in on an arc about ten miles long, centrally located between Holnicote Bay to the north and Oro Bay to the south. They had fortified and the Allies had targeted three enclaves at Gona, Sananada Point, and Buna. There in dark swamps, American and Australian troopers learned firsthand of the difficulties in rooting out entrenched Japanese soldiers. Men and military reputations fell before friendly forces walked the beaches of those three costly villages. By then it was 21 January 1943, exactly six months since the Buna struggle began. Seventeen days later Guadalcanal came to the U.S. forces, it too conquered in exactly six months. With momentum, north coast bases, and the drain of Guadalcanal now ended, MacArthur could plan for the future.

In that planning the 475th Fighter Group was conceived and born.[2]

FOOTNOTES

1. Frank Wesley Craven and James Lea Cate, *The Army Air Forces in World War II, vol. IV: The Pacific: Guadalcanal to Saipan, August 1942 to July 1944* (Chicago: University of Chicago Press, 1950), pp. 5-60 (hereinafter, Craven and Cate, *The Army Air Forces*); Letter: John S. Loisel to Author, October 1987 (hereinafter, Loisel Letter).

2. Samuel Milner, *Victory in Papua*, United States Army in World War II series (Washington, D.C.: Office of the Chief of Military History, 1957), *passim*; Lida Mayo, *Bloody Buna* (Garden City, NY: Doubleday and Co., 1974), *passim*; Ronald H. Spector, *Eagle Against the Sun* (NY: The Free Press, 1985), chaps. 7-9 (hereinafter, Spector, *Eagle*); Charles Willoughby and John Chamberlain, *MacArthur 1941-1951* (NY: McGraw-Hill Book Co., 1954), chap. 4 (hereinafter, Willoughby and Chamberlain, *MacArthur*); Walter D. Edmonds, *They Fought With What They Had* (Boston: Little, Brown and Co., 1951), *passim* (hereinafter, Edmonds, *They Fought*).

Chapter One

To The Southern Cross:
Amberly Field, May-August 1943

The 15 May 1943 activation of the 475th Fighter Group marked the beginning of MacArthur's drive to clear the Guineas of Japanese. Earlier in August 1942, even as the enemy moved on Port Moresby, the general had already planned for this strike force. In an act of remembrance, the general requested his new air force be designated the Fifth; this in honor of his old air command that fought — and died — under Philippine skies. Washington quickly acceded to his wish and on 3 September 1942, the phoenix rose. The Fifth Air Force was officially reconstituted.

Selecting commanding officers had already commenced before the Fifth had come into being. The C.G. (Commanding General) was veteran combat officer and long-time aviator, Lieutenant General George Churchill Kenney. Cocky, aggressive, competent, Kenney's abilities belied his diminutive five and one-half foot frame. Kenney liked to repeat his grandfather's admonition, "George, you're a little guy and you've got to remember that if you ever go after a big fellow, you're going to need a brick in each hand." In the Air Corps he did just that. A World War I fighter pilot with two kills, he held a number of important posts in the peacetime Corps and headed up the Fourth Air Force based at Riverside, California, before being summoned to the South Pacific.

Kenney had outstanding traits. He spoke with utter candor, with no equivocation or pause, and MacArthur delighted in his honesty. Typical of a man speaking with guileless conviction, Kenney brooked no pettiness, a mistake Major General Richard Sutherland, MacArthur's arbitrary chief of staff, made once and once only.

Kenney also had a keen technical sense honed by extensive experience in equipment. In 1939 he served as Chief of Production at Wright Field, site of the Air Corps' materiel development. The next year Kenney went to a Europe at war, observed air developments among the belligerents, and made valuable technical changes in American combat craft. This technical familiarity would bear ample dividends in the scrape-and-patch Southwest Pacific.

Most critically Kenney had an open, pragmatic spirit. His experiences as fighter pilot during the Great War, ground attack specialist during the intervening period, and technical expert during the 1930s, lent the general considerable balance in his approaches towards warfare. Furthermore, in that decade Kenney's duties precluded his presence at the Air Corps Tactical School (ACTS), the air arm's première center for strategic thinking, when the strategic bombing theory

came into being. There men like Major Harold Lee "Hal" George, Donald Wilson, and Lieutenant Kenneth Newton Walker hammered out the Air Force's leading tenet — daylight, target-select bombing. This is not to say that Kenney did not believe in that theory; instead, his practical and varied life tempered it, granting the freedom to carry out his Pacific mission in a no-nonsense manner, balancing all aspects of operations, including the recognition of the dominant role of fighter aviation.[1]

Operational control devolved upon Major General Ennis Clement "Whitey" Whitehead. Whitehead's operational career began in 1917, teaching American combat pilots at Issoudun, France, performing postwar test flying, and command of a variety of squadrons, including fighters. A career officer, he also had much experience in the technical end of aircraft development, especially from 1926 to 1931. He ably seconded Kenney as Deputy C.G. of the Fifth Air Force by July 1942. Tall and lanky, attesting to his athletic background, Whitehead commanded the twin strike forces of the Fifth's Bomber and Fighter Commands and he wielded them so deftly that the Japanese propaganda named him the "Butcher of Moresby." In 1945, General MacArthur lauded Whitehead, calling him a "field commander . . . [of excellent] caliber. . . ."[2]

Leadership for the V Fighter Command, of which the 475th FG was a part, fell to mustachioed, veteran pursuit pilot, Brigadier General Paul Bernard "Squeeze" Wurtsmith. Wurtsmith had a long association with fighter aviation including two postwar tours with Eddie Rickenbacker's old "Hat-In-Ring" Squadron, the 94th. After 1939 the European War had demonstrated amply the importance of fighter aviation. But commonly for pursuit specialists in the bomber-dominated Air Corps, Wurtsmith attended the ACTS late, graduating in August 1940.

In February 1942, Lieutenant Colonel Wurtsmith accompanied his 49th Group "down-under" in the defense of Darwin and later Port Moresby. The colonel led by example, flying combat with his men. More crucially he modified tactics that allowed his P-40s to hold their own against the Japanese A6M2 Zero-Sen fighter. Despite losses, the 49th successfully defended both vital ports. The enemy's bombers and fighters rarely raided without being contested, sometimes at punishing costs.[3]

In acknowledgment of his accomplishments, Wurtsmith received a brigadier general's rank in February 1943 and

Paul Wurtsmith, Commanding General of the V Fighter Command. (Anderson Collection)

shortly afterwards got Whitehead's nod to ramrod the V Fighter Command. With leadership in place, the Fifth Air Force began to plan for war in earnest. That planning had to account for the Fifth's strengths and weaknesses; the reconciliation of those attributes would produce a unit unlike any produced before.[4]

From the beginning the 475th possessed two distinctions: the first Pacific fighter group to be formed on foreign soil and the first in the Southwest Pacific Area (SWPA) to bear the designation "TE" — twin-engine — destined solely to fly Lockheed P-38 Lightnings. The Fifth Air Force's chief weakness centered on a lack of long-range, high altitude fighters. In October 1942, Kenney made this clear enough. In a letter to General H. H. "Hap" Arnold, Chief of the Army Air Forces, Kenney adamantly sought P-38s to take out "the Zero coverage up top-side while the P-39s and P-40s take on the bombers." The Lightning not only fought better, it had the requisite 800-mile range necessary to cover General MacArthur's ambitious and far-flung attacks slated for the Southwest Pacific. The activation of the 475th Fighter Group on 15 May the next year partially answered those pressing needs. Activation, however, guaranteed nothing. It only triggered the first moves in what was usually the slow creation of a unit.[5]

The first difficult step after activation was assembling personnel to man that unit. But, by 1943, the Army Air Forces (AAF) had formalized its methods of procuring, training, and assigning its men.

Many factors contributed to an airman's military occupation specialty (MOS): education levels, civilian jobs, personal preference, and chiefly, the Army's needs. But those factors had to meld with a series of standardized tests, the most crucial of which centered on the Army General Classification Test (AGCT) and Mechanical Aptitude (MA) test. Employed first in 1940, the AGCT sought to determine personal learning abilities with Grade I (130 and above), the fastest, and Grade V (59 and below), the slowest. The MA test measured abilities to master manipulative tasks. All of the examination results were recorded on each soldier's WDAGO Form 20, the comprehensive record of the man's military work experience.[6]

Crucial to the air arm's task lay the allocation of enlisted men from the Army's pool of potential soldiers. The very nature of air power, however, created problems. The highly technical nature of aviation created intellectual demands not met by the Army's normal distribution system. From 1941 on, under the Army's general distribution scheme, this problem intensified for the Army Air Force because of truncated courses caused by the war, resulting in a fifty percent failure rate in all its technical schools.

During 1942 Chief of the Army Air Forces, General Arnold, battled General of the Army, General George C. Marshall, over allocations. By August, Arnold won a pledge of 50,000 men scoring 100 and better on both the AGCT and MA tests. This preferential treatment continued until 1 June 1943, one month after the AAF passed its peak recruitment period of the war. In short, whether a pilot or not, Air Forces personnel represented the best of the Army's manpower pool.

After five weeks of basic training, excluding aviation cadets from civilian life, Army Air Forces standards classified recruits with only one man in five meeting the rigorous physical, psychological, and emotional standards set for pilots, the remainder going to technical, administrative, and service schools. Of those pilot trainees, 40 to 50 percent would "wash-out" of aviation training and go into other needed areas: navigation and bombardment.[7]

Pilot training varied during the war, but the traditional primary, basic, and advanced courses still held forth, averaging about seven months of training time. Shiny wings and flight time, however, only marked the beginning.

Fighter pilots had several essential "transitions" in their career. Of these, two crucial events occurred; first, the Air Forces divided the students into fighter and bomber pilots, and second, during advanced training, single-engined fighter pilots transitioned into combat aircraft. By 1944, approximately five weeks of training was required to master the intricacies of combat ready aircraft, including an officially mandated twenty hours of fixed gunnery training which, in reality, varied from class to class.

Pilots alone won no wars. Administrative officers were badly needed after the American war effort exploded in 1941.

In February 1942, Hap Arnold ordered Major General Walter R. Weaver to create an Officer Candidate School (OCS) for the Army Air Forces. Weaver drew exhaustively from three groups: aviation cadets who did not complete flight training, warrant officers, and enlisted men. Qualifying requirements included:

> . . . age limits of 18-36 years, American citizenship, demonstrated capacity for leadership, physical condition as required for commissioned officers of the Army of the United States, a score of 110 or higher on the Army general classification test, and such education or practical experience as will reasonably insure . . . satisfactory completion of the course of instruction.[8]

Until June 1944, the Army Air Forces' OCS was based at Miami Beach, Florida. Beginning with a twelve-week course, graduates of this precipitous climb to officer status wore the wry description of the "Ninety-Day Wonders" from start to finish. After June 1943, the OCS lengthened to sixteen weeks, its final address being Maxwell Field, Alabama, home of the pre-war Air Corps Tactical School. Before it finally closed down in June 1945, 30,000 officers had passed through the program.

For the majority of its life, AAF's OCS followed two curriculums. From February 1942 until January 1943 students took general classes addressing five basic areas: administration, messing, supply, transportation, and miscellaneous duties. After January 1943, the school specialized with an eight-week course on duties expected of junior officers. The remaining time centered on an assigned specialization in adjutant and personnel, supply, messing, intelligence, guard companies, or training. This remained the standard until October 1944, when greatly reduced attendance forced a return to the older general education system. By then, however, the bulk of the Air Forces' administrative officers had already graduated and had taken their valuable places in fields of conflict.[9]

For every combat pilot, four technical experts directly maintained his ability to fly, seven served his ground requirements, and, in the entire Army Air Forces, sixteen individuals, in one way or another, kept him flying. From 1938-1939 the Army Air Forces graduated 900 aircraft mechanics; by 1945 that number had risen to 700,000. Little wonder the AAF insisted on the teamwork concept. Generally speaking, their education followed the pattern of technical schools (with 314 different skills being taught by 1944), training in a squadron, then integration of the various specialist squadrons into a working unit capable of supporting a combat group. The myriad tasks necessary for the upkeep of an Air Force are too many to define here but the following lists some of the basic tasks and the maximum schooling available to each technician:

Airplane Repair and Maintenance	29 weeks
Armament	23 weeks
Communications	44 weeks
Weather	33 weeks
Motor Transport	10 weeks
Miscellaneous	9 weeks[10]

Once finished with the various schools, the newly-trained enlisted men (EMs) moved to their squadron and then group training phases, preparatory to shipping out to their combat units.

The AAF trained technicians for "echelons" or levels of maintenance. First echelons directly serviced fighters in the field and did minor repairs. This vanguard unit first reclaimed captured enemy airdromes or readied newly-built airstrips. Logistically, all equipment was air mobile for rapid deployment. Second echelons operated from established bases, performing more complex maintenance jobs and repairs such as full engine changes. While most tools could be shipped by air, some machinery at this level required ground or sea transportation. Levels one and two served the group's squadrons, absorbing the bulk of a base's maintenance and repair needs.

Echelons three and four tackled increasingly difficult jobs that required specialized knowledge, extensive and permanent facilities, regular supplies, and a secured base of operations. For the Fifth Air Force this meant the 4th Air Depot Group, Townsville, located on the northeast coast of Australia. The depots and sub-depots engaged in extensive repair and maintenance work. Distinct from the other two levels, they serviced craft from many units, received and conditioned new airplanes for the Fifth Air Force, salvaged damaged material ("cannibalizing" to the field forces), and carried out major combat modifications. Ground crews that served the echelons were enlisted men directed by noncommissioned officers. They represented the 80 percent that remained after pilot selection but they were already part of an elite group. While some blurring occurred between each echelon, basically the Air Force followed this scheme throughout the war.[11]

By spring 1943 pilots, administrative officers, noncoms, and EMs began the long move west and south, in time to link-up with veteran cadres in Australia. Together they became the 475th Fighter Group.

Beginning here, on the verge of overseas duty, the 475th's constitution differed in a number of ways. Because it had formed outside the continent, the group began in a fragmented state. This bore fruit both bitter and sweet. Cadre and new recruits took about a month before they met and began the process of forming a team. On the positive side, the neophytes of the 475th could not have asked for better leaders and teachers. Several Australian and New Guinea outfits contributed to the experienced cadre, including the seasoned veterans of Wurtsmith's 49th Group, the defenders of Darwin and by war's end the top-scoring group in the SWPA. The collection also included men from the 8th Group as well as the 35th Group. Among this assemblage was a core of men, members of a scattering of squadrons, now re-equipped and reconstituted after their bloody nightmare over Java, who became collectively and respectfully known as "Java men."

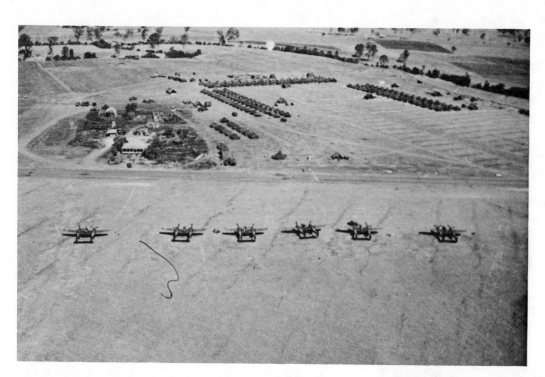

Forming up at Amberly, Australia, mid-1943. (Anderson Collection)

Merged together, veteran and neophyte began to form the group during their Amberly days.[12]

The 475th's C.O. was Major (later Lieutenant Colonel) George W. Prentice. Originally he had flown with the P-40-equipped 49th Fighter Group. When the 39th Squadron of the 35th Group received some of the first Lightnings sent to the Southwest Pacific Area (SWPA), Prentice was ordered to lead them after their senior officer died while practicing skip-bombing. Kenney picked Prentice for his operational experience in P-38s, experience not wasted on the all-Lightning group. Apparently Prentice had carte blanche because he brought with him several other 35th Group members, including Captains Albert W. Schinz and Meryl M. Smith, as the 475th's new executive and operations officers.[13].

Almost half of the 475th original personnel came from New Guinea units and, in some respects, it was less a group than a composition of older hands reinforced by stateside recruits like Captain Ronald C. Malloch, the 432nd's new intelligence officer, and Corporal Joseph A. Boch, also assigned to Clover Squadron as a radio mechanic. One hundred and seventy-five officers and men were drawn from New Guinea while one hundred and eighty came from America. For instance, in his roster of the 431st Squadron of the 475th FG, Master Sergeant Vincent F. Straus listed 187 personnel of which 68 formerly fought with his old 49th Group, approximately 36 percent of the squadron's complement.[14]

The 475th would habitually remain understrength, according to the AAF's Table of Organization. Authorized allotments of men and officers for a twin-engine fighter group stood optimistically at 1,037, but the group only approximated and retained that number for five months, April-August 1944. For the most part, the 475th averaged 885 men a month. Despite Official Tables of Organization, however, the group was well-equipped by standards of the theater.[15]

First C.O. of Hades Squadron, Major Franklin A. "Frank" Nichols, Dobodura, New Guinea. Nichols rose to the rank of Major General in the postwar Air Force. (Verle Jett photograph)

Gathering an air group in war resembled a caterpillar, slow, halting, with the feet at the back patiently waiting for those at the front to move forward. By 26 June 1943 the stateside contingent arrived at Amberly Field, just outside Brisbane, fresh from the 22nd Replacement Central Depot. Three weeks later the remainder of the group withdrew from New Guinea and merged with the newcomers at Amberly. Together they began to put things right.

Prior to the main group's arrival, an advance party had already begun to create order from chaos. Among them Captain Franklin A. Nichols, experienced P-40 pilot late from the 7th Squadron of the 49th Group, led a small contingent to Brisbane on 17 June. Shivering from the sharp climatic change from tropical New Guinea to the fall wet of Eastern Australia, his party of officers and men traveled by airplane and train to Amberly. There, they began to sort out supplies.

Even they had been preceded by an earlier arrival, the 75th's noncommissioned supply chief, Technical Sergeant Orville Joseph. Joseph had encountered a snag; important items had stalled at Amberly's Supply Department. With officers in tow and armed with bottles of Scotch whiskey, Joseph returned to Supply and arranged an amicable trade, exchanging goodwill and Scotch for priority on the group's supplies. Experience and know-how triumphed again.[16]

The sinews of war are often times subtler than at first glance. While aircraft dramatically dominated the 475th's purpose, thousands of items backstopped their efforts. From pencils to trucks, supplies had to be requisitioned, accounted for, and then distributed. Among other items, typewriters, which generated the tons of paper that fueled modern war, were avidly sought and jealously guarded, "More precious than jewels" according to a group history.[17]

Nor would these problems be quickly solved. On 19 October 1943, a month after the 475th began combat, shortages still appeared. Parachutes lacked first aid kits and dye markers; there was a shortage of rivets, sheet metal, and hand tools. Ironically, feast accompanied famine. Technical Inspector Lieutenant Henry J. Porter, III, noted a ". . . huge supply of instrument oil, compass fluid, and various greases . . .," as well as excess coolant pumps and, logically enough for the sweltering climate, wool clothing. Supplies, in time, sorted themselves out. In the meanwhile Lightnings began to arrive at Amberly.[18]

Lockheed's P-38 Lightning had risen from the fertile minds of H. J. Hibbard's design team ensconced at Lockheed's famed "Skunk Works" at Burbank, California. In 1936 the Army Air Corps released requirements for a high altitude interceptor capable of gunning down bombers above 20,000 feet, at speeds up to 360 miles per hour. The proposal's timing suggests that the Air Corps' new B-17 "Flying Fortress" had created a conundrum; if the U.S. produced a long-range bomber, so might a hostile power. Thus the Air Corps' very success in strategic bombardment capabilities spawned a need for a countermeasure — the P-38. The very features that made it a fine counter-bomber weapon also bequeathed to the fighter air superiority qualities as well.

The B-17's performance guided the Lightning's requirements: power for rapid climbs to altitude, fuel to intercept at extreme ranges, and a gun package that could bring down a bomber in the shortest time possible. Lockheed pondered the Air Corps' requirements and, like Boeing's decision that created the B-17, decided to gain requisite power by adding engines. Thus two Allison V-1710 series, inline engines pulled the Lightning to its outstanding performance levels. To quickly reach combat altitudes, the Army utilized turbo-superchargers employing exhaust gasses to compress the carburetor air which allowed superior performance at high altitudes. Two superchargers, however, stymied attempts at streamlining.

Twin engines, radical in itself, created the need for an equally radical airframe and Clarence L. "Kelly" Johnson was equal to the task. Out of six sketches, number four featured a central nacelle containing pilot and guns between the twin booms. Each boom also housed a supercharger behind its engine as well as a radiator battery, and the main landing gear. The combined fin and rudder assembly also stabilized the airplane by providing a large center of gravity. With the exception of an embarrassing touchdown in a New York ravine, Lockheed's thoroughbred averaged 340 m.p.h., with top speeds of 420 m.p.h., during her maiden flight on 27 January 1939.

Twin engines sped the Lightning to useful speeds but also gulped gas in huge amounts. The F and G models carried internally 600 gallons of 100 octane gas for a maximum cruising range of 1,425 and 1,150 miles respectively. Variants H through J carried 900 gallons for ranges of 1,950 and 1,750 miles. Twin powerplants also lifted external fuel cells but prior to the war American drop tank technology lagged badly.[19]

In the early 1920s, early Air Corps experiments produced

An H model P-38 on the Dobodura, New Guinea, flight line, 1943. 165 gallon drop tanks are already being carried. (Anderson Collection)

The heavies strike. Fifth Air Force Liberators crater an enemy air strip. Explosions run the entire length of the runway seen in the upper left. (Dennis G. Cooper Collection)

both the technology and tactics for drop tanks but, by the 1930s, several factors mitigated against extensive use of that innovation. Chief among those problems lay Depression-imposed austerity budgets that denied frills like aluminum tanks used once and then discarded. More seriously, the growth of strategic bombing thought and, by 1935, the "Flying Fortress" strategic bomber, allowed airmen radical visions of a new war, won and fought in the skies. The Boeing bomber was expensive. Given budgets, the Air Corps opted for the four-engine behemoth leaving scant monies for fighter aviation.

Drop tanks also suffered from their Army relationship. Commanders sought the direct support of ground operations by their aviation which diametrically opposed the strategic bombing theories. Disposable tanks extended attack aviation's radius of action, making them all the more desirable as a form of long-range artillery. Fearing the loss of bomber appropriations, the Air Corps minimized the role of disposable fuel cells in order to stifle Army interest in tactical air support.

The strategic bombing advocates also had to quell a rebellion in their own ranks. The notion of strategic bombing had not received uniform acceptance within the Air Corps, with resistance centering on a hawk-featured fighter pilot named Captain Claire Lee Chennault. A stubborn and, in ways, brilliant air tactician, Chennault challenged "bomber invincibility," the notion that unescorted B-17s could fight

their way to and from their target in the face of competent fighter opposition. The "bomber boys" retorted that "no fighter plane can be designed to escort . . . bombardment to their extreme tactical radius of action and there engage in offensive combat. . . ." Chennault took on the strategic bombing advocates at the Air Corps Tactical School but superior rank, constant pressure, and ill health forced retirement in 1936.[20]

Chennault went to China to forge a new air combat legacy but his troubling passage was not soon forgotten. To deny a further resurgence of the fighter arm, the Air Corps sharply curtailed drop tank use and refinement. Without range, fighters found no cooperative role with the strategic bomber, languishing through the remainder of the 1930s as a point defense weapon.[21]

The new war, however, drove home the need for long-range fighter craft. The global expanse of war made direct ferrying of replacement craft imperative. Drop tanks were rediscovered and over time became the obvious answer to short-legged fighter performance. Despite the Lightning's presence as early as 1942, the European Theater of Operations (ETO) continued to deny long-range fighter escorts. Europe represented the best opportunity to prove the strategic bombing theory, including the "bomber invincibility" notion, so in raid after raid the heavies waded through German flak and fighters alone. The prohibitive losses of 1943 forced reevaluation of the Air Forces' theory and triggered a frantic game of "catch-up," with P-51 Mustangs appearing in numbers only in early 1944.[22]

The late appearance of the long-distance escorts also spoke of the communication gap that yawned wide between the European and Pacific Theaters. Distance, both ferrying and combat, always loomed large over Pacific expanses. General Kenney groused that "engineers back home . . . were developing planes with no more range than was needed to make a fighter sweep across a ditch no bigger than Chesapeake Bay." By summer 1943, he had already ordered experimentation with, and production of, 110-gallon drop tanks for the P-47. Subsequent experimentation led to Australian production of tanks, the Lightning usually carrying 165-gallon cells with 300-gallon tanks occasionally used in 1945.[23]

Thus airmen of the SWPA were surprised, if not dismayed, when the Army Air Forces trumpeted the success of its first long-range fighter escort missions over Europe in early 1944. Over the watery tracks of the Pacific, P-47s and P-38s had already completed comparable missions the year before. With larger drop tanks, better fuel economy techniques, and the improved J and L model Lightnings, by war's end the P-38s flew 2,300-mile missions, a bone-wracking twelve hours in a 38's cockpit. With power and range, the Lightning needed only guns to make it a premier fighter, and guns it would have.[24]

The P-38's original role as a bomber destroyer gave it a deadly gun package at a time when conventional pursuits sported ineffectual arms. While aircraft evolved rapidly in the interwar years, aerial weaponry had difficulty leaving the 1914-1918 War behind. During the late twenties and the thirties, while greater horsepower, monocoque fuselage construction, and duraluminum materials made faster, tougher aircraft, weapon systems barely kept pace. When war flared in 1939, fighters, both Axis and Allied, carried relatively light armaments: the Messerschmitt Bf109 E-3 variant carried four 7.9 millimeter machine-guns and a 20 millimeter cannon; the Mitsubishi Zero-Sen A6M1 mounted two 20 millimeter cannons and two 7.7 millimeter machine-guns; the Supermarine Spitfire I sported eight .303 caliber machine-guns; and America's chief fighter, the Curtiss P-40B, had only just upped its arms from two to four .30 caliber machine-guns.[25]

At origin the sleek Lockheed craft carried a potent array of guns. While going through a number of variations, the 1941 D model Lightning nose-mounted a 20 millimeter Hispano cannon and four heavy Colt-Browning MG-53 .50 caliber machine-guns. This remained the weapons package for the Lightning family. Totally, the P-38 carried 2,150 rounds. The .50 calibers, alone, had a healthy 60 seconds of firing time. The 475th's common foe, the Zero-Sen A6M2 carried two Type 99 Mark I cannons with but 60 rounds per gun or 7.2 seconds of fire at 500 rounds per minute. Once those went dry the Zero had only two 7.7 millimeter machine-guns left.[26]

The positioning of the Lightning's guns also gave Satan's Angels a crucial advantage. With the central nacelle occupied by only the cockpit and nose wheel, the firepower could be concentrated in the nose. With engines in the wings, the nose sleekly tapered off providing the pilot with an excellent forward view for gunnery. A head-on view showed guns deployed in an arc covering the upper half of the craft's nose. While unremarkable to the casual viewer, it spoke volumes in explaining why the P-38 became the premier Zero killer.

The positioning of guns had been a perennial problem in fighter development. In the First World War, Anthony Fokker's invention of the synchronizing gear, allowing bullets to pass between whirling propellers, ushered in air fighting. Weapons were placed directly in front of the pilot allowing him to charge, fire, and clear jammed guns in a direct line of sight. The Allies attempted variations including a centrally-located machine-gun on the top plane which worked to a degree. The Germans also experimented with wing-mounted weapons but technical problems terminated this potentially fruitful method. Thus the war set seal on nose-mounted weapons.[27]

Centrally-located guns also concurred with the prevalent belief that in high speed combat, the ability to bring the converging fire of angled wing guns to bear on a speedy fighter was beyond the capabilities of most pilots. Even as technology produced metallic wings and the electronics to fire remote weapons, that prejudice lingered on, but single-engine fighters had limited space in the nose reducing the number of weapons contained there. Further, the interrupter gear slowed the rate of fire at a time when enemy aircraft required heavier firepower to bring them down. By the mid-thirties air forces reluctantly turned towards wing guns.

Experimentation and practice dispelled fears of the impossibility of fighting with wing-mounted guns but a secondary problem arose, concentration of firepower. Weapons had to be mounted to converge at a point in front of the craft. Without this convergence, bullets would have wider coverage but lack the knockdown punch of hundreds of rounds all in the target area. When angled, however, the apex of fire was set and only at that specific distance could the pilot expect to bring the full weight of his gunfire to bear on the target. When shooting from too close, or much more commonly, from too

Captain John J. Hood late of the 9th Fighter Group, 49th Fighter Squadron, and later member of Satan's Angels. (Anderson Collection)

far away, the dispersive effect created hits but with none of the concentration necessary to bring down a fighter. Thus a pilot flying a fighter with machine-guns in the wing had to be concerned about being exactly in range in order to shoot down his opponent.[28]

The P-38's nose guns vastly simplified that problem. With engines in twin booms, the central nacelle existed solely for the nose gear, the pilot and his equipment, and the weapons suite. Chiefly, to Lightning drivers, there was no concern for convergence. The push of the machine-gun and cannon buttons produced a stream of fire straight ahead and anything that flew into that maelstrom received the full force of the 38's armaments. This concentrated power was particularly effective against lightly armored Japanese fighters, lacking as they did self-sealing gas tanks.

Designed as a high altitude bomber destroyer, the P-38 found its attributes handsomely suited for the air war in the Pacific. And at Amberly Field the veteran cadre of what was to be the 475th, tasted the luxuries of civilization and investigated their new weapons. Master Sergeant Vincent Straus boresighted two or three Lightnings a day as they came to the depot from the "Eagle Farms," the receiving and assembly centers around Brisbane. Pilots, Captains Franklin

A. Nichols and John J. Hood, transitioned to 38s by the simple and honored tradition of taking turns sitting in the cockpit for half an hour while they memorized its instrumentation. Then, without much preamble, they started up, taxied to the runway, and took off. No young stateside jockey was going to show them how to fly a Lightning!

By 10 June many of the group had arrived from the U.S. and slowly the unit took form. For the pilots, familiarization and test flights ruled the day. The Lightnings suffered from nose wheel tires slipping off rims due to rough landings by inexperienced fliers. Also several pilots had problems with runaway propellers, a trouble never fully excised and which would have tragic consequences for the 475th in times to come. For the mechanics and technicians, stores had to be requisitioned and green members taught the intricacies of the P-38, most of whom had never seen one before. June faded to July and the group gained cohesion and coordination. Well it did. General Whitehead, based at the neat but unimposing Papua Hotel at Port Moresby, cut orders that the 475th should move out. On 10 August 1943, with only two months as a unit, Satan's Angels moved to New Guinea and their first taste of war.[29]

FOOTNOTES

1. Ronald W. Yoshino, "A Doctrine Destroyed: The American Fighter Offensive, 1917-1939" (Unpublished doctoral dissertation, Claremont Graduate School, 1985), pp. 328-30, 346, 353 (hereinafter, Yoshino, "Doctrine"); *Current Biography, 1943* (NY: H.W. Wilson Co., 1944), p. 373.

2. Douglas A. MacArthur, *Reminiscences* (NY: McGraw-Hill Book Co., 1964), p. 157 (hereinafter, MacArthur, *Reminiscences*); Flint O. Dupre, *U.S. Air Force Biographical Dictionary* (NY: Franklin Watts, 1965), pp. 254-260 (hereinafter, Dupre, *Dictionary*).

3. William N. Hess, *Pacific Sweep* (NY: Zebra Books, 1974), chap. 3 (hereinafter, Hess, *Sweep*); Edmonds, *They Fought*, pp. 42, 361, notes.

4. Dupre, *Dictionary*, p. 256.

5. Craven and Cate, *The Army Air Forces*, vol. IV, p. 101; Maurer Maurer, ed., *Combat Squadrons of the Air Force, World War II* (Washington, D.C.: U.S.P.G.O., 1969, rpt. ed., 1982), pp. 532-35 (hereinafter, Maurer, *Combat Squadrons of the Air Force*); File: Vincent F. Straus: Kiah Evans Papers (hereinafter, Straus File); Papers: Carroll R. Anderson, N.A., "Combat History: 475th Fighter Group, 1943-1945," p. 1 (hereinafter, Anderson Papers).

6. N.A., *The Official Guide to the Army Air Forces, AAF: A Directory, Almanac and Chronicle of Achievement* (NY: Pocket

Books, 1944), p. 112 (hereinafter, *AAF*); Craven and Cate, *The Army Air Forces*, vol. VI, p. 539.

7. Craven and Cate, *The Army Air Forces,* vol. VI, pp. 434-35, 545-56, 566-78; *AAF*, pp. 103-04.

8. *Ibid.*, pp. 680-81.

9. *Ibid.*, pp. 680-84.

10. *AAF*, p. 109; Craven and Cate, *The Army Air Forces*, vol. VI, pp. 631-73.

11. *AAF*, pp. 198-203; Craven and Cate, *The Army Air Forces*, vol. IV, pp. 102-05, 154, 629-31.

12. Survey: William D. Bean, May 1987.

13. Louis E. Lynch, et al., *Satan's Angels, 475th Fighter Group, 14th May 43-31st Dec. 44* (Australia: Angus and Robertson, 1946), pp. 11-12 (hereinafter, Lynch, et al., *Satan's Angels*); Straus File: Evans Papers, N.A. "First complete P-38 group arrives in New Guinea," N.D., p. 1 (hereinafter, Evans Papers: "First Complete P-38 group"); Letter: George C. Kenney to Carroll R. Anderson, 16 June 1967, pp. 1-2; Martin Caidin, *Fork-Tailed Devil: The P-38* (NY: Ballatine Books, 1971), p. 242 (hereinafter, Caidin, *Fork-Tailed Devil*).

14. Evans Papers: "First Complete P-38 group," p. 1; Straus File, "431st Fighter Squadron, 475th FG, 20 October 1943"; Alexander Balogh, Jr., Papers, "WDAG020"; Survey: Ronald C. Malloch, May 1987; Survey: Joseph A. Boch,

May 1987.

15. 475th FG, "History of the 475th Fighter Group," chap. 20, "Summary of Combat Record, Annex L" (hereinafter, 475FG, "Summary"); *AAF*, p. 21 has the "Official Table of Organization."

16. Letter: Vincent F. Straus to H.N. Madison, September 1986, pp. 1-2 (hereinafter, Straus Letter); Evans Papers: "First Complete P-38 group," p. 1; Dennis G. Cooper Papers: N.A., "The 475th FG: A Brief History," N.D. (hereinafter, "Brief History"). Originally the group had been slated for Charter Towers, Queensland, but shifted to Amberly because of its proximity to Brisbane supplies.

17. Lynch, et al., *Satan's Angels*, p. 12.

18. Report: First Lieutenant Henry J. Porter, III, to HQ-FISS Air Task Force, 19 October 1943, pp. 1-2.

19. R.L. Foss and Roy Blay, "From Propellers to Jets in Fighter Aircraft Design," *Lockheed Horizons*, 23 (April 1987), pp. 3-9 (hereinafter, Foss and Blay, "From Propellers to Jets"); Le Roy Weber, "The Lockheed P-38J-M Lightning," Profile Series (Surrey, U.K.: Profile Publications, N.D.), pp. 3-10, *passim* (hereinafter, Weber, "P-38J-M"); Anthony Shennan, *Lockheed P-38 Lightning: A History* (N.S.W., Australia: Historian Publishers, 1970), pp. 10-14 (hereinafter, Shennan, *Lockheed P-38*); Anthony Shennan, "Technical De-

tails — P-38L," in *Ibid.*, enclosure (hereinafter, Shennan, "Technical Details").

20. Craven and Cate, *The Army Air Forces*, vol. VI, p. 217.

21. Yoshino, "Doctrine," pp. 353-57; Craven and Cate, *The Army Air Forces*, vol. I, pp. 51-52; *Ibid.*, vol. VI, p. 40.

22. *Ibid.*, pp. 218-19; Yoshino, "Doctrine," pp. 397, note 48.

23. Craven and Cate, *The Army Air Forces*, vol. IV, pp. 199-200; Loisel Letter, October 1987.

24. Caidin, *Fork-Tailed Devil*, pp. 296-97.

25. William Green, *Famous Fighters of the Second World War* (NY: Hanover House, 1958), pp. 12, 27, 44, 51 (hereinafter, Green, *Famous Fighters*).

26. Green, *Famous Fighters*, p. 74; Murray Rubenstein, "The Curtiss P-40C vs. the Mitsubishi A6M2 Model 21 Zero-Sen," *Fighter Combat Study, Number One* (Biloxi, Mississippi: Gamescience Corp., 1976), p. 15 (hereinafter, Rubenstein, *Fighter Combat Study*).

27. Yoshino, "Doctrine," pp. 23-26.

28. As pointed out by both Ferdinand C. Hanson and John S. Loisel, the problems and complexities of air-to-air combat are oversimplified here as a complete analysis was beyond the scope of this work.

29. Straus Letter; Interview: John J. Hood, July 1987 (hereinafter, Hood Interview).

Chapter Two

"Harrying the North":
Dobodura and Wewak, August-October 1943

The tasks set before the 475th were derived from a series of compromises beginning at the Allies' Casablanca Conference, January 1943, extending down the Pentagon's halls, and finally lodging in the Southwest Pacific Area (SWPA). General MacArthur's Plan Elkton still hung fire as U.S. forces met and destroyed the Japanese on Guadalcanal and Buna. With both campaigns successfully concluded by spring 1943, the general looked to complete "tasks" two and three; to excise the enemy with twin drives up New Guinea and the Solomon chain, the capture of Rabaul being the endgame. Fates, however, that wreck the plans of mice and men could also work against generals.

On 12 March 1943 a series of meetings, collectively called the Pacific Military Conference, opened under the direction of the imperious Chief of Naval Operations, Admiral Ernest J. King. Present were the representatives of the SWPA's chiefs Nimitz and MacArthur. It was MacArthur's chief of staff, Major General Richard K. Sutherland, who outlined the year's program: in five steps the Navy and the Army would move towards Rabaul and after completely isolating it, would take the port itself. The accomplishment of tasks two and three, Sutherland emphasized, would require an additional five divisions, forty-five more air groups, and, mercifully, an unknown quantity of supplies, ships, trucks, and jeeps to support the operations.

The official Army history delicately attempted to describe the reaction to Sutherland's revelation: ". . . records do not disclose with what emotions the officers from the various Washington agencies received the information about the necessary reinforcements, but it is not difficult to imagine that some were surprised." Sutherland's "all-or-nothing" tone, warranted neither by his rank or demands, did little to sweeten the pill. Despite the Pacific commanders' insistence that their requirements represented "the absolute essential minimum," they left the conference with promises for only two or three more divisions and a small complement of airplanes.

The disappointing results arose from several sources, all with common roots in the Anglo-American agreement on the "Europe First" strategy. Focused on Nazi-occupied Europe, the American planners had simply assumed Rabaul would fall in 1943, taken by the men and materiel on hand in the SWPA. While all agreed upon unremitting pressure on the Japanese, the extraordinary demands, vagueness in schedul-

ing, and Sutherland's impolitic delivery took aback most officers present at the conference.

The worldwide scope of the Casablanca Conference also mitigated against a full thrust at Rabaul. At Casablanca the Allies agreed to open a round-the-clock air war against Germany, the British Bomber Command at night, the fledgling U.S. Eighth Air Force during the day. The solar-lunar offensive effectively bled off all available heavy bombers, a force Kenney had counted on for his part in the forthcoming battle for Rabaul. And the Navy could promise nothing in the way of aerial aid. Nimitz's ships had beaten the Japanese at Guadalcanal, but at a high cost. The admirals believed that in the narrow confines of the Solomons, carriers in particular were too vulnerable to surprise night engagements or worse, hostile land-based air strikes. Thus naval reluctance doubled the need for B-17s and B-24s at a time they were not to be had.

The Joint Chiefs of Staff stood their ground. Reluctantly the MacArthur-Nimitz team revised its plans. In essence, the resultant 28 March Directive authorized the completion of "Task Two" only. Nimitz would move up the Solomon chain and end his campaign by capturing the southeastern port of Bougainville Island. For MacArthur's part, he planned to clear Eastern New Guinea to Madang and then leap across to New Britain by investing Cape Gloucester.

An additional assignment directly reflected his failure to secure heavy bombardment units; MacArthur received orders to take the Woodlark and Kiriwina Islands lying off the southeastern New Guinea coast. Without substantial numbers of Fortresses and Liberators, the only bombing force available remained Kenney's medium bombers: B-25 Mitchells, B-26 Marauders, and A-20 Havocs. American possession of the two islands allowed the mediums, and their fighter escorts, to put the northern Solomons and Rabaul under air attack. Taken together Task Two would encompass thirteen separate operations, so many that they resembled the spokes of the overall plan's codename, Cartwheel. But before the wheel rolled an event occurred having implications for both the Americans and the Japanese.[1]

The Fifth Air Force had already moved against the Japanese after the investment of Buna in January 1943. With its fall the Fifth Air Force traveled north, but not before fighting a critical battle in the watery sound between New Britain and New Guinea. In March Army B-24 reconnaissance craft spotted a large Japanese convoy moving to reinforce MacArthur's next targets, Lae and Salamau. Kenney cut orders sending the full weight of the Fifth against the convoy. In a sense this was a test for his aircraft, tactics, and "kids."

Flying newly-modified, heavily gunned B-25 Mitchells, A-20 Havocs, and accompanied by RAAF Beauforts, the Americans and Australians savaged the convoy with mast-high skip-bombing attacks. With enemy ships damaged or sinking, the force returned, finishing them with bombs and the survivors with machine-gun fire. Above the carnage, P-38s wheeled about, fending off over 100 Japanese Navy fighters of the Eighth Fleet as they attempted to break up the bomber attacks. In four days much of the convoy had gone down and over 3,664 Japanese soldiers had died. A relative hush fell over the Guinea coast.

The Battle of the Bismarck Sea profoundly rocked the Japanese Army back at Rabaul. By mid-March they ordered that resupply of their New Guinea troops would only take place at night and then only by barge or lugger. This clearly denied sufficient materials to army units on the big island and, unacknowledged, essentially wrote them off. The Imperial Japanese Army left behind men who had nothing to lose save honor, and in the name of the Emperor that honor would be let at a very high price.[2]

The air-sea battle confirmed MacArthur's thinking that Kenney would be his cutting edge in the forthcoming campaigns. Denied artillery, heavy bombers, and naval guns and aircraft, General MacArthur settled for medium bombers and fighters deftly wielded by his airman, Kenney. On 6 May 1943, just eight days before MacArthur activated the 475th, he officially sanctioned Kenney's key role in a strategic outline conveyed to Washington:

> The general scheme of maneuver is to advance our bomb line towards Rabaul; first by improvement of presently occupied forward bases; secondly, by the occupation and implementation of air bases which can be secured without committing large forces; and then, by the seizure and implementation of successive hostile airdromes.[3]

As he wrote on, Satan's Angels' mission unfolded.

The success of MacArthur's plan hinged on fighter aviation. The same communique explained how he intended to isolate each intended target by air attacks on all "intermediate hostile installations" that could interdict or reinforce the besieged target. Next, fighters would gain air superiority over, and reduce, those objectives before an actual invasion took place. The final job of the Fifth's fighter arm would come during and after the American attack began, to intercept all Japanese craft attempting to disrupt the proceedings on the ground. The projected action would be directed against a rough arc of Japanese bases beginning with the Wewak airfields on New Guinea's north coast, Kavieng situated on the tip of New Ireland, Rabaul itself, and concluding with

A Douglas A-20 Havoc comes off its run against Japanese shipping. (Anderson Collection)

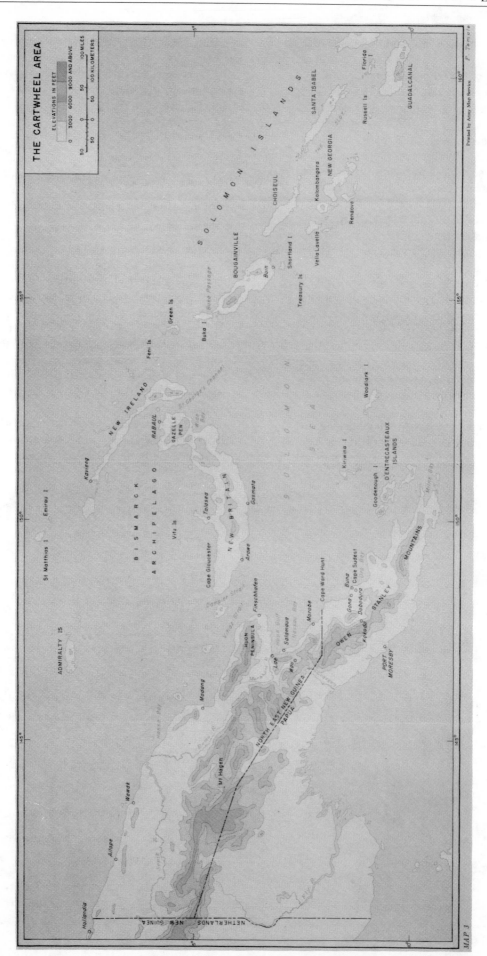

The Islands of Operation Cartwheel. From John Miller, Jr., **Cartwheel: The Reduction of Rabaul,** *United States in World War II series (Washington, D.C.: Office of the Chief of Military History, 1959).*

Kiriwina Island.

Buka Island just off the northern coast of Bougainville. MacArthur would follow this plan with amazing consistency so even before the 475th mobilized, its role had already been set down as tactical dicta.[4]

Responding to the Casablanca Conference's denial of long-range bombers, preliminary operations were directed at seizing and developing Kiriwina and Woodlark Islands as staging bases for raids against Japanese targets. From Woodlark, for instance, Rabaul lay 300 nautical miles away and

Captain Frank D. "Tommy" Tompkins, Clover Squadron's C.O. (Frank D. Tompkins photo)

Buin, at the southern tip of Bougainville, 225. Both islands were unoccupied by the enemy so landings were completed by 23-24 June, with airstrips operational by 18 July.[5]

With island airstrips readied to support strikes at major bases in the Solomons and Rabaul, MacArthur next tended to preparations for the main event, the capture of Lae. His notion of shore-to-shore invasions that bypassed and isolated hostile strongholds was radical enough, but an overlooked key to that strategy revolved around the need for air support based on fields deep within enemy territory. The Lae operation required such facilities: first, to cover the invasion itself and second, to act as a staging area for fighters covering the proposed Wewak attacks. This responsibility fell upon aviation engineer Lieutenant Everett E. Frazier.

In May 1943, Frazier staged out of Wau, an Australian airstrip located twenty-five miles south and east of the Japanese coastal enclave at Salamau. The officer trekked to the doorstep of Salamau without finding suitable ground for an advanced field. Backtracking, he fell in with an Australian officer and some natives. Together they walked northwest. Only fifty miles due west of Lae, Frazier came across a possible site with the romantic name of Marilinan. After surveying the area he walked back out of the bush on 9 June.[6]

At ADVON (Advanced Echelon) Fifth Air Force, Frazier briefed Kenney and his officers. Marilinan's gravest fault, he conceded, was the soil composition which would become a quagmire with the first September rains. Brigadier General Wurtsmith, the V Fighter Command's leader, flew back to Marilinan, reconnoitered the area and finally chose an abandoned strip at Tsili Tsili, four miles away, as the advanced fighter field. Under the noses of the Japanese, Army engineers covertly developed Tsili Tsili. They were aided by a decoying move, the renovation of the airstrip at Bena Bena some miles away near the Ramu Valley. In time Satan's Angels would come to know both fields well.

MacArthur sought to isolate Salamau while attacking her sister garrison at Lae with a shore-to-shore, seaborne invasion launched from Buna. Within easy interdiction range, the more northerly Japanese complex of Wewak airbase, with its three satellite fields of Boram, But, and Dagua, threatened the projected Lae invasion. The Fifth Air Force's assignment lay in shutting down those dangerous dromes and Satan's Angels had to defend the Army Air Forces bombers in that critical task. Therefore, while events both large and small set seal on the recapture of New Guinea, activities back at Amberly feverishly sought to transform that new group into a combat outfit.

The focus of training centered on the intricate task of melding veteran and neophyte pilots into a cohesive unit employing the new P-38. The "old" New Guinea hands had combat experience in the P-39s, P-40s, and for a quarter of them, P-38s. The stateside pilots had some Lightning time but no combat experience. Major Prentice handed this contradictory situation to his three squadron commanders: Amberly's earliest arrival and former 49th Group pilot Captain Frank A. Nichols, C.O. of the 431st Squadron; Captain Frank D. "Tommy" Tomkins, late of the 8th Group and now the

432nd's head; and Captain Martin L. Low, from Prentice's P-38-equipped 39th Squadron of the 35th FG, now leading the Angel's 433rd Squadron.

In short order the three officers implemented a vigorous training schedule roughly modeled after the Army Air Forces system. Lacking enough aircraft, they divided the pilots into two groups, morning and afternoon sections. While one flew, the other studied, reversing their roles at midday. During training the 475th laid groundwork for their early and sustained excellence in air combat.[7]

Continued flight training composed half of the two-month regimen at Amberly. Unlike Nichol's and Hood's earlier, highly irregular, one-hour checkout on the Lightning, a regular familiarization schedule cycled both old and new pilots through its intricacies. Generally speaking the air training consisted of both basic and combat flying because the pilots varied in ability, although all had survived the wartime Air Forces' wash-out rate of forty percent in pilot training. Veterans emphasized the fighting tactics for elements, flights, squadrons, and groups, but the flexibility of the SWPA air war could be also seen in the necessity of escort, bombing, and strafing exercises as well.

Prentice made no assumptions about his pilots' knowledge of their airplane. They studied aircraft functions under combat situations and at Amberly most took and passed an examination on the P-38's idiosyncrasies written by the group's Operations Officer, veteran pilot Captain Meryl M. Smith. The first third tested the pilot's knowledge of the operating limits of the Lightning, such as propeller adjustments, manifold pressures, and mixture controls among other items. The last two-thirds of the examination asked questions about common procedures and problems. A few examples demonstrate the nature of these concerns:

22. Why shouldn't maneuver flaps be used in combat?;
26. What would you do if your nose wheel blew out on landing?;

and a perennial topic of concern,

V. If [an] engine failed on takeoff, explain, in the proper order, the steps you would take.

This vital graduate course in combat flying would post big dividends for the 475th in the future.[8]

The Amberly interlude also imparted critical tactical information to the neophyte pilots. In a sense, the most important and difficult part of combat operations lay in the passing of experience on to the beginner. The way men fought each other in the skies largely reflected the theater of operations, the enemy's planes, pilots, and tactics, all superimposed on established doctrines that guided their own air force. Success generally went to that side which could most quickly modify its aircraft and tactics to meet and then defeat the opposition.

At the 475th's inception the New Guinea veterans acted as a collective intelligence. Their experiences were distilled and distributed at the blackboard, in "poop" sheets, and on the flight line. The message, in all its myriad forms, was simple: learn these rules and live. That the teachers were serious there was little doubt, knowing as they did the supreme price paid to secure them.[9]

The tale of America's air war in the Pacific had not been a happy one, partly because of obsolete fighters and faulty tactics. Both had their roots in the history of air warfare. The 1914-1918 War resulted in two approaches to fighter design: a light, nimble craft characterized by the Nieuports and Sopwith Camels, and powerful but less maneuverable machines as seen in SE-5s and Spads. This distinction was so well known that the U.S. Air Corps fighter texts of the 1920s and 1930s generically classified aircraft as from either the "Camel" or "Spad" schools.

The Japanese favored the "Camel" school because their earliest design influences came after World War I with the arrival of the British Semphill Mission in 1921, including Herbert Smith, a former designer from Sopwith, the firm that had produced the Camel. By the 1930s Japan's military men eyed expansive plans, the Army on the East Asian continent, the Navy in the Pacific. Long-range air power dominated the requirements for both bombers and pursuits, and given foreign influences and military demands, produced a long line of agile, long-range fighters.

By 1937 the relatively low horsepower of Japan's radial engines forced design compromises in order to comply with specifications. The resultant fighters, both from the Navy's supplier, Mitsubishi, and the Army's, Nakajima, were light, aerobatic, and far flying. As in all things technical, the A6M2 Zero-Sen and the Ki-43 Oscar traded off several assets to achieve their sparkling performance. Chief amongst them, armor, heavier armament, and self-sealing gas tanks.

The lack of those items, and the general non-use of parachutes, later bolstered an American belief in a Japanese indifference to life. From a different perspective, however, their choices were sensible. The original Japanese pilots in 1941 had vast experience, the Navy fliers, for instance, averaging 700 flying hours by the time they faced Americans in the Pacific. Combat to the Japanese simply meant winning, and that predicated on a superior, offensive aircraft that could beat safer but inferior pursuits. Parachute straps hampered movement in the compact cockpits of the Japanese fighters so they too were discarded. Furthermore, under the modern *Bushido* code the Japanese made no allowance for prisoners; a pilot downed was a pilot dead making all else superfluous.

As long as the caliber of pilots remained high and the Zeroes and Oscars stayed on par with the enemy aircraft the Japanese could hold to their philosophy, but as more of their veterans died in disputed heavens and as improved American fighters appeared, the deficiencies of their mounts became more apparent. That, however, came in the future. Early on the "Wild Eagles" of Japan rampaged under Pacific skies.

The Army Air Corps faced different problems. They too confronted the "Camel"-"Spad" dilemma. Through 1932, and the employment of the beloved Boeing P-26 "Peashooter," the air arm continued the dogfighting machine but two years later a hybrid pursuit, Consolidated's two-seat P-30, decisively ended the Camel tradition. A specialized airplane meant to escort bombers or serve as a rearguard to pursuit formations, the P-30's sleek, all-metal monoplane form brought American fighting craft into modern times. Envisioned to work at 15,000 to 25,000 feet, the P-30 also sported oxygen, a supercharger, and — an unheard of luxury — a heater. It acted as a prototype for fighters to come.[10]

With bigger engines like Allison's V-1710 series, U.S designers moved towards powerful aircraft that also carried essentials like armor, bulletproof glass, and self-sealing gas tanks. In the process, however, Army pursuits lost their nimbleness. At the start of the Pacific War, World War I's archetypes were recaptured in Japanese and U.S. fighter designs. The agile A6M2 Zero-Sen weighed 2,100 pounds less than the P-40C Tomahawk and 8,387 pounds less than the later J model P-38. Such radical differences emphasized correct tactics for each craft, the fit between design and employment spelling the difference between life and death in combat.

The Japanese fighters nicely conformed to the dominant dogfighting vision of aerial combat in the interwar years. Superbly aerobatic, the Zeroes and Oscars emphasized the classic twisting, turning evolutions of the Great War era. The American Air Corps also practiced the same classic tactics but over time their fighters got heavier, their maneuvers slowed. Without knowledge of Japanese craft or tactics the fighter arm went into battle unprepared to fly against the Japanese.

The early defeats of the Philippines, Java, and the Darwin-Port Moresby defense have been mentioned. Importantly, pilots like later Lieutenant Colonel Boyd D. "Buzz" Wagner survived, and in their survival painfully realized that given the technical differences and limitations between fighters, old ways had to be discarded. By the March 1942 air battles over Australia, the Yankee pilots had already begun to evolve successful counters.

Again and again a critical lesson came back to the Army pilots: you could not dogfight with Japanese fighters. Their turn, loop, and climbing abilities were extraordinarily quick, and attempts to stay with the enemy in any such evolutions courted a quick end. Instead, the Americans sought to use their heavier weight and firepower by plunging on hostile craft, firing, and then breaking off battle by diving away, only to climb again for another pass.[11]

While the tactics worked, minimizing losses, U.S. fighters severely limited offensive tactics because they lacked proper supercharging. Both the P-40 and the A6M2 variant Zero had a single speed, single stage supercharger, but again the enemy's lighter weight gave higher altitude performance. After May 1942, the P-39 Airacobra and P-40 Warhawk fared even worse, lacking any supercharging at all. The worn P-40s and 39s never got near their service ceilings, the Curtiss 'Hawks staggering to 20,000 feet, the 'Cobras 2,000 to 3,000 feet below that mark.[12]

Heights then often dictated the air combat over New Guinea. American veterans remembered those days. Seen from a distance the opposing forces approached, the Japanese forever higher than their enemy and flying in loose arrowhead "vics" of three. As the Zeroes swarmed down the American formations climbed to meet them in head-on attacks, fighters slowing as engines lost power in the thinner air. After the initial clash individual combat broke out, the Americans trying to gain altitude for hit-and-run strikes against the Japanese, the Japanese seeking to entice the Army airmen into a fight by maneuver. When either side found itself threatened they used opposite tactics to extricate themselves, the Japanese hauling into breathtaking climbs, the Americans breaking off by sharply diving away. This created a weird scene of machines hurtling up or down in the midst of a swirling melee. As always smoky plumes marked the paths of the losers. But from those fights came the lessons taught at Amberly.[13]

The foremost problem concerned transferring tactics created for the less capable P-39 and P-40 to the new P-38. The answer was simple. All those American aircraft commonly shared two factors, heavier weight and less agility than the Japanese opposition. Therefore much of the hard-bought tactics of earlier days applied to the Lightning as well. Now, however, with superior altitude and climb rates the P-38s could go on the offensive.

Fresh from the New Guinea air war, the veterans emphasized tactics that did the job and allowed pilots to come home again. Like all good rules the basics were simple and, though modified on occasion, essentially remained the same throughout the war. Amberly provided the time to contemplate and practice the pilot's role in air fighting.

Prentice and his lieutenants hammered home two cardinal rules, the two-craft element and constant vigilance. The element constituted the irreducibly smallest fighting unit in the Army Air Forces, a primary "shooter" guarded by his wingman. It received emphasis because the evolution of that simple formation had cost the air arm many men and airplanes before its adoption, and like all things of value it was jealously guarded and preserved. World War I spawned aerial combat and its romanticized practitioner, the ace, the solitary knight of the skies. The Great War eventually produced team tactics, but the airborne duelist embodied that conflict's notion of air fighting.

The strength of that image stayed strong as long as postwar fighters attempted to reproduce the lively fighters of the 1914-1918 period. Formation flying was practiced, but until the 1930s pilots assumed that once combat broke out fighting reverted back to the one-on-one melee of the previous war. By the mid-1930s the great protagonist of fighter aviation, Captain Claire Lee Chennault, advocated a trio of airplanes flying as a unit; and he toured the nation with his "Three Men on a Trapeze" exhibition that graphically demonstrated its possibilities. A number of problems, however, denied that configuration as the fundamental fighting instrument, including more powerful, less sensitive pursuits, immense training times necessary to perfect such coordination, and, most critically, the difficulties of keeping three craft in formation during combat.[14]

The development of the element is hard to trace. Werner

Molders of the Luftwaffe pioneered it during the Spanish Civil War but no evidence exists that the Air Corps noted or implemented that innovation. Sporadic squadron-level attempts at the two-fighter element occurred in the late 1930s, but it was not until World War II, and the subsequent Battle of Britain, that the Army Air Forces adopted that formation. By then, ex-RAF "Eagle Squadron" pilots sometimes returned to the states advocating the importance of mutually supporting pursuits.[15]

Plunged into the Pacific War, America's lack of experience cost her heavily in fighter pilots. Inexperienced and employing peacetime tactics, the Army had to learn from trial and error. Former 49th Group C.O. and Commander of the V Fighter Command, Brigadier General Wurtsmith receives credit for first implementing the two-plane element in the defense of Darwin early in 1942. From then to Amberly and afterward it remained the cornerstone of the Vth's fighter pilots.

A group pamphlet pithily summed up the second rule: ". . . put your head [on] a swivel." Constant watchfulness marked the fighter trade from its beginnings because the side that spotted the opposition first could maneuver to a killing position. The importance of the lesson redoubled because the

The jungle rimming Port Moresby. (Anderson Collection)

Lightning was a hefty fighter with an unmistakable silhouette, its passage clearly seen in tropic skies.

Pilots also received special caution on a blind spot particularly favored by the Japanese — a climbing attack from the rear. Warrant Officer Saburo Sakai, Japan's highest scoring, surviving ace, called the approach, "my own favorite tactic, coming up from under." The twin booms and horizontal stabilizer, plus the cockpit's position on and flanked by the wings, obscured much of the downward vision. Tactical formations were fashioned to maximize observation to the rear but it all came down to the never ending sweep of a pilot's eye.[16]

Other admonitions reflected accumulated air-fighting lessons passed on to the neophytes. Combat air speed received much attention because the P-38's chief advantages lay in superior altitude and swiftness. Altitude allowed a high vantage point, reaction time as the enemy labored to engagement levels, and speed in a diving attack. Barring the suicidal inclination of turning with a Zero or an Oscar, the next greatest threat came when a 38 driver allowed maneuvers to, unnoticed, slowly bleed off knots. Despite a superior terminal speed, the big eight-ton Lightning could not out accelerate Japanese fighters. Slowing down in combat gave the enemy an advantage of a sudden surge translated into evasive maneuverings or closing to firing range. The absolute minimum most veterans allowed was 200 to 250 miles per hour in all combat situations. One pass at speed, escape, maneuver to attack again, and live to fight another day: the classic dive and run maneuver that now formed the crux of the 475th's air fighting tactics.

Amberly was two months of flying and study. The rules imparted and absorbed at Amberly were deceptively simple and only the experienced pilot cadre knew they had been bought and paid for in American lives over the Philippines, Java, Australia, and New Guinea. Out of those two months came a well-trained fighter group that lacked but one thing, experience, and that came soon enough.

On 4 August the 475th received a terse radiogram from V Fighter Command. It was "mandatory," the message read, "that air echelon[,] your group[,] arrive SCARAMOUCHE August 10." It was signed by Wurtsmith. "SCARAMOUCHE" was the strangely theatrical codeword for New Guinea. To old hands, however, Wurtsmith's call to arms meant the 475th was simply going "north," a direction synonymous with war.[17]

By 5 August 1943 the 475th's water echelons had begun traveling north, their eventual destination the complex of airfields scattered around Port Moresby. The air echelons followed in C-47 transports and six days later reunited at their assigned fields: the 431st Squadron at Twelve Mile Strip; the 432nd at Ward's Drome; and the 433rd arriving by 16 August at Jackson's Drome. Simultaneously, Lightning pilots ferried 115 of their own fighters. Despite a few accidents, including the loss of a pilot and his craft at Mareba, Australia, most arrived safely at their respective bases.[18]

The names for the the Moresby fields were legion. All were named for their distance from the port. Some, like Ward's and

Working up a Lightning at Dobodura. Note the primitive conditions, but the "Line" kept 80% of the group's P-38s operational.

Below: A B-25 pulls off But Drone, part of the Wewak complex. End of the runway terminates on the sea. The indentation on the beach reveals huts and circular pits, possibly ack-ack positions. (Cortner Collection)

But Drone

Jackson's Dromes, honored persons. The Australians further confused the issue by also using native place names, such as Fourteen Miles Drome's alternate title Laloki, standing as it did on the banks of a like-named river.[19]

The move to the combat zone, the first of many, produced its usual share of dislocations. The 431st Squadron drew Twelve Mile Strip and immediately ran into problems. The single 4,800-foot runway hacked out of the jungle possessed enough length for takeoffs and landings, but just barely. Scattered trees at the end of the strip were an added inducement to clear the ground promptly on takeoff.

Under the best conditions Twelve Mile was marginal but most of the Wewak Campaign had to be fought from Moresby bases. The P-38s needed at least two 165-gallon drop tanks for a Wewak strike and the additional weight and drag made any launching from Twelve Mile a memorable event. After grazing a few trees, the pilots settled on as fast a takeoff as possible with 15 to 20 degrees of flap for increased lift. This proved satisfactory though no one ever took takeoffs for granted at that jungle field.[20]

Added to the problems manifested by its length, Twelve Mile had been designed for single-engine fighters, mostly P-39s and P-40s. The revetments and dispersal areas scattered around its perimeter were perilously small for the big Lightnings. In time the mechanics damaged three aircraft as they maneuvered them in the predawn dark preparing them for missions. Despite those mishaps, however, one crew chief estimated that usually 80 percent of the P-38s stood combat ready at Twelve Mile Strip.[21]

By 12 August the 475th had received orders to begin their

combat missions. Bad weather aborted that first mission and the next two followed uneventfully. On 16 August, however, the group was blooded over Wewak.

Fifth Air Force leaders had watched the Wewak complex carefully through July and early August. Their caution stemmed from two sources. Kenney wanted Tsili Tsili completed and stocked, ready to receive escorting fighters during the anticipated struggle to reduce Wewak. Equally important, when the Fifth struck Kenney wanted the fields filled with enemy craft so his raiders wrecked both airplanes and facilities. Bombing targets all around the object of his attention, the man bided his time.

On 30 July photo "recon" craft revealed only nineteen Japanese bombers at the dromes but Kenney's photo interpreters pointed out vigorous repair and construction at all four fields. Patiently the parent Fifth waited and was rewarded on 4 August with pictures now showing a mixed bag of over 100 craft scattered among all the strips except Boram. Kenney gambled and ordered no attacks. On 13 August circumstances galvanized the Fifth into action. Its two groups of painfully accumulated B-24s reported ready as did fifty-eight B-25s from its two medium groups. Tsili Tsili opened its runway and supplies to any escorting fighters. Gratifyingly, Wewak and its satellites brimmed with enemy craft, 199 bombers and fighters of the Japanese Fourth Air Army. Word flashed. On 16 August Wewak was to be struck.

The bombing attacks on Wewak were of limited success, at least in part because of a large number of aborted flights due to mechanical failures. On that day the 475th's Hades Squadron, the 431st, drew transport escort duty to Tsili Tsili, 300 miles from Wewak. At 1515, First Lieutenant David W. Allen, flying in the trailing high cover flight, sighted a bogey to the west of the field. The 431st smoothly wheeled towards the unidentified craft by making a swing around the strip. Five minutes passed, then a Japanese formation appeared above and to the left.

Here, at first combat, the months of Amberly training paid out handsome profits. These were no green pilots led by veterans, but instead a trained unit wise to the ways of air fighting. Allen's narrative clearly demonstrates the sophisticated skills imparted in Australia. The first and second flights attacked. The lieutenant's flight, responsible for guarding their comrades' struggle below, visually cleared the area and then, seeing no more intruders, dove into the fight.

Allen's first kill spoke of lessons imparted and learned:

Entering the combat I was able to get a couple of snap shots at two Zeroes before I shot the right wing off and [sic] Oscar who was turning into my flight leader.

The Oscar did not burn, but went down spinning. The report indicates at least two facets of the Pacific air war. Allen's "snap shots" at the two Zeroes indicate a firm adherence to the no dogfighting rule. There was no maneuvering with the Japanese. Commonly, American pilots usually got no more than one burst at each enemy airplane either in a deflection shot, as the hostile aircraft fleetingly flashed across the P-38's

axis of flight, or as the Lightning closed from the rear. Even in the classic tail-chase position, single bursts ruled the day because the Americans fired at a turning Wild Eagle only as long as they could lead the Japanese in their gunsights. As the enemy's turn tightened and he slipped from view, the Army airmen broke off combat and with their surplus speed pulled away for another pass. Allen's notes show a clear understanding of, and adherence to, the standing tactical rules.

Secondly, the passage highlights the essence of the 475th's success, teamwork. Despite the confusion of battle Allen saw veteran flight leader Captain Harry W. Brown in trouble and destroyed his attacker. Nor was this an isolated incident. A moment later a Japanese fighter made a high-side pass on the lieutenant, but even as he turned into the attack, a P-38 broke clear and fired on the enemy craft. Allen concluded his flight by shooting down a "Kate-type" divebomber on the way to the squadron's rendezvous point. Taken together, Hades Squadron's combat debut revealed a fighting machine honed razor sharp. The Japanese left behind ten fighters and two bombers shattered in the jungles around Tsili Tsili. The 431st sustained only two damaged fighters and Satan's Angels were now opened for business.

The 17 August Wewak strike again saw no action but the 432nd Squadron's Diary recorded a problem that was to plague the group for months. Most pilots in the 475th, veteran and beginner alike, had accumulated little flight time in the Lockheed Lightning. Despite good internal gasoline storage and drop tanks, the fliers had not yet experimented with the fuel mixtures and rpm (revolutions per minute) settings that conserved fuel on long-distance missions. Flying out of Moresby and having to cross the towering Owen Stanley Range, out and back, made cruise control instruction even more pressing. Mission 6 uncovered this fact when five of the sixteen escorts, almost one-third of the squadron, had to land at Tsili Tsili for, as the 432nd's diarist deemed it, "a spot of petrol." One of the group's most experienced pilots, Major Albert W. Schinz, led the pack that topped off their tanks, indicating a general problem with long-range missions. The problem of efficient gas usage would not be solved until 1944 with the arrival of civilian Charles A. Lindbergh.[22]

Whereas the Tsili Tsili raids of the sixteenth and the Wewak attack of the seventeenth encountered "nil" opposition, Mission 7 on the eighteenth saw Wewak swarm with defenders. The Japanese response puzzled the men of the Fifth Air Force, with major attacks going uncontested while other seemingly secondary strikes provoked vicious responses. Basically this resulted from stretched enemy air resources and the twin drives of MacArthur and Nimitz to the east in the Solomons. This forced the Japanese to shift their aircraft rapidly from Truk in the Central Pacific to Rabaul, and then to either theater the Americans chose to attack. On the eighteenth, the Japanese were present in force.[23]

That raid would distinguish itself on several counts. B-25 pilot Major Ralph Cheli won the Medal of Honor when he insisted on completing his strafing run on Dagua despite a flaming right engine and numerous hits that wrecked his craft. He crashed in the ocean upon completing his attack.

"Satan's Angels" in route formation, April 1944. Notice "Tail-end Charlie" in the trailing flight is missing — again. (Cortner Collection)

There were no survivors. On a happier note, the 432nd drew first blood when Captain William M. Waldman splashed a Zero as it attacked American bombers over Wewak. Mission 7 also introduced one of the stellar 475th pilots to combat for the first time. His name was Lieutenant Thomas B. "Mac" McGuire, Jr.[24]

The 431st Squadron, to which McGuire belonged, got briefed the night before, part of a maximum effort that would send seventy-four Lightnings out to protect the Fifth's medium and heavy bombers. Group formations were discussed with two dominating the mission. By mid-1943 fighter formations had grown in sophistication and efficiency. On the way to their rendezvous with the bombers Satan's Angels adopted a "route formation," stepped up diamonds of four flights with flight two above, behind, and flanking the leader's diamond; flight three configured the same but opposite two flight and, 100-150 feet lower than the leader's group. Flight four was "Tail-End Charlie," highest of all the flights and trailing behind, responsible for protecting the squadron from stern attacks. Route formations afforded maximum vision, concentration of firepower, and critically on long flights, ease of flying. Group missions simply reproduced squadron formations, substituting whole sixteen-ship squadrons for flights.[25]

After rendezvousing with the bombers the 475th took up escort positions anywhere from fifty to twenty-five miles from the target. Bomber altitudes varied with target and weather conditions but usually flew at 15,000 to 20,000 feet. On Mission 7 McGuire's 431st Squadron flew point, a vanguard position 5,000 feet lower than the main force and a distance ahead. Theirs was a spoiling mission, to report enemy defenses, trigger any aerial ambushes, or at least force defending enemy interceptors to commit to combat at lower altitudes. Behind them the B-25s flew on, a squadron of P-38s now on each flank 2,000 to 5,000 feet higher, with wingmen spread wider now and slightly trailing their leaders, poised to follow them in attack. The entire mass had cover from the trailing high squadron that protected all from attacks from the rear and broke up Japanese thrusts from above.

At 0945 the Hades Squadron swept over Wewak first and was immediately jumped by Navy Zeroes. McGuire's flight provided rear coverage but counted only three aircraft having sent the fourth limping home with mechanical problems. At 8,000 feet a Zero rolled in for a diving pass forty-five degrees off the front. With its deadly gun package, Mac confidently turned his P-38 head-on into the attack. The fighters passed.

*Francis J. Lent later became a captain and an eleven victory ace.
(Anderson Collection)*

Nicely judging his timing McGuire reefed his mount around and fired two long bursts that torched the Zero, sending it down.

Meanwhile McGuire's wingman, future ace Lieutenant Francis J. Lent, called for help; another Zero had latched onto his tail and they swept through space in a deadly game of tag. McGuire located his hapless comrade and drove the enemy off with several bursts. Again teamed up, Mac went into a left-hand circuit, spotted another Zero and attacked. With Lent faithfully guarding him, McGuire chased the frantically twisting fighter towards the waiting flak at Dagua, getting off several shots until one burst scattered tiny sparks of bullet strikes all around the Zero's canopy. As he broke off, Lent reported seeing the Navy craft nose down and crash in flames Number two.

Pulling up and away, McGuire and Lent made another head-on attack on a Zeke (the Allied codename for a Zero) but the Japanese steadfastly held a collision course despite exchanges of fire linking the two approaching craft. A split second before impact, Mac dove beneath the onrushing fighter, both feeling and seeing their left wings brush in passing. Together leader and wingman closed on another Zero over the sea off the end of Dagua's runway but it escaped and the two retired, the light and heavy ack-ack described as "intense."

Engaging yet another Zeke that attempted to outclimb the Lightnings, Lent bore in, hammering pieces off the stumbling fighter until it exploded in midair. Low on fuel and ammunition, McGuire and Lent cautiously withdrew from the violence surrounding Wewak. As three Mitchells turned off their bomb runs, the two P-38s fell into escort positions for the trip home.

Ten minutes out of the target area a fast, inline-engine fighter pounced on the formation. It was the best Japanese Army fighter produced thus far in the war, Kawasaki's Ki-61 *Hien* or Swallow. Upon its combat introduction in New Guinea five months earlier, the sleek fighter sported a copy of one of the world's best liquid-cooled engines, the Daimler-Benz twelve cylinder DB601-A. Faster and heavier but less handy than Zeroes and Oscars, its arms still lacked punch with the standard twin 7.7 millimeter machine-guns and two 20 millimeter cannons or 12.7 millimeter machine-guns. The Allies codenamed it "Tony" and did not underestimate its strength.[26]

McGuire noted the Tony "appeared quite fast," the mot-

"Harrying the North," the Fifth Air Force batters Wewak. (Dennis G. Cooper Collection)

ed green, yellow, and brown fighter starting a pass at the -25s but the P-38s turned into his attack. McGuire fired nort, economical bursts, hits splashing the sleek fighter until fell off smoking, the bomber boys later confirming its crash nto the ocean. After topping off tanks at Marilinan, McGuire ew home to Moresby. A three-victory start marked his, and ne 475th's, rise to greatness in the Southwest Pacific Area.[27]

The raids against Wewak continued through the end of ugust. A major engagement took place on the twenty-first, 1ission 10. Heavy clouds caused the high cover to separate om the B-25s. At 1005 the low flight was struck hard by apanese defenders, their calls for help reaching the 431st's 3lue, White, and Red high cover flights just as they reached ne target area. Diving, they encountered hostile craft stacked rom 3,000 to 9,000 feet. The three flights immediately ttacked; after the initial pass the squadron and group contin- ed their team tactics with good effect, but mistakes were still eing made.

First Lieutenant David Allen saw two P-38s fail to turn nside an Army Oscar. He picked up the airplane just as the ightnings broke off the attack and with the speed he picked p in diving, fired a long burst as the enemy aircraft swung round in front of the big onrushing fighter. Burning, the apanese fighter plunged down. Allen nailed a Zero out over ne sea but left it smoking when jumped by another Zeke. A quadron mate confirmed its crash. Allen used standard vasive procedures: a jinxing dive to gain initial speed and hen a shallow, erratic climb back to height. West of Dagua,

the lieutenant spotted his squadron C.O., Captain Frank Nichols, closely pursued by one Zero with one more on the way. Again teamwork paid off when Allen rolled left and into the enemy fighter, opening fire at very close range with murderous results: "the ship [fell] apart just behind the cockpit." By 1025 the raiders departed and Mission 10 ended.[28]

By month's end the Fifth Air Force had completed its primary mission, neutralizing the Wewak dromes. Kenney claimed 200 aircraft destroyed on the ground, but the AAFHQ reduced this to 175. Postwar Japanese records halved that claim. However, Japanese air commanders also stated that their air resources never recovered from the raids and that afterwards "the prospects of the New Guinea opera- tion [were] much gloomier." Sporadic attacks would contin- ue as the enemy occasionally staged out of the strips, but never again as a permanent base of operations. Well educated at Amberly and well led in combat, Satan's Angels' debut made them a group to contend with. Sixteen missions com- posed of 257 individual sorties gained the neophyte group forty-one victories at the cost of three of their own pilots and planes. Counting auxiliary missions accomplished during the Wewak campaign, the 475th raised the score to fifty-three confirmed kills.[29]

The collapse of Wewak paved the way for MacArthur's successful invasion of Lae on 4 September. From that day on bomber escort missions were laced with combat air patrols over the invasion sites, sixty sorties flown on the first day

The 475th Fighter Group, 431 Squadron, over Lae, New Guinea, late in March 1944. (Anderson Collection)

alone. The only two Allied fighter control stations on the north coast lay at Dobodura and Tsili Tsili. Their ranges were too distant for effective radar coverage of Lae. A radar picket destroyer, the *USS Reid*, codenamed "Duckbutt," steamed along the invested beaches and provided early warning and directional information for the Army fighters in the skies above.

Lae set the stage for a series of quick moves which the 475th protected. On 5 September American paratroopers jumped into Nadzab, northwest of Lae, locale for a future airbase and a barrier to any escaping Japanese troops who chose the Markham Valley route. Satan's Angels flew protective cover for the C-47s of the 54th Troop Carrier Wing as they delivered the 503rd Paratroop Regiment to its drop zones, little realizing that Nadzab would be their home in the near future.

The ground campaigns came to unexpectedly swift ends. On 13 September Salamau fell to a combined American-Australian force, with Lae succumbing three days later. The generally weak Japanese defense encouraged MacArthur's planners to move up their timetable, reslating Finschhafen for 22 September. Finschhafen lay at the tip of an easterly bulge called the Huon Peninsula. Sixty-four miles north of Lae, the port was the nearest point to New Britain Island, home of Rabaul and MacArthur's ultimate goal under his Cartwheel plan.

On D-Day 22 September, shortly after noon, three P-38 squadrons were relieved of beach patrol duties by two more Lightning units. Just as they broke to return to base, the *Reid* reported a large group of bogies inbound at seventy miles. The original patrol had an hour's fuel remaining so all five squadrons climbed above the invasion convoy and waited.

The Japanese came in strength, approximately 20-30 twin-engine "Betty" bombers and 30-40 fighters. Clover Squadron, the 432nd, dove to 5,000 feet, two flights scissoring in among the bombers and the American anti-aircraft fire. By air combat standards it was a very long fight, over forty-five

minutes. When the enemy finally cleared the area, they lef eighteen fighters and bombers behind. The 432nd lost tw P-38s and one pilot. In total, the 475th Lightning patrol dispatched ten bombers and twenty-nine fighters. Wurtsmith sent a commendation to the group and the day closed with huge party. With local air supremacy secured, ground troop captured Finschhafen by 2 October. Task Two of Cartwhee was nearly complete.[30]

While Satan's Angels carried war to Wewak, the wate echelon sailed to Oro Bay, gateway to the group's home fo the next seven months, Dobodura. By 14 October the ad vanced party surveyed the site for their future base, an ope Kunai grass plain bound on one side by low, steep hills and o the others by the shallow arms of a stream that flowed amon vine-encrusted trees and dense underbrush. Later in the da the 433rd touched down, the first of the Dobodura-base 475th group. While the 431st and the 432nd Squadron harried the north, "Dobo" slowly took shape.[31]

The Army Air Forces had begun building Dobodura i support of the Buna operation in November 1942. The futur home of the 475th lay fifteen miles from Buna Station, a hug grassy plain capable of supporting several runways an dispersals. In a month and a half four strips crossed the Kuna expanse. From then on Dobodura grew into the major ad vanced base for North Coast air operations.[32]

The "Fightin' Blue Devils" (also later known as Possun Squadron) of the 433rd Squadron moved directly to Dob from Amberly. In lulls between Wewak and the opening o the Rabaul campaign, the other two squadrons departed th Moresby dromes and flew across the Owen Stanleys to thei new nest at Dobodura, the 432nd on 31 August, the 431st on October. Once there, all worked to establish a home.[33]

Dobo proved a better base than Moresby. Takeoffs an landings were easier and its location limited the suprem hazard, the requisite crossing of the Owen Stanleys to an from targets. While hardly a tropical paradise, the base ha been established for a time and the 475th would remain ther

Hades Squadron being briefed on escorting General Douglas MacArthur over the Nadzab drop zone. (Anderson Collection)

A rare inflight photograph of a Clover Squadron P-38 taken by C. J. Rieman from inside his own Lightning. Nice detail shot of the old style turbocharger intakes on the H model fighter is seen in the foreground. (Anderson Collection)

475th mess facilities at Oro Bay, just before moving to Dobodura. (Anderson Collection)

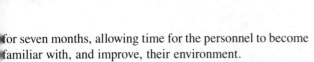

Typical personal tent at "Dobo," October 1943. This one belonged to Sergeant James Fazzi. (Anderson Collection)

The theater at "Dobo." (Anderson Collection)

for seven months, allowing time for the personnel to become familiar with, and improve, their environment.

The headquarters, administrative facilities, clubs, mess, and living quarters were located two miles from and to the side of the dispersal areas and the runway. Headquarters occupied the corner of a rough rectangle, the living areas of the 431st and 432nd Squadrons side-by-side and laying out one long side, the 433rd filling in the short arm opposite to headquarters. The group worked hard to reproduce, no matter how crudely, the amenities of life. Pilots faced extreme stress with every flight and a comfortable base helped alleviate some of the tension. For the noncommissioned officers and

The alert shack, Dobodura. All 475th squadrons rotated alert duty, aircraft and pilots ready for takeoff to defend the base from air attacks. (Cortner Collection)

Dobo. Despite it all, teams sprang up and the crack of bat and catcalls echoed strangely across the Kunai plains. Eb bett's Field had come to New Guinea.

For more serious entertainment the group erected a officers club appropriately named the "Club 38," its addres 475th Dobodura. An open-side, "T" shaped, raised tent, i time it boasted a bar overseen by a traditional mural o fashionably bare ladies, ample seating, and an orchestra "pit." From somewhere they even liberated a striped canop for the entrance, its jaunty welcome curiously out of plac against a jungle backdrop.

Other fundamentals, though, went wanting. The availabil ity of female companionship and liquor was extremely lim ited leaving only one other human drive available, food. Th government provided plentiful food for its G.I.s, but it cam

enlisted men, it was long hours of labor and even longer hours of monotony with no relief to be found in the jungle conditions at Dobodura.

As a team, the group labored to improve the camp. They threw a dam across the stream creating a swimming hole, a relief from the tropical heat at the field. Special Services worked hard to lessen the burdens of the group. Movies came and were screened at the theater, built opposite the 433rd's frontage. They also got sports equipment including gear for America's hallmark — baseball. Major complaints centered on the effect of the humid climate on equipment; mold grew on mitts and rotted lacings, bats deteriorated. More seriously, the baseballs absorbed the moisture making them extremely heavy. To be struck by a line drive was no laughing matter at

Beginning "Club 38," Dobodura, 1943. Much of the work was done by New Guinea natives pictured to the left. (Cortner Collection)

The "demi-mondaines" mural over the bar at "Club 38". (Dennis G. Cooper Collection)

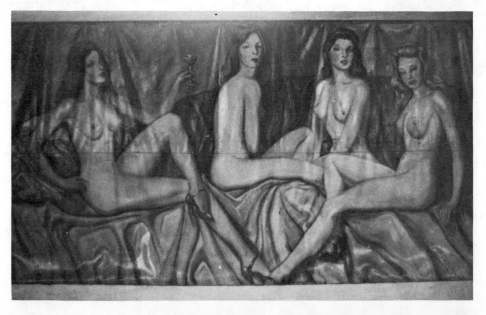

in the form of cans or powder. This helps to explain the comment of a member of the 433rd Squadron, Staff Sergeant Emmett M. Maiers: "Not enough to eat." The 475th's cooks bore the wry title of "The De-canning Section." Prepared without care, meals became a grimly monotonous function akin to washing hands or breathing. At Dobodura, things took a turn for the better. For instance, Cook Corporal Gordon D. Hoxie went to a two-week training course for the preparation of dehydrated foods while at Dobodura. He would soldier on with the group until separated at Korea in November 1945.[34]

Armaments men work on the business end of a Lightning, Dobodura, October 1943. (Anderson Collection)

Based at Moresby, the sheer numbers of men, without liquor to barter, made it difficult for cooks at the distant fighter fields to supplement the standard mess fare. At Dobo, the docks of Oro Bay lay close by and allowed for "scrounging" trips. Men like Sergeant John Ovlasuk daily drove to the docks and supply dumps searching for anything that would spice up the food. Meals also benefited from a brisk trade with the New Guinea natives. The personnel often varied the menu when they went "fishing," their bait, pole, and tackle a standard Army issue hand grenade! Except for holidays like Thanksgiving or Christmas, chow time never elicited much praise, but the cooks and bakers of the 475th did their best with what they had.[35]

Dobodura also had its share of problems and maintenance sat high on the list. Supplies of aircraft parts habitually stayed low, never more than thirty days' supply on hand and service tool kits were virtually nonexistent. Of particular note the H model Lightnings had badly designed drop tank hard points. Upon release the nose of the tanks whipped down and the tanks slashed upwards tearing holes in the wing's trailing edge. The group's sheet metal men worked long hours repairing the damage.

Armaments specialists, like later Technical Sergeant Michael May of the 432nd Squadron, also learned their trade at Dobo. Repairs on guns remained constant and pilots had to be tactfully scolded for overly long bursts that wilted lands and grooves to a mirror-like finish. In September the .50

calibers had problems with jams and shell casings that split their barrels and necks. Ammunition had to be belted up: incendiary, armor piercing, and the favorite amongst many of the Lightning drivers, "the blue-nosed one," Armor Piercing Incendiaries (API).

Tracer bullets remained the center of controversy. The tracer had a white phosphorus mixture in its base that ignited in flight, its trail a wispy white during the day, a fiery streak in the dark. Interspersed among standard rounds, usually at one tracer for every five other bullets, it marked the path of machine-gun fire in aerial gunnery. Or so the theory went. Pilots were divided over the tracer's practicality. It had two major faults. First, as the phosphorus burnt out over distance, its absence changed the bullet's ballistics causing erratic flight. At best the careening trails negating the rounds very purpose — guidance; at worst, the pilot fired at the wrong point in space, missing his target. A second problem involved firing the phosphorus-laden bullet in combat. Men like Prentice argued that tracer fire alerted enemy pilots if the shot missed, causing instant evasive action. The 475th's first C.O. felt so strongly about this point that he forbade tracers completely. Eventually Prentice relented, but the issue still divided pilot opinion.

Lieutenant Morgan Potts, Group Armament Officer, reported a more serious problem involving the Lightning's 20 millimeter cannon. Frequent stoppages hampered early combat. The armorers found a round chambered, its primer cap dented. Upon inspection, no abnormalities could be found on the shell casings, and when test fired the cannons worked normally. Not until December 1943 did they find the culprit, the primers of Lot Number 58424's 20 millimeter shells were of uneven constitution, in some cases double the standard

Lieutenant Donald G. Revenaugh, 433rd, catches a Japanese Helen bomber on his gun camera moments before bringing it down. Rear gunner is seen silhouetted just forward of the vertical stabilizer. (Anderson Collection)

thickness. With the removal of that batch, most cannon problems ended, and the P-38s were given back their heavy-weight punch.

Gun cameras also fell in the armorer's province. Used to verify kills, the original nose-mounted cameras vibrated so badly that nothing could be discerned, heartbreaking when a score depended on film confirmation. The group's armorers jury-rigged cameras on the belly tank shackles and while not a perfect solution, vastly improved the number of confirming frames. Lockheed finally responded by switching their cameras to the same location beginning with the J variant. Other problems arose but gradually the armorers of the group solved them all and contributed greatly to the 475th's success.

Between missions, then, Satan's Angels settled in at Dob-odura. A rhythm established itself as men struggled to adjust to foreign soil. Clothes were turned inside out before going to bed and all shook their shoes before putting them on in the morning because the five-inch scorpions and centipedes inflicted a jolt that could numb a limb for hours. Men sweated out allotted tasks in sun or shade by day, wrote letters, drank coffee during a ceremony called "Smoke" or "Smoko," and slept under a mosquito net at night. Pilots perspired in the cockpit waiting to take off and at altitude then shivered in their damp, sweat-soaked "uniform." The weather was always watched, no matter what the "Met" officer reported. And as summer faded to autumn, men in high places mandated changes that launched the 475th on its next campaign — Rabaul.[36]

FOOTNOTES

1. John Miller, Jr., *Cartwheel: The Reduction of Rabaul*, U.S. Army in World War II series (Washington, D.C.: Office of the Chief of Military History, 1959), pp. 11-19 (hereinafter, Miller, *Cartwheel*); Spector, *Eagle*, pp. 222-26; Craven and Cate, *The Army Air Forces*, vol. IV, pp. 129-35.

2. Edwin P. Hoyt, *Japan's War: The Great Pacific Conflict, 1853 to 1952* (NY: McGraw-Hill Book Co., 1986), p. 323 (hereinafter, Hoyt, *Japan's War*); Miller, *Cartwheel*, p. 41; Spector, *Eagle*, p. 228. The North American B-25 was the dominant medium bomber of the Fifth Air Force. For details of its evolution see Roy Wagner, "The North American B-25 A to G Mitchell," Profile 59 (Berkshire, U.K.: Profile Publications, rpt. ed. 1971), pp. 1-5, and especially p. 8.

3. Miller, *Cartwheel*, p. 28.

4. *Ibid.*; Spector, *Eagle*, p. 228.

5. Miller, *Cartwheel*, pp. 49-59; Craven and Cate, *The Army Air Forces*, vol. IV, pp. 164-65.

6. Spector, *Eagle*, p. 233.

7. *Official History of the 475th Fighter Group*, 4-4710-99 (Maxwell AFB, Montgomery, AL: United States Air Force Historical Research Center, N.D.), frame 652 (hereinafter, *Official History*). The USAF Historical Research Center is the current designation of the Alfred F. Simpson Historical Research Center at Maxwell AFB. Works published before the redesignation will retain the original name as publisher. Lynch, et al., *Satan's Angels*, p. 12; Hood Interview.

8. Hood Interview; *Official History*, frame 688, p. 40, Annex H-3.

9. *Ibid.*

10. Yoshino "Doctrine," pp. 318, 376; Lloyd S. Jones, *The U.S. Fighters: Army-Air Force, 1925-1980's* (Fallbrook, CA: Aero Publishers, 1975), p. 74; Gordon Swanborough and Peter M. Bowers, *United States Military Aircraft Since 1908* (London: Putnam, 1963), pp. 148-49; Ray Wagner, *American Combat Planes*, new rev. ed. (Garden City, NY: Doubleday and Co., 1968), pp. 192, 194; Rene Francillon, *The Mitsubishi Ki-21*, Profile series (Surrey, U.K.: Profile Publications, N.D.), p. 14; Rene Francillon, *The Nakajima Ki-84*, Profile series (Surrey, U.K.: Profile Publications, N.D.), p. 3; Rene Francillon, *The Mitsubishi A6M3 Zero-Sen ("Hamp")*, Profile series (Surrey, U.K.: Profile Publications, N.D.), pp. 3-4; Rubenstein, *Fighter Combat Study*, pp. 2-4; Saburo Sakai, *Samurai!* (NY: Ballantine Books, 1957), pp. 122-23 (hereinafter, Sakai, *Samurai!*).

11. Rubenstein, *Fighter Combat Study*, pp. 11-15; Hood Interview.

12. Hood Interview; Rubenstein, *Fighter Combat Study*, pp. 8, 17-19; Loisel Letter.

13. Hood Interview; Interview: John S. Babel with Author, August 1987 (hereinafter, Babel Interview); Edward L. Maloney, ed., *Fighter Tactics of the Ace's[sic]-S.W.P.A.* (Corona del Mar, CA: World War II Publications, 1978), pp. 43-45 (hereinafter, Maloney, *Fighter Tactics*). *Fighter Tactics* was a much needed reissue of a V Fighter Command confidential publication, A-3 Section, V Fighter Command, *Twelve to One: Fighter Combat Tactics in the SWPA* (N.L.: N.P., 1945). Maloney's edition deleted information on American night fighters and added some photos and information.

14. Claire Lee Chennault, *Way of a Fighter: The Memoirs of Claire Lee Chennault*, ed. by Ray Hotz (NY: G.P. Putnam's Sons, 1949), p. 29.

15. Richard H. Kohn and Joseph P. Harahan, eds., *Air Superiority in World War II and Korea* (Washington, D.C.: Office of Air Force History, 1983), p. 21; Hood Interview.

16. Sakai, *Samurai!*, p. 158.

17. *Official History,* frames 687-88, 713; Hood Interview; for Saburo Sakai's favorite tactic see Sakai, *Samurai!*, p. 150; Henry Sakaida, *Winged Samurai: Saburo Sakai and the Zero Fighter Pilots* (Mesa, AZ: Champlin Fighter Museum Press, 1985), p. 67; File: Leland F. Howerton, "Combat Report of Captain R.D. Van Auken, 13 June 1942" (hereinafter, Howerton File).

18. Straus File: "A Brief History," p. 1; *Official History*, frame 591; Craven and Cate, *The Army Air Forces*, vol. IV, p. 169.

19. Pat Robinson, *The Fight For New Guinea: General Douglas MacArthur's First Offensive* (NY: Random House, 1943), p. 68 (hereinafter, Robinson, *The Fight For New Guinea*).

20. Hood Interview; Letter: John S. Babel to Author, August 1987, p. 4 (hereinafter, Babel Letter).

21. Robinson, *The Fight For New Guinea*, p. 68; Straus Letter, p. 3.

22. Miller, *Cartwheel*, pp. 198-99; Straus File: "Combat Report of 1st Lieutenant David W. Allen, 16 August 1943,"; M.F. Hawkins, *Nakajima B5N "Kate,"* Profile series (Surrey, U.K.: Profile Publications, N.D.), pp. 3-10, *passim*; Lynch, et al., *Satan's Angels*, p. 13; Craven and Cate, *The Army Air Forces*, vol. IV, pp. 178-80; Also note 432nd Squadron Diary, *passim*. On 21 August "many of our planes" had to stop at Marilinan to refuel. For Charles A. Lindbergh's stay with the 475th see chapter 6.

23. Hood Interview; Lynch, et al., *Satan's An-*

gels, p. 13.

24. *AAF*, p. 328; Craven and Cate, *The Army Air Forces*, vol. IV, p. 180; 432nd Squadron Diary, 18 August 1943; Hal Bamford, "Attack on Wewak," *In the Name of Congress* series, no. 14 (November 1959), pp. 34-35.

25. *Official History*, frames 682-3.

26. Green, *Famous Fighters*, pp. 106-109; Maloney, *Fighter Tactics*, *passim*.

27. Straus File: "Individual Combat Report of 1st Lieutenant Thomas B. McGuire, Jr.," 18 August 1943; Hess, *Sweep*, pp. 116-17.

28. Straus File: "Individual Combat Report of First Lieutenant David W. Allen, 21 August 1943"; *Ibid.*, McGuire, 21 August 1943.

29. Miller, *Cartwheel*, p. 199; *Official History*, frame 656; Lynch, et al., *Satan's Angels*, p. 13.

30. Miller, *Cartwheel*, pp. 217-221; Craven and Cate, *The Army Air Forces*, vol. IV, pp. 186-92; Lynch, et al., *Satan's Angels*, p. 14; Hess, *Sweep*, pp. 123-24. For Wurtsmith's commendation see *Official History*, frame 743.

31. *Official History*, frame 659.

32. Craven and Cate, *The Army Air Forces*, vol. IV, p. 119.

33. Lynch, et al., *Satan's Angels*, p. 13; 432nd Squadron Diary, 31 August 1943; *Official History*, frame 658; Letter: Theodore W. Hanks to Henry C. Toll, 8 June 1986.

34. Survey: Overton W. Long, May 1987; Survey: Pierre C. Schoener, May 1987; Survey: Emmett M. Maiers, May 1987; Survey: Gorden D. Hoxie, June 1987.

35. Hood Interview; Straus Letter, p. 5; Lynch, et al., *Satan's Angels*, pp. 79-82; *Official History*, frames 747-48, 750, 757-59.

36. *Official History*, frames 688-89, 690-93; Hood Interview; Babel Letter, p. 4; Survey: Michael May, June 1987; Survey: Leonard E. Midkiff, May 1987.

Chapter Three

"Hardships": Rabaul, October-November 1943

Later, new pilots would ask lanky Captain Chase Brenizer, Jr., of the 433rd Squadron what the Rabaul missions were like. Brenizer would answer with one word: "Hardships," he intoned in his Carolina drawl, "hardships." October opened with no hint of the coming campaign against Rabaul. Bad weather grounded the group from the fifth to the eighth, with the rest of the days through the tenth filing by with alerts, barge-hunting sorties, and constant escort missions to Wewak, Finschhafen, and other points on the Huon Peninsula. Compared to mid-September, the action had slowed.

The 431st was in transition. By 4 October personnel began their move to Dobodura and, while waiting for completion of Airstrip Number 12, bunked in the 432nd's operations and alert buildings. The conditions bore a striking resemblance to "a quiet[,] little madhouse." To the relief of all Hades Squadron vacated the premises five days later.[1]

Also early in October Prentice reassigned the original 433rd Squadron commander Martin Low and promoted Captain Daniel T. Roberts, Jr., to that slot. A former 80th Group member and originally Operations Officer of the 432nd Squadron when Satan's Angels formed at Amberly, Roberts had already established his reputation as a first-rate flier with seven kills to his credit. Slim and soft-spoken, Roberts ". . . was an altogether remarkable man. He did not smoke or drink; he did not use profanity, when its usage was almost universal. He pulled his squadron together and brought it up to superior performance by the power of his personality and by his very able leadership." Victories validated that observation: through August and September the Blue Devil's lagged behind both the 431st and 432nd in kills, with none in the former month and eleven in the latter. In October, with Roberts at the helm, the 433rd outshot the other two squadrons with forty-four victories. His untimely death one month and six days later was a tragedy for his squadron — and the 475th.[2]

The 432nd Squadron's C.O., Major Frank D. Tomkins, remained dissatisfied with the unit's performance, so training flights ruled the tenth day of October. Despite the troops' grousing, Amberly had taught the importance of practice, and practice they did.

On the afternoon of the eleventh, the group's operations and intelligence officers were summoned to H.Q., First Air Task Force, at Dobodura. There they received thorough briefings on the next day's mission. Returning to camp that evening, they gathered the squadrons; on the morrow, the 475th would raid Rabaul for the first time.

* * *

Rabaul. Next to Truk, the "Gibraltar of the Pacific," Rabaul commanded the most respect, a fortress sheltering Japan's southernmost airdromes and harbors. Located at the head of the contested Solomon Group to the south, and New Guinea to the west, the capture of Rabaul had been MacArthur's focus and comprised Task Three of his Cartwheel plan. But in August, while Satan's Angels entered combat for the first time, the general had received devastating news, Rabaul was to be bypassed.

MacArthur was furious. All of his men's efforts and sacrifices, from Buna to the Huon, had aimed at that target. Now faceless men meeting at the Allied Quadrant Conference, Quebec, rendered all that for nothing. The decision even contained a mean twist, the planners suggesting that MacArthur isolate and bypass Rabaul, a strategy that he had pioneered and used so well during the New Guinea campaign.

The Combined Chiefs of Staff, however, had to husband resources for the anticipated D-Day Invasion of France. They also believed Nimitz's oceanic Central Pacific drive offered savings in lives, resources, and, most critically, time. Generals and admirals eyed an assault on Rabaul with great misgivings. The Japanese "to the last man" defense against even the slightest Allied incursions did not bode well for a final, and some thought apocalyptic, struggle for the greatest enemy bastion in the South Pacific. The officers at Quadrant disbelieved MacArthur's intelligence estimates, rightly it later proved. Postwar interrogations revealed that Rabaul contained 100,000 men and up to its isolation in January 1944, had a minimum of six months supplies cached in well-built cave and tunnel systems. Chief U.S. Navy historian, the late Samuel Eliot Morison, predicted that the invasions of "Tarawa, Iwo Jima, and Okinawa would have faded to pale pink in comparison with the blood which would have flowed if the Allies had attempted an assault on fortress Rabaul."[3]

MacArthur's concern was not for Rabaul as an end in itself. His long, loving association with the Philippines influenced each move he had made for it was there MacArthur faced his darkest and bitterest moments, coming out of those islands just weeks before they fell to the Japanese. To go back to the

Philippines went beyond just another military operation; to the prideful general it was a promise made and to be kept, an act of personal redemption.

Rabaul's invasion, indeed the entire New Guinea campaign, simply cleared flanks for drives west and north to a Philippines languishing under enemy occupation. Hence MacArthur's alarm at the proposed isolation of the fortress, thinking that the Joint Chiefs of Staff (JCS) intended to stall his advance while sending Nimitz through the Central Pacific route, a campaign that did not necessarily include the liberation of the Filipino people. Much to the general's relief, his fears proved groundless.

MacArthur's presence and the sacrifices of his men helped prevent the scrapping of the Elkton plan aimed at approaching Japan from the south. More importantly, the JCS favored two axes of attack thus forcing already dwindling enemy responses and resources to widely separated fronts, and allowing the Allies a flexibility of action emphasizing that area which produced greatest success. Reassured, MacArthur produced a revised plan called Reno III on 20 October 1943.

Reno III fully satisfied Quadrant's basic demands. The Allies would neutralize and occupy Japanese bases west along the top of New Guinea, concluding with Vogelkop on 1 October 1944. From there MacArthur would enter the Philippines through the southern island of Mindanao.

Before any of those plans went forward, however, MacArthur had to ring Rabaul. Its potential menaced the general's supply line, especially at the narrows of the Vitiaz Straits between New Guinea and New Britain. Simpson Harbor could lodge, protect, and sortie elements of the Imperial Navy sent from Truk. Enemy air power posed the most dangerous threat bound by nothing except range.

The Americans planned to encircle Rabaul, then reduce it to impotence. Subsequent operations centered on doing exactly that with three basic campaigns occurring simultaneously. To the south, Vice Admiral William "Bull" Halsey continued the Solomons campaign begun at Guadalcanal a year before. Under the revised plans the last of the Solomons, Bougainville, arcing directly south of Rabaul, was slated for capture thereby bringing Rabaul under air attack.[4]

With the east face of New Guinea, from Buna to the Huon Peninsula, closed to the Japanese, MacArthur welded the ring shut by taking bases that isolated Rabaul to the north; Hansa Bay on 1 February 1944, the Admiralties on 1 March, with Kavieng on New Ireland also falling to Halsey's forces on that latter date. While the two campaigns sealed off Rabaul, the race for Western New Guinea, and the Philippines, continued unchecked. But all this lay in the future. For the 475th Fighter Group Rabaul loomed an unparalleled challenge.[5]

Surrounding Rabaul was not enough; its dromes and aircraft constantly threatened air raids and had to be neutralized. Simpson Harbor's expanse had to be emptied, and kept empty, of Imperial Japanese Navy units. A communique issued by a joint meeting of South and Southwest Pacific air commanders, dated two days before the first October attacks, ordered both air arms to "attack airfields and shipping at Rabaul with the object of destroying shipping and neutralization of enemy air." Only "Kenney's Kids" could do this.

As early as 25 January 1942, the Allies had made sporadic attacks on Rabaul but the lack of long-range escorts and prohibitive American losses forced the Fifth to switch to less effective nocturnal raids. One offshoot of that earlier campaign, photo reconnaissance, continued unabated. This offered Kenney's intelligence officers an intimate knowledge of the Rabaul complex, its workings, and its pattern of move-

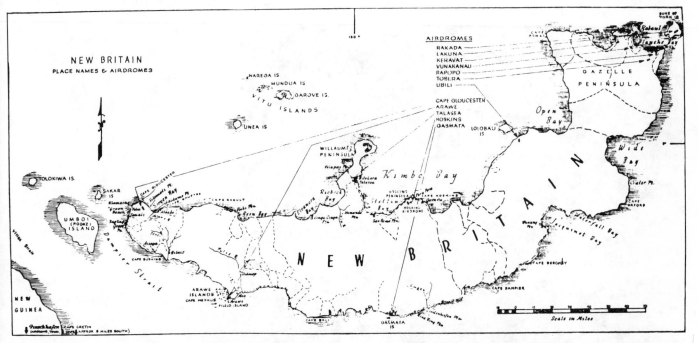

*The Island of New Britain. From Wesley Frank Craven and James Lea Cate, **The Army Air Forces in World War II**, vol. IV (Chicago, IL: University of Chicago Press, 1950), p. 315. Copyrighted 1950 by the University of Chicago. All rights reserved.*

ments, both aircraft and ship. This information made a crucial difference during subsequent raids.[6]

Rabaul lay on the extreme northeastern part of New Britain, a long island lying like a huge seal perpendicular to, and due east of, the Huon Peninsula, recently conquered by the Allies. The principle targets for the Fifth included Rabaul's main harbor, Simpson, and a cluster of airdromes that circled and protected the area. Four major fields would feel the blast of Fifth Air Force bombs: Lakunai, Vunakanau, Rapopo, and Tobera. Lakunai and Vunakanau existed before the war — Lakunai on the eastern shore of Simpson, Vunakanau inland and guarding southwesterly approaches to Rabaul. Rapopo lay fourteen miles southwest and had sprung up during the war, receiving its first Japanese aircraft by December 1942. Tobera formed a southerly apex between Rapopo and Vunakanau, a concrete strip completed in August 1943, just two months previous. Between the four fields, the enemy had hardstands for 166 bombers and 265 fighters. Additional reinforcements could be expected from any number of outlying bases, such as the Shortland or Buka Islands, respectively south and north of Japanese Bougainville, and New Ireland, northwest of Rabaul, could contribute craft from fields like Borpop or Kavieng. Collectively, Japanese air defenders would be formidable over Rabaul.

The book of hazards only began with hostile interceptors. The flak at Rabaul was already legendary by the October start time. The Japanese Army and Navy manned anti-aircraft positions around the airdromes and harbors, the soldiers responsible for 192 guns, the sailors for 175. Both air and gun defenses received aid from an extensive radar system established by the Southeastern Fleet at Rabaul. With a ninety-mile range and positioned on southwest New Britain, Kavieng and Cape St. George on New Ireland to the northeast, and south at Buka, it formed an early warning net that gave the enemy a thirty- to sixty-minute indication of approaching

strikes. Taken together, Rabaul had earned its dangerous reputation.[7]

As Satan's Angels leaned forward, listening intently to the briefing, the first mission to Rabaul unfolded. Kenney, as at Wewak, waited for a number of factors before launching the Fifth's real blow at the island fortress.

Kiriwina Island, occupied before the Wewak campaign and standing flank guard to New Guinea's coast, had finally signaled ready to act as a staging and refueling point for the trip north. Royal Australian Air Force engineers had completed two airstrips and all supporting structures by mid-October. Faced with the 750-mile round trip to Rabaul, Kiriwina was essential as a rendezvous point for the bombers and their escorts, and a refueling point for all craft, particularly P-38s stretched thin by the long haul north.[8]

Kenney's intelligence personnel also intently watched Rabaul. Major Karl Polifka, commander of the 8th Photo Squadron, sent his F-4 reconnaissance Lightnings to photograph a gradual build-up in Simpson Harbor. On 1 October "a heavy cruiser, one light cruiser, ten destroyers, five submarines, and twenty-six merchant vessels were rocking at anchor." Of more interest to the 475th, enemy airstrips held 124 assorted bombers and 59 fighters, the latter category more than doubling, to 145, ten days later. By 11 October then, Rabaul represented a ripe target. Only one factor intervened, the weather.

Tropical weather remained a problem with autumnal changes exacerbating an already complex situation. Kenney had slated the initial attack for 15 October, but the "Met" officers pointed to a break on the twelfth. Fully aware that the northwest monsoon season threatened and that any clear weather was good weather, the Fifth moved up the date to the twelfth. The briefing continued. Call signals were designated; times of rendezvous and altitudes were checked and rechecked; routes were reviewed. The raid was on.[9]

An air reconnaissance photograph of Kavieng Drome, New Ireland, February 1944.

Clover Squadron P-38 damaged on the first attack against Rabaul. (Anderson Collection)

and one Betty over Vunakanau but other than that the skies remained empty of enemy airplanes. In the 432nd Squadron, only one pilot fired his guns. "Naturally," the Squadron Diary laconically concluded, "all of our pilots were a bit disappointed."

The long distance emptied fuel cells at an alarming rate and many escort craft took on gas at Kiriwina. Some pilots were already wondering about the run to Rabaul. If this initial mission with few interceptions created fuel problems, how empty would tanks be when the Japanese chose to fight? The AAF fliers chose not to dwell on that notion long.

A more substantial problem surfaced on the first trip out. The 475th insisted on good radio discipline, and considering its fearsome objective, recommitted itself to the practice of

The Fifth Air Force attacks Simpson Harbor, Rabaul, 1944. The white dots to the left are masses of parafrag bombs suspended beneath tiny parachuts which allowed the bombers to release at low altitudes and escape their own bomb blast. (Cortner Collection)

Fifty-five Lightnings of the group rolled out of Dobo at 0730, squadron leaders making a wide, slow circuit around the field, with successive P-38s cutting inside the leader's turn, forming as quickly as possible. On the twelfth the 475th escorted the B-25 gunships on a low-level strike aimed at shutting down Vunakanau and Rapopo while the heavies attacked shipping in Simpson. Catching up to the Mitchells at 1,000 feet, the 475th flew just above the bombers in loose "string" formations of four, making easy S's over the mediums with a slightly higher group of 38s guarding the backs of the low units. Reaching the New Britain coast, the main force dropped to zero altitude, skimming the waters of Saint George Channel and then roaring inland at the mouth of Warangoi River, the bombers, with their escorts, splitting to attack the two fields. After ten minutes of parafragging and gunning both strips, the Americans quickly withdrew. The surprise was total and complete. Escorts took out one Oscar

radio silence. Nothing could be done about Japanese radar but at worst they should have been forced to scramble interceptors as the Fifth flew its last ninety miles. Radio transmissions, however, could warn the enemy at distances beyond radar range which posed a problem preventable by silence. But on this initial attack on Rabaul first an accompanying RAAF Beaufort squadron, followed by the B-25s, transmitted miles from the target. Steps were taken to prevent a recurrence of such a security breach.[10]

The raid proved successful but poor weather conditions blocked a return to Rabaul until 18 October. This would be a constant problem during that campaign. Devastating damage hurt the Japanese but periods of bad weather granted them time to regroup, repair, and reinforce. Despite storms to the north, Satan's Angels had plenty to do; the Wild Eagles had decided to strike back.[11]

The Japanese flew south three days later possibly believing

Lieutenant Warren J. Cortner in front of his "Home, Sweet Home," Dobodura, 1943. This was a fairly sophisticated dwelling, raised off the ground on a permanent floor and frame. Conditions could, and would, be more private in the future. (Cortner Collection)

that the 12 October attack was a prelude to an invasion. They sought out Oro Bay, a logical shelter for an American invasion fleet. Over 40 fighters accompanying 20-plus dive bombers showed up on Dobodura's radar plot and a red alert sounded at 0815. Along with alert aircraft poised to intercept enemy aircraft on short warning, many other 475th fighters wheeled down the strip eager to engage the Japanese. Among the first was Major Charles H. MacDonald, slated to lead the 475th in less than two months. MacDonald and another headquarters pilot, Captain William H. Ivey, careened down to dispersal in a jeep, "stole" two Lightnings belonging to the 433rd "Possum" Squadron, and took off.

Hades Squadron also rose to challenge the Japanese. Mac McGuire cruised at 19,000 feet when, at 0840, he spotted a pair of Val divebombers below. Rolling into an attack, McGuire leveled out at the six o'clock position and fired dead ahead at a Val. Hits sparkled over the craft and flames soon followed the smoke as it smashed into the bay. The American fired at the other Val but the dive from the chilly air at 19,000 feet to the warmth at sea level fogged his windshield so, because of poor defrosters, he fired without the benefit of his

gunsights. The enemy's fixed-gear craft smoked slightly but slipped from sight. Another "sightless" pass on a Zeke resulted in smoke but no flames as it too vanished in the press of combat. McGuire claimed one certain and two probables.[12]

By combat's end, fifty-one of Satan's Angels had fought at various stages of the battle, beginning at Oro and tangling as far out as the Huon Gulf. MacDonald and Ivey scored doubles and collectively the group claimed 21 bombers and 15 fighters for 5 Lightnings damaged. The smart money said the Japanese would return.

On 17 October radar again warned of approaching bogies. The 431st and 433rd Squadrons scrambled to intercept. The day before the 432nd had attempted to escort bombers to Western New Britain, but dense clouds had shut down the targets. Low on fuel, they diverted to Lae. On the way home the next day the 432nd spotted 15 to 20 Zeroes, part of the Oro Bay attack force, but lack of fuel again forced them to discreetly decline combat. By then 432nd's sister squadrons were already climbing to intercept.[13]

Scrambling at 0930, control ordered the 431st to "angels 20," 20,000 feet. Adding 3,000 feet for luck, Hades Squadron sighted the same group of Zekes seen earlier by the returning 432nd sweep into Oro Bay. Dropping tanks, the squadron climbed slightly and turned for a head-on attack. While not the maneuver of preference, the P-38 drivers did not hesitate meeting Japanese craft head to head, their heavier guns tilting odds in their favor. With hostile attacks imminent the head-on attack was mandatory, offering as it did minimal targets and the business end of a fighter.

In the first pass Mac McGuire turned slightly left and triggered .50 calibers and the single 20 millimeter cannon. A Zero to the right of the enemy formation shuddered, emitted smoke, and rolled into a dive. McGuire's Lightning pitched forward snapping out bursts down to 13,000 feet. The Japanese fighter never recovered, going into the bay at the vertical. Having lost his flight and wingman McGuire climbed and at 21,000 feet saw two Mitsubishis slide into position for an almost no deflection shot at Red Flight. The ace bore in for a stern attack, firing as much to frighten the pursuing Zekes as to bring them down. Responding, a quartet of hostile fighters chased him down again to 14,000 feet before breaking off.

In quick succession McGuire fired at two passing Zeroes with no results, then was bounced by three more coming in on his left rear quarter. In order to evade the attackers McGuire dove almost vertically for 11,000 feet, coming dangerously close to compressibility speed before wrenching his craft out at 7,000 feet. As he climbed once again, the pilot spotted a loose formation of seven Zekes stalking a lone Lightning. Unhesitatingly McGuire turned on the leader who had begun an attack run on the hapless Lockheed. With superb skill McGuire led the attacking Zero, fired a long burst, and saw flames break out as the Mitsubishi waded into his cone of fire.

McGuire could have broken off the attack. Instead, he offered himself up — it almost killed him. In the middle of alerted Zeroes, the Lightning "pulled up slightly and to the right getting a direct tail shot" at the stricken enemy. McGuire's one best hope, speed, bled off as he closed to point blank range and pressed his weapons' buttons. His target burned and fell off to the left. Unfortunately Japanese fighters sprinted faster than the heavier Yank craft and by the time the lieutenant finished firing, a Zeke had sliced in to 100 feet, closing fast.

McGuire was in trouble. He had lost his flight and wingman early on. One enemy approached his 6 o'clock position while five other Japanese ships jockeyed for their turn, and the pilot had run out of speed. As Mac began the standard diving escape, the P-38 took hits and the left engine erupted in flames. The right engine began to smoke as machine-gun and cannon rounds raked McGuire's canopy. A 20 millimeter exploded in the radio compartment and a 7.7 machine-gun slug hit his wrist while other shells blew up, spraying his right side and hip with fragments as they chewed up the base of the control column. Wounded and with no elevator control, the lieutenant escaped the cockpit and fell into space.

McGuire landed in the sea twenty-five miles out and paddled about for thirty minutes. His raft had been holed by the shrapnel and would not inflate but luckily PT 159 rescued the pilot and took him to the tender *Hilo*. The Navy patched McGuire up, lent him a jeep, and upon arrival back at Dobodura, he met Sergeant Vincent F. Straus and asked for another Lightning. Standing before the men, McGuire's arm was bandaged, he had two black eyes, as well as assorted punctures. Straus convinced McGuire that enough was enough. The lieutenant made his report and then recuperated for a few days at the hospital.[14]

The various attacks by the Japanese, including two against Finschhafen on the seventh and nineteenth, yielded nothing. The Fifth claimed 100 victories but more importantly, no shipping had been hit. As the two sides traded blows, Kenney concentrated on Rabaul. Thwarted by weather, he planned the next strike for 18 October, but a front of towering cumulonimbus clouds choked off the heavies and P-38s. The medium Mitchell gunships drove under the weather and struck runways and shipping off of Cape Gazelle.[15]

The monsoon season continued to shield Rabaul from the nineteenth to the twenty-third and Kenney fretted over the delays. His worst fears received confirmation on 19 October when photo recon showed that enemy aircraft numbers had risen to almost pre-strike levels, 211 craft scattered about Rabaul's airdromes. Worrying his weathermen, the general received word that a break in the storms would occur on 23 October. Satisfied, Kenney began to lay on a raid for that day.[16]

Despite the consequences, not all personnel minded the interlude. The 432nd ran combat air patrols up to the Huon Gulf and, while uneventful, the missions gave them flight time without casualties. For ground crews, the break allowed them to refurbish worn Lightnings. The Rabaul missions had wreaked havoc on 475th fighters with men working day and night to "keep 'em flying." Well that they attempted to catch up. The last week of October would see Satan's Angels airborne constantly.

Repairing group Lightnings prior to the climactic November raids on Rabaul, Dobodura, October 1943. (Anderson Collection)

The weather broke on 23 October. Everyone knew a maximum effort mission lay ahead. Fifty-seven big, slab-sided Liberators, escorted by 100 Lightnings, were sent to bomb the build-up of aircraft at Lakunai and Vunakanau. Escorting heavies soon took on its own pattern and rhythm. After forming up over Kiriwina by 1025, the air groups took on a stately air as the B-24s and 17s swept forward accompanied by their Lightning consorts. Usually the combat box formations stacked at 25,000 feet with escorts low and in front, on either flank, and with a rearguard approximately 2,000 feet higher than the bombers. The P-38s flew gently weaving formations that uncovered blind spots and allowed them to stay with the slower bombers.

It was cold at the 25,000- to 27,000-foot mark. Waiting to take off, pilots perspired in the Dobodura heat, their damp clothing cooling at altitude. Most distracting, they had cold feet. Eventually the upper torso would dry out and warm in the sunlight streaming through the canopy, but feet stayed cold. The H model Lightning had a flexible hose that blew warm air out of the instrument panel, where it was unneeded. The pilots disconnected the tube and positioned it on the floor to warm their feet, some going as far as to stuff the end into their boot tops!

Originally the pride of some fliers, the envy of others, Australian fleece-lined flying boots kept feet warm. However, reports of parachuting pilots losing their shoes with the shock of the main canopy opening caused some of the Satan's Angels to revise their thinking. The more pedestrian, but securer, G.I. boot became the preferred footwear. Feet might chill but would be shod for any emergency trek out of the jungle.

On the trip north the Lightning escorts watched their charges. The older Boeing B-17s kept tight formation, their design and thick wing comfortably gripping even the thin air at 25,000 feet. The Liberators, on the other hand, had more difficulties. The radical, high-lift Davis wing insured speed and great range (the farthest of any U.S. four-engine bomber before Boeing's B-29 Superfortress), but when fully loaded its thin airfoil caused directional instability, the B-24s skidding and slipping at high altitude. Imprecise control multi-

A squadron of P-38s in a string formation. (Anderson Collection)

plied the chance of midair collisions forcing the Liberator pilots to spread their formations. The pilots of the 475th maintained that B-24s took higher losses because of their loose formations, breaking up easier at hostile contact, and dispersing the escort aircraft over a greater area. For instance, McGuire commented in his after-action report that the Liberator formations were ". . . spread out very much too far. . . ."[17]

By 1943 the V Fighter Command's escort tactics far outstripped those of the Eighth Air Force, European Theater of Operation. The Eighth commanders insisted on close escort that tied fighters to lumbering four-engine craft, sacrificing their forte — speed and initiative. They would not change tactics until January 1944, when Major General James H. "Jimmy" Doolittle took command of the Eighth.[18]

The 23 October mission demonstrated the growing tactical sophistication of Kenney's Kids. Beginning on that date the V Fighter Command introduced "sweeps," groups of P-38s ranging far in front of the main force, covering hostile dromes in an attempt to engage and destroy the Japanese interceptors before the heavies arrived. At minimum, air battles at lower altitudes would allow the bombers to release their explosives unmolested and clear the target as the enemy labored to climb to their altitude.

At high noon the 431st and the 432nd Squadrons flew over Lakunai and Vunakanau but found them blanketed in clouds.

As they orbited, waiting to rejoin the incoming Liberators, approximately fifty enemy aircraft attacked. Danny Roberts' 433rd rode high guard at 25,000 feet and watched as the two Lightning squadrons tangled with the Japanese. Individual combat broke out and the skies filled with twisting craft from 17,000 to 21,000 feet as the 432nd engaged. Charles Mac-Donald quickly shot one down. Lieutenant Campbell P.M. Wilson made a stern attack against an Army Oscar, firing continuously as his range closed from 200 to 100 yards. Pouring smoke, it went into a spiral before splashing into the sea. Lieutenant Howard A. Hedrick was attacked by another Nakajima. Banking left and climbing, Hedrick took the Oscar on a head-on pass, the P-38's .50 caliber hits lighting up the aircraft, the .20 millimeter exploding large pieces from the enemy. When the long burst ended, the Japanese pilot bailed out and his craft disappeared. Captain Frederick A. "Square Loop" Harris, the 432nd's "Ops" Officer also scored a victory in the same battle.

Hades Squadron was led by Captain Verle E. Jett and circled north to south slightly higher than the bombers. Lieutenant David W. Allen spotted a dozen bogies climbing from the direction of Kavieng but contact never occurred. At 21,000 feet Allen and Jett fired at a Hamp, a more powerful, faster rolling Zero, but saw no results. Its partner made a hard starboard turn and then dove. Lieutenant Edward J. Czarnecki followed and never returned. Shot down in Simpson

Harbor, he escaped ashore and would return to Brisbane four months later.

The overall situation became complicated when Roberts saw another formation of thirty-five hostile fighters approaching the now occupied Lightnings below. On command the 433rd released their drop tanks and dove into the maelstrom. Roberts took one Zero from the six o'clock position, carefully measuring out three bursts and then a fourth into its wing tanks as it banked into a turn. The blazing craft fell off into a dive. By then the 433rd's leader was already hunting his second score, another Mitsubishi coming in with its nose and wings lit up. Turning into the enemy, the captain fired, saw flames as the Zeke half rolled and then plunged downward.[19]

While the fighter sweep kept the Japanese busy, the escorted Liberators roared over Rabaul. Seeing their primary targets obscured by clouds, the B-24s hastily improvised a secondary objective, Rapopo. Despite some confusion, most of the heavies hit the field claiming twenty aircraft destroyed on the ground.[20]

Escort Lightnings, including Satan's Angels' 431st Squadron, were fully occupied. As the B-24s made their runs, escort pilots saw 25 or 30 Zeros dive in long lines out of a towering cloud to the west. As the P-38s wheeled to meet them, Captain Marion F. Kirby was concerned. As he lined up on an onrushing Zero, Kirby remembered hearing that Japanese pilots sometimes sacrificed themselves by crashing into American aircraft. Just to play it safe, he thumbed the buttons on his yoke as the two fighters rushed at each other. The Zeke flew through Kirby's fire and, to his relief, broke left at the last moment and disappeared. A few minutes later the captain shot down a Zero in a more conventional style.

Lieutenant Allen lost a chance at downing two Hamps

Later 431 Squadron C.O., Major Verl Jett. (Anderson Collection)

rising to intercept because he would not leave his leader, thus demonstrating the tight teamwork that made Satan's Angels so effective. After one last pass at another Hamp, the 431st Squadron cleared the retreating Liberators, disengaged, and turned for home. Limping 38s were guarded by comrades and most Lightnings gassed up at Kiriwina before returning to Dobodura. They claimed thirteen enemy aircraft with a loss of only one Lockheed. Lieutenant Henry L. Condon II had no success over Rabaul but upon landing a cable informed him "he did have one son to his credit." The 23 October mission was over.[21]

Vunakanau, one of the Japanese fields defending Rabaul. The parafrags are drifting down over revetments holding Mitsubishi "Betty" medium bombers. (Cortner Collection)

Another view of Vunakanau under attack. Note the frontal shot of a B-25 Mitchell at the head of the right-hand road. (Cortner Collection)

The following days balanced missions against aircraft availability, all arbitrated by the weather. Weather or no, Kenney pushed the missions. Unknown to all but his top commanders, Halsey was set to move up the Solomons and expected the Fifth to pin down Japanese air power in the north, freeing his polyglot, COMAIRSOLS (Air Command, Solomons) to cover the landings. This helps to explain Kenney's scheduling of attacks against Rabaul despite marginal weather conditions. It also explains the fragmented nature of the last raids of October.[22]

On the twenty-fourth, Kenney had the big bombers stand down while the Mitchell gunships again flew to Rabaul, the 475th going with them. The counterair regimen still ruled the day with Vunakanau, Rapopo, and Tobera slated for strikes. Japanese combat air patrols usually took to the air by noon and the twenty-fourth's early takeoff intended to catch the interceptors on the ground but the landing of bombers on Kiriwina to refuel dragged on, slowing down the outbound assembly. When the B-25s finally swept over their targets Japanese fighters were already up and hunting.[23]

The enemy got one strafer before the escorts could break up initial attacks, but as fights erupted over Rabaul the Mitchells struck hard claiming 4 grounded aircraft at Tobera, 21 at Rapopo, and 27 at Vunakanau. Topside, escorting Lightnings entered skies alive with hostile interceptors.

On this mission the 80th Squadron of the 8th Fighter Group teamed up with Satan's Angels, the two units fighting side by side. As the Americans came in at 11,000 feet, a group of approximately fifty, dark-colored Zekes and Hamps struck the twin-engine clan. The danger deepened because the enemy pilots were eager and, uncharacteristically, worked in pairs.

Heretofore, the light Japanese fighters had encouraged individualistic tactics and American teamwork had taken advantage of that fact. In 1942, even the elite Lae Wing suffered from the lack of aerial discipline. Warrant Officer Saburo Sakai's words betrayed his frustration after his nine Zeroes encountered seven B-26 Marauders and only shot down one because of a lack of teamwork:

> I fairly exploded in anger back at Lae. I jumped from my cockpit . . . and shouted at every pilot to stand and listen. For perhaps fifteen minutes I cursed their clumsy stupidity, pointing out to each man his errors and stressing that only a miracle had brought them all back to Lae alive. From that night on we held sessions every evening to improve our teamwork.[24]

Luckily for the U.S., most Japanese units were less self critical. Teamwork never received wide acceptance on the operational, let alone the doctrinal, level of the enemy's air arms. But there were exceptions.

On that morning of the 24th, Satan's Angels knew they had a fight on their hands. As Lightnings tacked onto the dark hued fighters, Japanese wingmen would swing in behind or make a charge from the flank forcing the American off the attack. The P-38 pilots also measured Japanese tactical skill by their clever use of clouds dotting the sky. Enemy craft used the cottony masses as ambush points or escape hatches intermittently moving in or out as combat dictated. Slowly however, hard fighting, superior aircraft, and better team work began to favor the Americans.[25]

The 475th came in over the target area very low, allowing the defense forces a diving start which opened the battle. The

A B-24 Liberator, this one from the 43rd Bomb Group (Heavy). (Anderson Collection)

American formation dissolved into flights, then elements, as the fighting scattered them apart. Lieutenant Zach W. Dean of the 432nd shot a Zeke and a Hamp out of the air and became an ace in the process. Captain Frederick A. Harris and Lieutenants James R. Farris, Grover D. Gholson, and Elliot Summer each downed enemy aircraft, with Farris having an engine shot up during his combat.

As usual, mechanical difficulties lessened group performance. Standing rules dictated that any incapacitated craft was escorted home because of possible hostile fighters or forced ditchings during the long over-water flight back. Thus any wounded Lightning doubled its loss by withdrawing from combat an escort for the return to Kiriwina.

Squadron C.O. Major Frank Tomkins left with a hung-up drop tank; Howard A. Hedrick, who downed an Oscar the day before, took an escorted ride to Kiriwina with a malfunctioning supercharger. Farris limped in on one engine, and Lieutenant Raymond J. Krantz overnighted at Kiriwina while mechanics changed a generator. Mac McGuire crashlanded in a shot-up Lightning. The pace of combat was beginning to tell on the 475th's aircraft. In a few days, this would be brought home sharply to the group, but six confirmed kills to zero losses was reason enough to celebrate on the twenty-fourth.

The next day Kenney directed Whitehead to send up another strike, sixty-one Liberators accompanied by eighty-one P-38s. Heavy weather turned eleven B-24s and seventy-one escorts back to base but a communications failure sent the rest of the bombers and two flights of the Hades Squadron, led by MacDonald, on to the target. Clawing over a front at 22,500 feet, the fighters slid down to Simpson Harbor. The skies lit with a manmade storm of fire and metal, even the warships in the harbor throwing up flak of every caliber. Worse, over sixty Japanese interceptors had gathered to contest the air over Rabaul.

MacDonald's seven Lightnings were the B-24s' only defense. The major decided on bluff. Quickly the twin-boom fighters rose to their standard high cover position over the lead box. Two perilously thin strings of Lockheeds wove above their bombers. From all appearances it was business as usual. The enemy seemed to buy the mock escort, or were skittish thinking that the seven fighters were bait for a Lightning ambush, a trick the Japanese often used themselves. Whatever the reason, the opposition acted tentatively with halfhearted passes easily driven off. MacDonald flamed a Zeke that pressed an attack but the bomber train moved on, dropped their bombs, and departed. Only as the last squadron, the 403rd of the 43rd Bomber Group (H), cleared the target did the Japanese attack and down one Liberator.

MacDonald and the two flights of the 431st carried off a brave and remarkably successful ruse. Together, the raids of 23-25 October had been entirely effective despite hostile opposition and bad weather. MacArthur radioed Kenney a congratulation which he passed on to his Kids:

> Please accept my heartiest congratulations for yourself [Kenney], General Whitehead and all forces involved on the superb double strike at Rabaul. It gives me a sense of great security to have such an indomitable unit in my command.
>
> MacArthur

Kenney, with characteristic flair, added his own thanks: "A sweet job. Never give a sucker a break. . . ."[26]

Weather limited attacks for the next three days. On 27 October Halsey opened his campaign against Bougainville with an uncontested occupation of the Treasury Islands, part of Bougainville's chain. Now pressure mounted because the Japanese would not tolerate an invasion of Rabaul's southern outpost. To split Japanese air resources Kenney had to continue his offensive against Rabaul and two days later the weather cleared.[27]

The 475th used the three days respite well. Again the mechanics' constant tinkering brought wounded airplanes back on line. Missing pilots returned and new fliers joined the roster. Perry Dahl, then nineteen years old, joined the 432nd and sparked speculation that he might be the youngest pilot in the Southwest Pacific Theater. Local orientation and test hops continued.[28]

The 29 October strike proved disappointing on several counts. The 475th had launched a two, three, and a four craft flight when P-38s of the 39th Fighter Squadron, 35th Group, intervened during takeoff and delayed the rest of Satan's Angels. By the time the remainder of the group became airborne, the escorts and bombers had vanished. They dashed north, but unable to locate the strike force, the Lightnings returned to Kiriwina.

Only nine P-38s crossed Rabaul at 1235, guarding a small group of approximately eighteen aircraft. As they withdrew, the truncated group attacked a number of Zekes, only probables being reported. On the plus side, all craft returned safely but Rabaul remained a lethal threat to American interests in the Pacific.[29]

While Rabaul's shadow fell on all that the SWPA forces endeavored to do, conversely the enemy also feared American actions. The linchpin was Bougainville, just south of Fortress Rabaul. The Japanese knew its capture would render Rabaul useless, subject to continual air attack from both New Guinea and the south. Thus by September, the enemy had already planned to smash any invasion of Bougainville's shores. Given shipping losses in the waters of the Solomons and New Guinea, and still awaiting a climactic naval clash in the Pacific, the Japanese opted for an aerial resolution to their dilemma.

Kenney was anxious. He knew that Halsey planned the invasion of Bougainville at Empress Augusta Bay on 1 November, that the admiral's air forces would be occupied fully trying to control the skies over the landing beaches, and that on 1 October MacArthur had promised "maximum air support," meaning all out attacks on Rabaul. The Satan's Angels understood this. Rabaul veteran Marion F. Kirby pithily translated the official 2 November order: ". . . occupy the Jap Air Force over Rabaul," into ". . . keep the Japs at home . . . in other words 'occupy them.' " Nobody knew, could have known, that the Rabaul campaign was nearing its end.[30]

The 2 November mission capped the Fifth Air Force's campaign to neutralize Rabaul. It also dealt that organization its sharpest losses to date, a tariff paid in part by the 475th Fighter Group. All that Satan's Angels knew, however, was that they had been granted a respite after the 29 October raid. Although Kenney alerted his air arm on the 30th, 31st, and on 1 November for impending attacks, monsoons blocked the Fifth from Rabaul. On the latter date, Halsey's forces landed on Bougainville and immediately came under air attack. The Fifth had to strike soon. A preliminary report on the second gloomily repeated the now familiar forecast of impenetrable clouds west of Rabaul but pitting his will against nature's, Kenney ordered two F-5s of the 8th Photo Squadron to sweep Rabaul again. The results showed clear weather. The 2 November raid was on.

On that day tiredness permeated the 475th, both men and planes. For two and one-half months they had fought and beat the best the enemy had mustered but the unrelenting pace exacted a toll. Despite improved conditions at Dobodura, it was still not home. The main fare revolved around reconstituted foods. A 431st driver got to the point where he would not eat before a mission, preferring instead hard candy from the highly prized "K" rations and a canteen of water.[31]

A lack of sleep also reduced performance. Often the Japanese would field nocturnal raiders called affectionately "Washing Machine" or "Bedcheck" Charlie. Essentially a nuisance, one man did comment that he felt the nocturnal raids helped to relieve the boredom. Loitering over Dobo, the aircraft droned back and forth sporadically dropping bombs that destroyed needed sleep. Without much accuracy, there was a tendency to doze through the raids until that one close bomb that woke men with a start. The men of Sergeant Carl Begh, Jr.'s tent, part of the 431st Squadron, no longer minded Charlie until a string of bombs walked towards them one

Dig it deeper! Sergeant Louis Fazzi works on a slit trench bomb shelter in back of a sleeping tent. (Anderson Collection)

night. Into the long unused slit trench they dove — and into a large colony of mice, no more inclined to face the bombs than they. Mice and men cohabited the shelter until the "all-clear" sounded.[32]

Illness fed off marginal diets and low bodily resistance. The tropics bred diseases that, by the standards of the time, were exotic and deadly. Scrub typhus and dengue killed men, malaria and dysentery incapacitated them. Early on, lack of adequate medical supplies and minimal prophylactic measures hampered disease control with unscreened mess areas near latrines and untreated swamp areas within the camps.

The 475th's medical records show a steady rise in pilot man-days lost due to illness once the group entered combat. In August it was 1 percent; in September, 2 percent. With the intensification of combat, severe living conditions, physical extremes in temperature and atmospheric pressure, and intense anxiety, totals tripled by October to 5.9 percent. By the eve of the 2 November mission, Satan's Angels were wearing thin.[33]

On the practical side men that flew often did so while ill.

A P-38 hit in a Japanese bombing raid, Dobodura. Another Lightning stands in the center foreground. (Anderson Collection)

Master Sergeant Vincent F. Straus. (Vincent F. Straus Collection)

John Hood, a professional from the early Moresby days, estimated that by September's end every one of the 431st Squadron had had malaria. The question was not whether one had the "bug," but to what degree. Indeed, Hood would soon rotate back stateside with a worsening case of malaria. Replacement pilot John Tilley flew continually with chronic dysentery.

After the Rabaul campaign the medical problems continued: 5.8 percent in November; 6.9 percent in December; to fall only in January 1944 to 2.9 percent. In fact, at no time during the first seven months of fighting did the 475th combat casualty rate ever surpass the rate of illness. By the November raids, disease was an unwanted co-pilot on many missions.[34]

Sick rates contributed to and fed off of another constant, stress. While difficult to pinpoint, combat's unceasing pace played havoc with human constitutions and the 475th's employment in both the Wewak and Rabaul campaigns demonstrated that facet of the military experience. The aviator differed from the soldier in that the pilot's world revolved around relatively brief but intense exposures to external danger interspersed with long hours of boredom often seen as a countdown to the next mission. By November the strain was beginning to show in the group.[35]

All suffered but stress hit the veteran cadre of the 475th hard. They had already spent a year of combat in the worst of conditions. Despite the profitable, and restful, two months at Amberly, the recommitment to battle already increased their tired state. Combat fatigue manifested itself in many guises most commonly in slowed reflexes, and more dangerously,

impaired judgment. Mac McGuire pushed very hard and the records confirm this. Getting "shot up" (aircraft damaged but flyable) or "shot down" commonly occurred but the shock, psychologically, was traumatic. In slightly less than two months Japanese fighters hit and severely damaged McGuire's craft three times, on 29 August, 28 September, and 24 October. In each instance he flew home, although in the last fight his craft barely reached Kiriwina Island forcing McGuire to crashland, another harrowing experience.

Over Oro Bay, 17 October, McGuire rescued a fellow pilot and got shot down and wounded for his pains. This made four close calls, averaging one every two weeks. As related above, McGuire returned shortly after his rescue on the seventeenth and demanded another P-38 so he could continue to fight.

While admirable in intent, an experienced hand like Sergeant Straus thought this a bit much. Later he wrote the story's aftermath. The wounded McGuire completed his combat report and then went to the base hospital at Dobodura. "He stayed for a few days[,] not long, because this man [McGuire] was always ready for action, maybe to [sic] eager."[36]

More commonly tired pilots simply lost their edge and slowly, almost imperceptibly, became more and more vulnerable in combat. On 28 September 1943, the 431st tangled with Japanese interceptors over Wewak. For John Hood it was a good day with two confirmed kills. It was also the day he came closest to dying.

Hood had come out of New Guinea as a cadre for the 475th. He was stricken even then with malaria. Furthermore, September was Satan's Angels first full month of combat and they lost eight ships, a four-fold increase over August and not to be exceeded until the tough November attacks against Rabaul. But escort missions had to be flown and the twenty-eighth was no exception.

Hood had just flamed his second kill and watched it fall off to the side. In the process he made two cardinal errors; he did not clear his tail and the captain's maneuvering had dropped his speed. Hood had just begun to attack a Zeke when he felt a jarring sensation, controls leaping in his hands. A Zero had made a textbook stern attack, walking 7.7 and 20 millimeter fire from the tail to the engine which burned fiercely. It seized up, the torque created by its mate going at combat speed flipping the Lightning over causing the Zeke to overshoot the stricken craft and probably saving Hood's life. The burning P-38 dove into solid overcast at 19,000 feet.

Hood righted his mount and limped home on one engine, leg jammed full rudder to keep the eight-ton fighter from slewing to the side. His mechanic counted over seventy-six holes in the craft and for a month afterward, every time Hood thought of the incident, the leg that had cramped tight on the rudder bar would begin to twitch. Hood was hospitalized with severe malaria just before November and went home for recuperation.[37]

And just as the strain of combat made its mark on the men of the 475th, so too had the aircraft suffered. The task of keeping men and machines in the air fell to the group's maintenance personnel. Men like Staff Sergeant Teddy W.

Hanks, crew chief for Danny Roberts' Lightning, carried heavy responsibilities. A mistake on the ground could kill "his" pilot on a mission so all hands worked all hours to insure the P-38's readiness at the start of a mission. Under open skies, in the heat or rain, sick or well, the maintenance men labored without fanfare or glory.

While support personnel worked as long or longer hours under the same conditions as the pilots, their's was a less anxiety prone environment and the group's medical records displayed an interesting phenomena. The pilots' periods of illness spiked about a month after combat intensified, for instance October after September's first full month of fighting and casualties, and December after November's raids against Rabaul. Ground personnel, however, became ill on a much more even basis: 1 percent of man-hours lost to illness in August; 2.6 percent in September; 2.2 percent in October and November, and then, as soon as the pace of missions slackened, 1.5 percent in December down to 1.2 percent in January 1944. In short, less anxiety and a relatively even pace of work drastically flattened the curve of their instances of sickness.[38]

Unhappily, some officers did not respect or acknowledge the work done on their behalf by the men. The men, however, continued to do their best. Most pilots, however, regarded their ground crews highly and maintained congenial relationships with them. Dismounting his fighter after a mission, Danny Roberts often smiled at Hanks saying, "We got another one, Sergeant."[39]

At first the men did not know the Lightning well. The older line technicians had worked primarily on P-39s and 40s, relatively simple machines compared to the P-38. The newer men, rushed through training stateside, also had only the slightest of acquaintances with the 475th's fighter. This accounted for the "snafus," craft that dropped out of a mission due to malfunctions. Standard procedures dictated replacement fighters on every mission, taking the slots of those forced to return to base. For instance, the 432nd counted seventeen airplanes unable to continue or incapacitated during missions in the months of September and October.[40]

The group's maintenance personnel faced three fundamental problems on the eve of the November raids, beyond standard maintenance: combat damage, a lack of replacement parts and aircraft, and breaking-in problems in newly issued craft. Combat damage took up much time and demanded rapid fixing, often by the next day. Its repair became the specialization of the first echelon and its support.

A major problem concerned lack of adequate spare parts on the squadron levels. Parts were jealously guarded by the squadron's line personnel and came from unidentified sources no one cared to talk about. Not until January 1944 did maintenance equipment come in volume to the group. Despite the problems, equipment officers, NCOs, and men steadily improved their skills. In June Allison engines had to be changed, on average, after every 150 hours of flying time. By December that time extended to 300 hours, doubling an engine's life. Much had been learned in six months.

The solution to the 475th's greatest problem, however, lay

beyond their grasp, new fighters. Kenney constantly battled Washington for replacements for worn or shot up Lightnings but he bucked the whole tide of "Europe First" commitments that sent the newest craft to U.S. air commands in Britain and the Mediterranean rimlands. While the November missions poised to start, the European Theater of Operations staggered under heavy bomber losses suffered at Schweinfurt and Regensburg on 14 October 1943. This triggered a frantic scramble for long-range fighters, fighters slated for Kenney and the SWPA.

Kenney received, in compensation, a promise that Halsey's P-38 allotment would go to the Fifth Air Force, along with 350 shorter-range Republic P-47 Thunderbolts. In reality the Southwest Pacific would receive no more than forty-five Lightnings from October through November. The forthcoming Rabaul Campaign would be fought with perilously few long-ranged 38s and its aftermath would witness Lightnings plummet from "212 in September to 150 in February 1944." The resources for Rabaul stretched very tight.[41]

And then there was the enemy. Japanese actions created a situation that exacted heavy losses from Satan's Angels yet bled themselves white in the process. The fear of a Bougainville invasion forced the Japanese to shift again. In August all Army air units flew from Rabaul to Wewak, and the Fourth Air Army died there defending north coast bases. The Imperial Japanese Navy's 11th Air Fleet filled the vacuum created at Rabaul. Commanded by Vice Admiral Jinichi Kusaka, the fleet had concentrated its 200 aircraft at Rabaul in October.

In order to stabilize the Southeast Asian area of operations, the Japanese then decided to reinforce Kusaka by stripping air elements off their 3rd Carrier Fleet at Truk, 173 aircraft and 192 pilots strong. Rested and refitted, the pilots of Carrier Division I arrived on 1 November, the same day the 3rd Marine Division landed at Cape Torokina, Bougainville, and the day before the Fifth planned to hit Rabaul. The Japanese were determined to defend Rabaul at all costs.[42]

In later years survivors of the 2 November mission referred to it as "Bloody Tuesday." The assignment seemed simple enough, "occupy" the Japanese. Strike plans envisioned a sweep by each P-38 squadron of the 8th and 49th Groups followed by flak-suppressing Mitchells directed to attack ack-ack batteries. Simultaneously other B-25s were to take out airstrips and shipping in Simpson Harbor. Satan's Angels drew an assignment to escort the strafers of Major Benjamin Fridge's 345th Group as they cleared a path through the gun batteries surrounding Simpson Harbor, and then turning east, attacked Lakunai's strip.[43]

As the 475th rolled out at 1058, sharp-eyed ground personnel counted off their squadrons: the 433rd at 15 airplanes, the 432nd's numbers slightly worse at 13 Lockheeds. All were appalled as the 431st raised runway dust, only 9 craft taking off, down 45 percent of its usual squadron strength. On the long, watery, outbound trip two 433rd Lightnings "snafued" and had to return, escorted by a third squadron mate. This reduced Danny Roberts' "Fightin' Blue Devils" to 75 percent strength, 12 ships. Now 22 percent understrength, the group flew on to fight the reinforced Japanese Naval air arm at Rabaul.[44]

For Hades Squadron, the day started wrong and stayed that way. The 431st had stood alert duty for the two previous days and looked forward to some rest on 2 November, their first scheduled day off. Now they were taking part in a maximum effort against Rabaul. At takeoff Captain Marion F. Kirby, the squadron's leader for the mission, could not get his engine started and as the captain fumed, the eight craft of the 431st lifted off. Powerplants finally caught and as Kirby skimmed the runway, he set course for the squadron's rendezvous point. The P-38 raced to catch the others but Kirby thought his fighter accelerated too slowly so, in time honored tradition, he tested the airspeed indicator by tapping on its face, perhaps too vigorously. He knocked the glass completely off and damaged the instrument itself. Now Kirby had no inkling of his speed, certainly not enough to navigate for the squadron. Drawing up to the 431st he signaled First Lieutenant Lowell Lutton, his wingman, to lead the squadron, a small act that would have major consequences in the moments to come.

The 475th set a familiar course for New Britain's south coast, the lowering ceiling pressing them down to wave top heights. By the 2 November raid an earlier problem was solved; radio discipline had been improved. As the two groups rendezvoused and merged, not a single electronic impulse betrayed that roaring mass driving on towards Rabaul.[45]

Clearing Cape Gazelle, the Mitchell gunships turned west down the St. George Channel heading towards the throat of Simpson Harbor at the terminus of Blanche Bay. Half way down the channel the sheltering overcast lifted. The Lightnings climbed a few thousand feet above the wave-hopping mediums, extending into their attack formation, sinuous lines that crossed and recrossed above the B-25s. Then things unraveled fast.

At the mouth of Simpson two Japanese destroyers challenged the onrushing forces with blazing guns, their main batteries raising tall plumes in front of the Mitchells, their secondaries filling the sky with ropey lines of tracers and explosives. Surprise literally went up in smoke and flame. During this encounter Lieutenant Lutton ordered the 431st to jettison their belly tanks.[46]

In retrospect this boded ill for the squadron. Kirby, with veteran instincts, felt the move premature. With external cells gone, all that remained were the internal fuel cells meant for takeoff, combat, and landing. Any prolonged combat would make for a very dry trip home. Once done, however, all concentrated on the job at hand as they entered the storm of Simpson Harbor.[47]

The lead 39th Squadron encountered little opposition on their initial run through the target area, but once alerted, newly-arrived Japanese Navy pilots rose to fend off the intruders. The 80th flew into a cauldron of silver interceptors eager to fight. By the time the 475th arrived with the mediums, the skies blossomed with flak and over a hundred Japanese interceptors milled about.

The B-25s swept the dockside anti-aircraft positions with white phosphorus bombs, euphemistically called "Kenney Cocktails," that sent out burning, white tendrils and billows of smoke. Once finished, the Mitchells lifted over the low hills and struck Lakunai. Satan's Angels encountered a much lower ceiling inside the harbor forcing them to dive from approximately 4,000 to 1,500 feet to provide cover for the bombers. It also stripped them of one of their chief tactical advantages, height. Without it, diving and climbing escapes became restricted to a thin band of clear air just above the ocean's surface. The eight leading strafers of the 345th took heavy Japanese fire and three never returned to base.[48]

Danny Roberts led Possum Squadron, providing close cover for the skimming Mitchells, his Lightnings feinting, criss-crossing, dodging nasty pods of flak as they stayed with the gunships on their run. Though losing one man, they sacrificed kills to insure the bombers' safety.

The 432nd saw a break in the overcast which rapidly filled with Zekes, Oscars, and Tonys. Climbing to 4,000 feet they met the enemy in swirling, confused battle. Lieutenant Grover D. Gholson doubled with an Oscar and a Zeke, while Lieutenant Arthur L. Peregoy got a Zeke losing his combat "virginity" in the process.

White Flight lost their squadron in the melee and as they emerged from the overcast, they immediately engaged the enemy. Lieutenants Howard A. Hedrick and John J. Rundell narrowly missed a collision with a Tony. Squadron mate Lieutenant Leo M. Mayo picked up the action from a distance and firewalling his Lightning, dove to cut off the Japanese Army fighter. As the 432nd trailed behind, Mayo closed rapidly, fired, and in the narrowing distance, watched the craft disintegrate. Instantly Mayo's P-38 plowed into a large chunk of the fighter, losing the right wing and forcing the Lieutenant to bail out. Two comrades circled, guarding him on the way down.

Hedrick stayed above protecting the two fliers aiding Mayo's lonely descent off of Mope, New Britain. Suddenly four hostile fighters bounced him, shot out his left engine, and closed for the kill. Desperately employing every trick he knew, Hedrick whipsawed ahead of the pack avoiding Japanese rounds. One overshot him and staggered as his fire crumpled the airplane, promptly forcing it down. Hedrick soon evaded his pursuers and settled in for the long trip to Kiriwina.

Members of Satan's Angels examine a 345th Bomb Group Mitchell just prior to the Rabaul Raid. (Anderson Collection)

Hades Squadron pilots at Dobodura. Left to right: Robert F.
"Pappy" Cline (later C.O. of the
432nd), Marion F. Kirby, Frederic F.
Champlin, Franklin H. Monk, Vincent T. Elliot. (Anderson Collection)

The nine aircraft of Hades Squadron were badly outgunned but rose, unhesitatingly, to break up enemy formations. The ensuing fight gave eloquent testimony to the group's insistence on teamwork. The 431st took bad losses, but they would have been heavier without the superb mutual support lent to each other in the fire-swept space above Simpson Harbor.

Marion Kirby's memories of Rabaul, especially the 2 November missions, were unforgettable. Later he described the difference between the Wewak and Rabaul missions; "I never fired my guns on a Wewak mission . . . never quit firing them going to Rabaul." Crossing inland to cover the 345th Mitchells, the ceiling closed to 1,500 feet. Turning left, Kirby saw a B-25 streaming flames from its right engine, three Japanese fighters attacking it in succession. Kirby disrupted them with a pass that sent one of the interceptors down in flames. As he banked for a second run the captain was momentarily distracted by a unique sight, an extinct volcano (one of several ringing Rabaul) alive with ack-ack fire directed *down* at his P-38 flying below. Diving, Kirby shot down a second hostile plane, its pilot parachuting free, only to be jumped by the last Zero. As he jinxed to throw off the Japanese, a second P-38 intervened. Lieutenant Frederic F. Champlin fired, finishing off Kirby's attacker. The strafers left sixteen Japanese craft destroyed at Lakunai and ran for home. Kirby was very low on fuel and gladly left the area as well. But he was not the only 431ster to see action.

Lowell Lutton, now squadron leader, flew to the aid of some besieged Mitchells. Alone, Lutton's gunnery fired up a Zeke but drew two attackers in return. Lieutenants Ed Wenige and wingman Franklin Monk dove to clear Lutton's tail. Monk forced one Navy fighter out of the attack, Wenige shot down the other and then reuniting, the two sped across the bombers, running interference.

Hostile interceptors lost patience and concentrated on the Lightnings. Guarding their leader's stern, Wenige and Monk turned into a pair of Zekes making a high side pass on Lutton from the one o'clock position. They repeated their earlier performance, Monk bluffing one while Wenige downed the second. A third interceptor bore into the attack. Wenige slid in to take him but pressed gun buttons produced no comforting fire and noise. Here American teamwork shone brightly again with Wenige sliding under the Zeke, exposing it to Monk's guns which destroyed it. Breaking through five more Japanese fighters, the two Lightnings fought their way out of Rabaul. Lutton, however, never made it back; his gallant fight over Simpson exhausted his fuel forcing him down.

The 2 November battle lasted a long forty minutes and the sixty enemy defenders harried the Lightning rearguard for another fifty-four miles out to sea before quitting. Typically, and unfortunately, weather built up over Kiriwina forcing exhausted pilots to detour on low levels of fuel. Upon landing, some Lightnings had just enough gas to wet the tip of a dip stick. The 2 November mission was over.

The Fifth took heavy losses: nine fighters and eight heavies with a Mitchell and three Lightnings so badly damaged as to be useless. The 475th took its heaviest casualties and losses in its short career. Roberts' 433rd lost a man, as did the 432nd. The outnumbered 431st suffered most of all. Of the nine men who went into Simpson Harbor, only six came out, a casualty rate of one-third of the squadron, and making up fully one-third of the total 475th losses for the day. But they had also made the enemy bleed, the 431st with nine confirmed kills and the 432nd with five. But Rabaul was not finished yet.[49]

On 5 November, three days after Bloody Tuesday, a Japanese build-up at Rabaul aimed at Halsey's Bougainville campaign forced a desperate expedient, a carrier raid against the most heavily defended target in the Southwest Pacific. Halsey asked for, and Kenney agreed to, a simultaneous Fifth Air Force mission aimed at again splitting Japanese defenses, the first major joint mission in the SWPA.

Again the Fifth struck docks and airstrips while the Navy went after Japanese shipping in the harbor. Light enemy air opposition surprised many P-38 pilots, the 432nd encountering only ten Japanese, dispersing them with no victories or losses. Dick Bong of the 8th Group scored the only hit of the day.[50]

Attacks were planned for the sixth but were thwarted by the weather. On 7 November, the fronts cleared enough for the Liberators and sixty-four Lightnings to return to Rabaul. The 475th had moved temporarily to Kiriwina in support of the B-24 mission. From there they lifted off on the morning of the seventh, rendezvousing with the Liberators near Gasmata, New Britain. The results were spotty. The 432nd and 433rd encountered light opposition, inflicting no damage. The 431st shot down four interceptors and in the fight Marion Kirby again had a close brush with calamity.

As Kirby turned starboard into an attacking Zero, his wingman, Lieutenant Charles R. Samms, properly allowed his leader to cross over him and then fell into a low, trail position. Samms followed too closely. Kirby fired and a rain of brass casings whipped out the chutes and slammed into the lieutenant's canopy, the Plexiglas exploding and blinding the wingman. In his pain Samms reflexively triggered his weapons. He was so close to Kirby's belly that the leader could feel the muzzle blast jar his airplane. Talking calmly, Kirby reassured his blinded wingman and, after leveling him out, verbally guided Samms free of the combat area. The lieutenant recovered his sight on the way to Kiriwina where they made an uneventful landing. Thus ended the 475th's last mission in the November campaign.[51]

Rabaul's back had been broken. While the Fifth sometimes miscalculated damage inflicted, they, and Halsey's air arm, had reduced that great bastion to impotence. At minimum it had prevented the Japanese from mounting any kind of lasting air offensive against the Bougainville operations. More than that the 475th's struggles over Rabaul destroyed irreplaceable Japanese pilots and craft. Rabaul would continue to be targeted through February of the new year but by mid-November 1943, Halsey's growing air forces took responsibility for its neutralization. By the second week in November, Satan's Angels drew a much desired respite.[52]

The group's aircraft supplies had been drawn down to critical levels. At the beginning of the November raids, the 475th had 31 Lightnings, 24 craft less than mid-October. By 16 November the total had fallen to 24 serviceable fighters, reduced three days later to 6. Combat damage, primitive repair facilities at Kiriwina, and, of course, Lightnings lost in battle forced drastic measures. Fifth Air Force stripped P-38s from the 9th Squadron, 49th Fighter Group, and the 39th Squadron, 35th Fighter Group, and turned them over to Satan's Angels, bringing them near normal strength. The two fighter-less squadrons received the "Jug," Republic P-47 Thunderbolts in exchange, an uneven one in their estimation.[53]

As fighters wore down, so did the pilots. In that small circle of men downed comrades were missed, but were missed subtly, slowly, in a time honored manner; no one prepared eulogies, no services marked their passing. Instead, footlockers were put in order and their places made ready for replacements. But the stress on the 475th's pilots began to show its deleterious effect.[54]

Kill ratios also spoke to the difficulties of reducing Rabaul. From August through January, Satan's Angels averaged a 10.9:1 ratio of victories over the Japanese. During November, group losses reduced the numbers to 2.7:1. Only in January 1944 would casualties become less, and that due to reduced contact with the Japanese. Lowered kill ratios hinted at a growing weariness among the 475th's pilots.[55]

Combat fatigue, already growing before the November raids, continued to erode the health of the fliers. By the conclusion of October, after a month's combat and the beginning of the long, over-water flights to Rabaul, the loss of man-days among pilots to illness rose from 2 percent to 5.9 percent. By December's end, a month after the November raids to Rabaul, that ratio rose to 6.9 percent, tapering to 2.9 percent only in January.[56]

On a personal level, the effects were subtle but no less real. Group leadership recognized the problem of fatigue, especially in the hard-hit 431st Squadron, and atypically sent half of each squadron at a time on much desired leaves to Sydney beginning the second week in December. Unfortunately war did not stop because of the 475th's problems, so while some officers enjoyed Australia, the depleted squadrons worked doubly hard, testing the proverbial "cure or kill" axiom. Marion Kirby felt the strain both as a pilot and a leader. Shorthanded, he selflessly led a mission described as "very routine." "Routine" except he had flown one too many missions. Later Kirby recalled that last flight: ". . . every little air pocket became a hole in the sky, both engines ran as smooth as glass but my imagination saw props flying off, pistons coming out of the sides of the engines, oil flying everywhere." The mission lasted slightly less than four hours; to Kirby it was the longest flight of his life. He returned home soon afterward.[57]

So the 475th rested and regained strength. Despite losses, Satan's Angels could look back with pride on their accomplishments since thrown into battle in August. They had flown over 557 missions composed of 6,069 sorties, by January 1944. In that same time, the 475th destroyed 285 Japanese craft for a loss of 38 Lightnings to enemy action.

The Angels had also forged bonds with the V Bomber Command. Escort missions far outstripped other types of assignments and forced the Japanese to fight for their airspace, resulting in heavy enemy losses. Simultaneously the mediums and heavies excelled at anti-airfield strikes, destroying the "wild eagles" in their eyrie. Without the 475th's protection, however, none of this would have been.

After the 2 November raid a number of grateful "bomber boys" called the 475th, expressing deep appreciation for protection rendered on that day. In Kiplingesque style, Technical Sergeant R.H. Bryson summed up that appreciation best in a poem entitled "Lightnings in the Sky." The last stanza reads:

> Sure, we're braver than hell,
> On the ground all is swell,
> In the air its a different story.
> We sweat out our track, through fighters and flak,

We're willing to split up the glory.
Well, they won't reject us, so heaven protect us,
And, until all this shooting abates,
Give us courage to fight 'em,
And — one other small item —
An escort of P-38s.

Absorbing the worst the enemy could inflict, the 475th never quit. The future held great promise, but the original cadre — half veterans, half novices — had won Satan's Angels a brilliant beginning.[58]

FOOTNOTES

1. 432nd Squadron Diary, 4 October, 9 October, 10 October; Straus File: "Brief History," p. 2.

2. Henry C. Toll, *Tropic Lightning* (Manhattan, KS: Sunflower University Press, 1987), pp. 4-5 (hereinafter, Toll, *Tropic Lightning*); Hood Interview; Lynch, et al., *Satan's Angels*, p. 30.

3. Spector, *Eagle*, pp. 276-77; Craven and Cate, *The Army Air Forces*, vol. IV, pp. 312-13.

4. Craven and Cate, *The Army Air Forces*, vol. IV, chap. 8; John Costello, *The Pacific War* (NY: Ransom, Wade Publishers, 1981), pp. 228-29 (hereinafter, Costello, *Pacific War*).

5. Craven and Cate, *The Army Air Forces*, vol. IV, pp. 194-95; Spector, *Eagle*, pp. 276-79.

6. Craven and Cate, *The Army Air Forces*, vol. IV, pp. 138, 317.

7. *Ibid.*, pp. 312-13.

8. *Ibid.*, pp. 316-17.

9. *Ibid.*, pp. 9-10, 318; Miller, *Cartwheel*, pp. 229-30.

10. 432nd Squadron Diary, 12 October 1943.

11. *Official History*, frame 660; Craven and Cate, *The Army Air Forces*, vol. IV, p. 321; Willoughby and Chamberlain, *MacArthur*, pp. 119-20.

12. Straus File: "Individual Combat Report of First Lieutenant Thomas B. McGuire, Jr.," 15 October 1943; Letter: John Tilley to Author, July 1987 (hereinnafter, Tilley Letter).

13. 432nd Squadron Diary, 16-17 October.

14. Straus File: "Individual Combat Report of 1st Lieutenant Thomas B. McGuire, Jr.," 12 October 1943; Straus Letter, p. 6; Lynch, et al., *Satan's Angels*, p. 15; Miller, *Cartwheel*, p. 230.

15. 432nd Squadron Diary, 18 October 1943; Craven and Cate, *The Army Air Forces*, vol. IV, p. 322.

16. *Ibid.*, p. 323.

17. Hood Interview; Letter: Marion F. Kirby to Author, July 1987, p. 4 (hereinafter, Kirby Letter); Tilley Letter, p. 8; Straus File: "Individual Combat Report of First Lieutenant Thomas B. McGuire, Jr.," 16 September 1943.

18. Yoshino, "Doctrine," pp. 372-73, 397, note 48.

19. Hess, *Sweep*, pp. 132-33.

20. Craven and Cate, *The Army Air Force*, vol. IV, p. 323.

21. *Official History*, Annex G-1, frame 24; Straus File: "Individual Combat Report of 1st Lieutenant David W. Allen," 24 October 1943.

22. Craven and Cate, *The Army Air Forces*, vol. IV, pp. 88-89, chap. 8.

23. *Ibid.*, p. 323.

24. Sakai, *Samurai!*, pp. 88-89, also see p. 153.

25. Craven and Cate, *The Army Air Forces*, vol. IV, p. 323; 432nd Squadron Diary, 25 October 1943.

26. *Official History*, frames 662-63; Craven and Cate, *The Army Air Forces*, vol. IV, pp. 323-24; 432nd Squadron Diary, 23-25 October 1943; Lynch, et al., *Satan's Angels*, p. 15; File: Teddy W. Hanks, "Commendation," 26 October 1943 (hereinafter, Hanks File).

27. Craven and Cate, *The Army Air Forces*, vol. IV, pp. 324-25; Robert Ross Smith, *Triumph in the Philippines*, vol. 10, *The War in the Pacific, United States Army in World War II Series* (Washington, D.C.: Office of the Chief of Military History, 1963), p. 232 (hereinafter, Smith, *Triumph*).

28. Craven and Cate, *The Army Air Forces*, vol. IV, pp. 324-25; 432nd Squadron Diary, 25-28 October 1943; Survey: Perry Dahl, enclosure.

29. Craven and Cate, *The Army Air Forces*, vol. IV, pp. 324-25; 432nd Squadron Diary, 29 October 1943.

30. Miller, *Cartwheel*, pp. 229-32; Craven and Cate, *The Army Air Forces*, vol. IV, p. 250; Kirby Letter, p. 1.

31. Tilley Letter, p. 3.

32. Letter: Carl E. Begh, Jr. to Author, July 1987; Also see Tilley Letter, p. 2; and 432nd Squadron Diary, month of October.

33. *Official History*, frames 751-52.

34. *Official History*, "Man Days Lost: Flying Personnel," frames 751-52; Hood Letter, p. 1; Tilley Letter, p. 1; Craven and Cate, *The Army Air Forces*, vol. IV, pp. 268-69.

35. Letter: Henry C. Toll to Author, June 1987, p. 2 (hereinafter, Toll Letter); Kirby Letter, p. 12.

36. Straus Letter, p. 6.

37. Hood Interview; Maurer Maurer, ed., *USAF Credits for the Destruction of Enemy Aircraft, World War II* (Maxwell AFB, Montgomery, AL: Albert F. Simpson Historical Research Center, 1978), pp. 346, 653 (hereinafter, Maurer, *USAF Credits*).

38. *Official History*, "Man Days Lost: Ground Personnel," frames 753-54.

39. Hanks Letter, p. 8; Tilley Letter, p. 5; *Official History*, frames 694-95; Survey: Fred Champlin; Survey: Gwynne White; Survey: Ralph Smith; Survey: Leland F. Howerton.

40. 432nd Squadron Diary, 1 September-28 October; Survey: William Bean; Craven and Cate, *The Army Air Forces*, vol. IV, p. 319.

41. Craven and Cate, *The Army Air Forces*, vol. IV, p. 196.

42. Miller, *Cartwheel*, pp. 233, 248; Craven and Cate, *The Army Air Forces*, vol. IV, pp. 253, 314-15.

43. Kirby Letter, p. 1; Craven and Cate, *The Army Air Forces*, vol. IV, p. 325; Edward Jablonski, *Air War*, Bk. 1, "Outraged Skies" (Garden City, NY: Doubleday and Co., 1971), p. 36 (hereinafter, Jablonski, "Outraged Skies.")

44. *Official History*, "Engineering's Contribution to Victory," frame 672; 432nd Squadron Diary, 2 November 1943; Hess, *Sweep*, pp. 136-37; Craven and Cate, *The Army Air Forces*, vol. IV, pp. 324-25; Jablonski, "Outraged Skies," pp. 35-36.

45. Kirby Letter, p. 1-2; Steve Birdsall, "Target: Rabaul!" *Air Force Magazine* (September 1975), p. 110 (hereinafter, Birdsall, "Target: Rabaul!").

46. Kirby Letter, p. 2; Craven and Cate, *The Army Air Forces*, vol. IV, p. 325; Jablonski, "Outraged Skies," p. 36; Hess, *Sweep*, p. 136.

47. Kirby Letter, p. 2.

48. Craven and Cate, *The Army Air Forces*, vol. IV, p. 324; Hess, *Sweep*, p. 136; 431st Squadron History, Summary, p. 7.

49. 432nd Squadron Diary, 2 November 1943;

Kirby Letter, p. 2; Kirby File: "Recommendation for Award of Silver Star"; Lynch, et al., *Satan's Angels*, pp. 52-54, 58; Maurer, *USAF Credits*, pp. 653-57; Jablonski, "Outraged Skies," p. 36; Hess, *Sweep*, pp. 136-39; Charles L. Brammeier, *USAF Fighter Operations* . . . (unpublished paper, Air Command Staff College, 1987), p. 25 (hereinafter, Brammeier, "Fighter Operations"); Birdsall, "Target: Rabaul!," pp. 108-13.

50. 432nd Squadron Diary, 5 November 1943; Hess, *Sweep*, p. 139; Craven and Cate, *The Army Air Forces*, vol. IV, p. 327; Miller, *Cartwheel*, pp. 352-53.

51. Kirby Letter, p. 3; 432nd Squadron Diary, 7 November 1943.

52. Miller, *Cartwheel*, pp. 232, 255; Craven and Cate, *The Army Air Forces*, vol. IV, p. 323.

53. *Official History*, Annex G-1, frames 665, 724-25; especially see "Engineering's Contribution to Victory," frames 671-72. See the effects of this drawdown of group strength in Straus File: "Individual Combat Report of 1st Lieutenant David W. Allen," 17 November 1943.

54. Group Interview, 24 July 1987, Glendale, CA.

55. *Official History*, frames 724-25.

56. *Ibid.*, frames 751-52, 739-40.

57. *Ibid.*, frame 665; Kirby Letter, p. 3; Yoshino, "Doctrine," p. 343, note 57.

58. *Official History*, frames 722-25; Lynch, et al., *Satan's Angels*, p. 50.

Chapter Four

Transitions: Dobodura to Nadzab, November 1943-February 1944

Major Warren R. Lewis, left, and Captain John S. "Long John" Babel, right. (Anderson Collection)

Important changes filled the interstice between the Wewak-Rabaul campaigns and the 475th's entry into the Philippines. Combat slowed after November and, both rationally and intuitively, Satan's Angels used the time to reforge themselves preparing for future actions. The Fifth Air Force as a whole coiled to strike north in advance of MacArthur's continued offensives, seeking to complete the isolation of Rabaul and then, pushing east, clear the rest of New Guinea of the enemy.

Changes of leadership marked time's passing. Veterans of the hard, early days of the Moresby defense received overdue stateside rotations. Combat also took some of the 475th's finest. On 9 November 1943, Captain Danny Roberts died.

Roberts had taken over a dispirited 433rd Squadron on 3

October 1943. Combat leadership is not an easy thing to understand. Later a senior pilot and ace, Captain John S. Babel, explained that it was not a simplistic matter of "good" or "bad" command, but a complex matrix that came together as a style. The 433rd's former leader had a style unsuited for that unit. Group C.O. George W. Prentice selected "Captain Dan" to remedy that situation.[1]

Prentice had confidentially asked Roberts to take over the 433rd on 25 September, just after he had touched down from an escort mission to Finschhafen. The captain assented. In his diary entry for 26 September Roberts wrote: "Today the Col. [Prentice] asked me to take a squadron and whip it into shape. . . . This is a break but it will be hard work."[2]

Typical of a skilled leader Roberts began by interviewing squadron personnel, officers and noncoms alike, impressing on them the importance of firm, humane leadership. In 1984 former Chief Warrant Officer Donald E. Wagner, the 433rd's Engineering Officer, remembered Roberts well and gave a clue to his effectiveness: ". . . that Danny was the best listener [he] had ever known." Before terminating the conversation with Wagner, the new C.O. again emphasized that without maintenance, the squadron's work went for nothing.

He was as good as his word. The next night, 4 October, Babel noted the first meeting between the pilots and their new C.O. Roberts reemphasized his cardinal belief — teamwork — both in the air and on the ground. Enlisted men were crucial to the 433rd's, and the group's, missions; he expected them to be treated in that light. To that end Roberts dropped the previously existing ban against fraternization between officers and men and announced that, effective 1 November, promotions for the EMs could be expected. Morale skyrocketed in Possum Squadron.[3]

The pilots were a different story. Danny Roberts' special skill centered on his self-confidence and his ability to impart that sense of assuredness in an "almost mystical" manner. Briefings, remembered Babel, were inspirational, always emphasizing teamwork. The young C.O. would ritualistically end the meetings with, "Stick together like a pack of wolves and we'll all come home!"

Flight line crew chief Theodore W. "Teddy" Hanks had drawn Lightning number 197, the "Old Man's" craft, Danny Roberts' own. Hanks clearly remembers the first 433rd mission Roberts led. The captain started down the end of the flight line greeting each man with a nod or a few words. Approaching 197, Hanks rose and Roberts greeted him in a

One of the last pictures taken of Danny Roberts. (Dennis G. Cooper photo)

warm, sincere manner. Teddy Hanks took an instant liking to his new boss.[4]

The 433rd responded to their new squadron leader by posting their highest score to date, forty-four in October alone — and the highest single month's kills in the group's history. Roberts led by example. He came to Possum Squadron as a seven-victory ace. In the ensuing days the captain shot down six more Japanese fighters for thirteen, thereby leading the 475th in kills.[5]

By 9 November the group was continuously raiding in advance of MacArthur's next assignments, the complete isolation of Rabaul by the investment of Western New Britain and the continued march across New Guinea's north coast. On that day the B-25s of the 38th Bomb Group staged a low-level, antishipping strike against Alexishafen, just south of Madang, the 475th escorting them to and from the target. The 432nd still showed the wear of the Rabaul missions, fielding only twelve P-38s for their top cover assignment. Roberts' 433rd flew the low position as the Mitchells attacked from the land side, hit their targets and then escaped out to sea, homeward bound.

Over the ocean a mixed bag of between fifteen to twenty Japanese interceptors rose. The 432nd, enjoying a height advantage, slid into them destroying seven enemy fighters before breaking off the attack. Possibly the remnants of that hostile group reformed because Roberts' Possums, down low, got bounced by Japanese fighters coming out of the sun. In the ensuing fight, Lieutenants Jack A. Fisk and John Babel each scored one. Roberts saw a Hamp low over the water and blew it up. While reassembling his brood, a Zeke 52 singleton swept past the 433rd running hard for the Alexishafen strip and the protection of friendly flak and fighters. Events blur from this point on.

Sergeant Teddy W. Hanks, crew chief for Danny Roberts, Dobodura, New Guinea. (Ted Hanks Collection)

Official records indicate that Roberts dove in pursuit. His wingman, Lieutenant Dale O. Meyers, spotted the Zeke at the same time and pulled in tight onto his leader's left because the enemy craft was probably weaving from side to side at the time of the accident. Suddenly the Japanese "banked sharply right." The two Americans followed. At least one source believed that the wingman responded too slowly, striking Roberts' left fuselage boom and severing it just behind the wing. However, this could only happen if, in a right turn, the wingman turned faster than the 433rd's C.O., ramming him at that point, apparently unable to drop below Roberts in an attempt to slide to the other side.

Roberts' Lightning number 197 had developed a hydraulic leak, and so it was a replacement craft, number 198, that fell off and exploded less than 400 feet above a swampy patch of ground near Alexishafen strip. Meyers' craft also burst into flames and went in. No parachutes appeared and at that collision's altitude, none could have opened in time to save the pilots. Officially the USAAF concluded that Roberts died in an aerial collision with his wingman.

Teddy Hanks, Roberts crew chief, believed otherwise. Over the years Hanks gathered evidence and produced a different interpretation based on a number of factors. In the aftermath of a terrible, but swiftly unfolding event, a mix-up in specific aircraft identification possibly took place. Three P-38s went down during Roberts' last mission to Alexishafen.

Hanks' version differs in several respects. Pilot re-creations of the event were not specific on aircraft identification numbers. Personally, Meyers was a good pilot and had flown wing to Roberts several times before, indicating his knowledge of the C.O.'s combat practices and a mutual trust. Conversely, the third missing man had recently come aboard and, despite ace status (five or more hostile aircraft downed in aerial combat), was still gathering experience.

A scenario unfolds with Roberts rendezvousing with his squadron after its first sharp fight. Unseen, Meyers was brought down either in the initial Japanese attack or by the later, single Zeke which then passed in front of the 433rd triggering the tragic collision. Roberts chased the aircraft, joined by the second P-38, no longer an element but two Lightnings fixated on the same target. When the Zeke whipped into its turn, the newly-arrived "wingman" reacted quicker than Roberts and sliced into the C.O.'s fighter.

On 28 August 1950, the Roberts family received a letter from the Office of the Quartermaster General, U.S. Army, concerning the final resting place of the 433rd's leader. It explained that in June 1944 a Search and Recovery team of the American Graves Registration Service had found two graves in the area of Roberts last combat. The wreckage of a P-38 was found nearby, having fallen, according to locals, "about" a year before. The aircraft's serial numbers, 42-66596, matched those of the new pilot, not the late wingman Meyers. The Army Air Forces found no trace of either Meyers' ship or Roberts', which had reportedly exploded in midair. His remains were later positively confirmed, as were those of the man who piloted Lightning 42-66596.

Whatever the circumstances, the results remain the same. Often in war the best are taken first. Captain Daniel Tipton Roberts, Jr., was gone. A brilliant battle leader, he performed miracles in thirty-seven days and "Captain Dan's" passage left a void — and a worthy tradition — for his squadron and the 475th.[6]

November 1943 also saw the long overdue rotation of veteran pilots who had served since 1942. The Army Air Force ticketed Satan's Angels commanding officer, George W. Prentice, for a well-deserved trip home. From January 1942 onward, Prentice had flown combat missions, first in P-40s, then as the 39th Squadron's commander, 35th Fighter Group, the first unit to receive P-38s in the SWPA. After taking over the 475th in June 1943, Prentice commanded Satan's Angels through 307 missions, 3,452 sorties, 230 confirmed victories. This in three and a half months.[7]

Slim, with a small, clipped mustache, Prentice carried himself with military bearing. Charles H. MacDonald, Prentice's executive officer, later commented that Prentice "looked like he should have [had] a swagger stick" to complete the picture. Prentice immersed himself in his new duties. So busy was the 475th's C.O. that he flew infrequently, his three kills all coming before assuming control of the group. The colonel's insistence on training at Amberly largely figured in the group's initial and continued success, as did

The 475th Group's first C.O. Colonel George W. Prentice. (Anderson Collection)

his operational experience which insured smooth missions. Most critically Prentice led, his organization discreetly reflecting his standards.

Sometimes doing right came hard especially if it meant changing personnel for the good of the group, but Prentice never shrank from that responsibility. If the pilots demanded teamwork, it was because their C.O. lived by and acted on that concept. If a comradely spirit typified the unit, it started at headquarters and percolated down. Prentice stressed repeatedly, "Headquarters exists to serve the squadrons," and to this end Prentice gave himself to the group. On 28 November, the 475th gave the colonel a "going home party." Group intelligence officer, Captain Dennis G. "Coop" Cooper spoke for many when he described the departing Prentice as an "officer's officer."[8]

Lieutenant Colonel Charles H. MacDonald moved up to command the 475th. By 1939 he had earned his wings and on a bright Hawaiian morning, MacDonald flew a P-40 surveying the smoke and flame of Pearl Harbor as he hunted for Japanese raiders. Returning to the states, the then major commanded a P-47 squadron that activated in New Guinea by May 1943. By early summer MacDonald joined the 475th at Amberly, now attached to headquarters.

Each war produced its share of warriors and leaders, but the combination of the two in one man proved rare. Charles H. MacDonald would rank with some of the ace commanders of World War II: Colonel Hubert "Hub" Zempke of the ETO's 56th Group, RAF wing commander John "Johnny" Johnson, and the Luftwaffe's Adolph Galland. In MacDonald's case, the key stemmed from a maturity that allowed him to control his aggressive, self-confident nature selflessly enough to place the group's welfare first.

MacDonald came aboard in October as Prentice's executive officer, gaining promotion to lieutenant colonel in the process. While they worked well together, there was little time for any close relationship. In administering the 475th the colonel wisely followed at least one of his predecessor's examples, that of insisting on the importance of all hands in the unit and that headquarters still existed "to serve the squadrons." MacDonald held out that same courtesy to his pilots. Later Fred Champlin of the 431st Squadron nicely summarized that important melding of respect, familiarity, and concern that MacDonald so easily wielded:

> Col[onel] Mac was . . . easy to talk to, easy to socialize with, and a leader in the air[,] . . . everyone wanted to be a member of his flight or at least part of the formation. He considered all members of all three squadrons his personal responsibility. His pre-mission briefings and tactics . . . gave consideration first to the pilots and second to the successful completion of the mission.[9]

Thus "Colonel Mac" led the 475th on the ground and in aerial battle until July 1945, a gifted leader in either sphere.[10]

His move sparked shifts at lower levels, especially among the squadrons. Squadron leadership came through a filtering process, sheer survival topping the list. Both training and combat took a heavy toll of men. Those who survived, still had their wits about them, and wished to continue flying combat were few and could become leaders, especially in the pre-Dobodura days. Aggressive flying clearly figured importantly in leadership roles with seven of eleven 475th squadron C.O.'s gaining ace status. Outstanding command qualities, skilled flying, tactical planning, and the ability to sustain morale also admitted men to the inner circle. Three squadron commanders scored from two to four victories, and had excellent leadership qualities. A fourth C.O.'s tenure was brief and he obtained no confirmed kills.[11]

MacDonald, himself, never scored a kill before coming to Satan's Angels. Once part of the group, he began his illustrious career with two Japanese fighters on 15 October 1943 and steadily increased his tally from then on. By the time the colonel took command of Satan's Angels, he was one score over ace and when he fought, the Pennsylvanian had a marked propensity for multiple kills. Of his 27 victories, 12 came as doubles and 6 as triples, 18 craft for 8 days flying, an amazingly efficient record.[12]

MacDonald used his time wisely; the change in command corresponded with an influx of "new guys" replacing homeward bound veterans. This transition provided a crucial test for the new commander. There would never again be a two-month breaking-in period as at Amberly. Missions mounted drawing in the experienced and neophyte alike. MacDonald coped the best he could.

Breaking-in beginners followed a loose group policy administered by squadron commanders. A new pilot presenting himself to the colonel for the first time would soon face the

Lieutenant John A. Tilley of Hades Squadron, later at Hollandia in Dutch New Guinea, June 1944. (Anderson Collection)

first of several informal but crucial hurdles. First Lieutenant John A. Tilley was one of those "yardbirds," a fledgling pilot. MacDonald set Tilley down and briskly questioned the lieutenant on gunnery, particularly a major concern of Mac-Donald's, deflection shooting. Satisfied that Tilley knew enough, or at least was no more ignorant on the subject than anyone else, Colonel Mac informed him that a check-out flight was next — flying wing to "Mac" McGuire.

With little time available the 475th's leadership chose a simple, traditional expedient; take the new pilot up and try to fly his wings off. Later Major John S. Loisel, ace and last commander of the 475th, explained this methodology: "A good combat outfit will not coddle the weak pilot." Satan's Angels preferred to lose the replacement before combat rather then when the cards were on the table. As Tilley trudged up to the flight line only one thought consoled him, the lieutenant had whipped his instructor in the final dogfight test during operational training just before shipping out.

In his words, the check-out flight was "a wild one." Later Tilley wrote, "I've never worked harder staying on someone's tail. That guy [McGuire] was probably the best fighter pilot I've ever flown with, but he couldn't shake me off his tail." Back on the ground, McGuire informed Tilley he was "combat qualified." While relieved, even the lieutenant felt his operational introduction was a bit brief. Later Tilley confided that "it wasn't [un]til many missions later that *I* thought I was combat qualified."[13]

Once assigned a squadron, the neophyte flew wing position with some of the most experienced men in the group. There the yardbirds could observe the flying and tactics of skilled men and acclimate themselves to combat as they guarded their leaders. Furthermore, the leading edge of the squadron was safer than the exposed "Tail-end Charlie" position.

As the yardbirds accumulated experience they flew wing for the flight's second "shooter," the number three pilot. This meant the neophytes occupied the last slot, a position of maximum responsibility and vulnerability. Most did not relish this assignment. As they seasoned, and survived, the pilots moved forward to the number three slot and then flight leader in the front.[14]

Luckily, the intensity of combat slackened in December and January. Group losses, an indicator of enemy contact, dropped to their lowest point since the first half month's fighting in August. Newer pilots could fly "milk runs," relatively benign missions that risked little hostile interception. It was on those missions that the veterans could spot and correct the myriad mistakes that came with inexperience.

Transitioning to combat flying meant breaking habits learned in training and the acquisition of new skills. John Babel's chief complaint centered on the tight, spit and polish formation flying of the new members. Earlier used to hone a sense of precision control, in the combat zone it became a positive hazard, making instantaneous maneuvers impossible without a collision.

Lack of observation constituted another deadly sin. The group's imperative of "put your head on a swivel" made sense on the ground, but in the cockpit, over enemy territory,

and surrounded by the veteran pilots, beginners concentrated on just flying. As operational time mounted and the men loosened up, their powers of observation increased until they too visually swept their share of the sky. Other problems included a lack of navigational skills, crucial in the long oceanic flights that inevitably accompanied 475th missions, and dangers created by the few "hot" pilots eager for ace status, even at the cost of squadron integrity. Coaching usually cured the former problem, the Japanese the latter, the group's records occasionally noting "last seen pursuing enemy aircraft."[15]

For a nation that prided itself on marksmanship, Army Air Forces gunnery suffered during the war. This partly sprang from the urgent need for pilots, training being, as MacDonald later observed, "a numbers game." Lack of gun training also stemmed from fighter aviation itself. The task of teaching men the intricacies of military flight had always required time and given the press of the battlefield, luxuries like gunnery always suffered.

Poor aerial marksmanship also showed in the old pre-war hands as well. Early Army Air Corps fighters, like the Curtiss P-36 Hawk, had sights provided by U.S. Army Ordnance, with reticles suited only for fixed targets. Christmas tree in shape, a vertical line was scribed by graduated lines representing yardage. Pilots corrected for distance by raising the airplane's nose. This sight, however, made no allowance for firing at an aircraft moving across a fighter's front, called deflection shooting. Thus pre-war gunnery training was still "by guess and by God."

Veteran Marion Kirby graduated five days after war was declared and quickly went to the SWPA. His first gunnery practice came in combat firing at Japanese craft. Victories came as a surprise to him, partly because of modesty, partly because he considered himself a "poor shot." Another yardbird lieutenant arrived at the 431st as a replacement pilot just after the Rabaul missions. No one in gunnery instruction, or in the group, informed him of "bullet drop," gravity's pull on a fired bullet causing it to fall off at the end of its flight. He assumed that sights were sights; place a target on the reticle and it should fall. No Japanese aircraft fell. The lieutenant experimented by pulling closer to his target before firing and began to score. Only in 1978, while sighting in a hunting rifle, did he learn about bullet drop. Ironically, the lieutenant's ignorance of bullet drop forced upon him the correct solution, fly closer to the target.

MacDonald abhorred poor gunnery. A fine marksman himself, the colonel had benefitted from a pre-war course taught by Royal Air Force veterans. His growing string of victories attested to his abilities as a gunner. In April 1944 the commander wrote and distributed a handout entitled "How To Be An Expert Aerial Gunner . . . In One (1) Easy Lesson!" It addressed several basic problems. Pilots could not judge range. Without individual sights, armorers adjusted each gun to fire straight ahead, all barrels converging on a twelve-inch circle and boresighted at anywhere from 200 to 300 yards. In combat, however, the urge to fire at anything in front of the craft was overwhelming, frittering away rounds hat made few or no hits. Even attacks from dead astern went for nothing if firing took place outside effective range.

Multi-ace Mac McGuire summed up the solution best, "Go in close, and . . . when you think you are too close, go in closer." MacDonald advocated the same thing.[16]

Chiefly MacDonald concerned himself with the problem of deflection shooting, firing at aircraft as they crossed the axis of flight. Accurate deflection shooting often spelled the difference between ace and average pilots. For instance, Danny Roberts had a reputation for making those difficult shots count. A good deflection shooter himself, MacDonald espoused the solution to pass gunnery, aim at the rear of the target, pull the sight through it until proper lead was established, then fire. The colonel later explained that this technique was distilled from his shotgunning experience. All these lessons, MacDonald asserted, so "we won't have so damn many probables and damaged."[17]

While the colonel put his group in order, the war ground on. The Allied Quadrant Conference of August 1943 reconfirmed the cross-Channel invasion in the next year but the Combined Chiefs of Staff's plans for the POA (Pacific Ocean Area) horrified Washington, D.C. The Anglo-American plan read with slug-like deliberateness: 1945-46, capture the Philippines, Formosa (Taiwan), Malaya, and the Ryukyus; 1947-48, reduce and take Japan. This timetable predicated itself on the fall of Nazi Germany in 1944.

The U.S. Joint Chiefs of Staff rejected this plan, countering with a green light for Nimitz's Central Pacific drive, the reduction of Rabaul by air, and a continuation of MacArthur's western drive across to Dutch New Guinea.

While the SWPA area held two U.S. Air Forces, the Fifth and the Thirteenth, even the air arm in Washington began to favor Nimitz's island thrust. Boeing's new strategic bomber, the B-29 Superfortress, opened vistas of a direct air assault on Japan staged from Pacific Islands like the Marianas. Thus a chief supporter of MacArthur's Southwest Pacific strategy, the Air Forces, moved towards favoring Nimitz. Through all the discussions at Quadrant, and later at Cairo's Sextant Conference, not a single word issued on an invasion of the Philippines. This worried MacArthur considerably, but for the present more immediate problems occupied his time.[18]

Operation Dexterity had been confirmed by 22 September 1943. In order for the Army to move west unimpeded into Dutch New Guinea and east to secure the vital Vitiaz Straits, MacArthur had to secure the western end of New Britain. After some debate, the general decided to strike Arawe on New Britain's south coast, Cape Gloucester at its tip, and finally, Saidor on the New Guinea coast opposite the Gloucester landing sites. Much of the 475th's efforts would fly in support of those operations.[19]

Missions to New Britain began with Gasmata. A previously slated invasion site, later substituted by Arawe, Gasmata drew two escort flights on the 22nd and 24th of November. On Z-Day, 15 December, the 475th ran escort and support missions to the Arawe beachhead. Little happened until 1800. With thirty Zekes at 16,000 feet, 8,000 feet above the 432nd, the squadron got separated and only two pilots made contact. In that fight they made two or three passes before deciding "discretion was the better part of valor." Lieutenant William T. Ritter returned with his Lightning peppered with small caliber holes.[20]

On the eighteenth, the 433rd ran into a string of bad luck. For Lieutenant John F. Knecht, the problems started five days before. While taxiing onto crowded Dobodura strip, Knecht drifted in front of a B-24 loaded with bombs. The heavy's outboard engine chewed up the trailing edge of Knecht's right

The end of Wewak. After months of Allied attacks, Wewak, seen here early in 1944, had been reduced to impotence. Wrecked enemy fighters are strewn about in the right of the photo. (Cortner Collection)

Lieutenant William G. Jeakle, "Ops" Officer for Possum Squadron, back after being downed over Arawe beachead.

wing leaving a swath of torn aluminum, the B-24's engine finally lodging in his inboard wing panel between the powerplant and the nacelle. The Liberator's propeller stopped a scant two feet from Knecht's cockpit. On 18 December Knecht was shot down on a raid over Arawe, landing in the midst of a PT boat squadron supporting the landings. They immediately fished him out of the sea. His twin brushes with the reaper engendered some discussion as to whether he was the luckiest or unluckiest man in the group. John Babel's diary described the occurrences in a single word, "close!"

On that Z-Day plus one mission, the squadron ran into a Japanese bombing mission and broke it up. Major Warren R. "Louie" Lewis, now head of the 433rd, bagged two, while Captains John Babel, Charles A. Grice, and Lieutenant Austin K. Neely got one each. On that same mission, bad luck struck again.

In a swirling dogfight, Lieutenant William G. "Jake" Jeakle and wingman Neely fought for their lives. Jeakle, an original member of the squadron and later operations officer for the 433rd, took out one hostile craft but in the maneuvering his wingman swung in behind too tightly and severed the

"Close!" John F. Knecht's P-38 with a B-24 propellor lodged in its inboard wing section. (Ted Hanks Collection)

Lieutenant John F. Knecht's Lightning after colliding with a B-24's propellor, Dobodura, 1943. (Anderson Collection)

An AAF PBY "Catalina," an Army Air Force PBY Catalina, the type used by the Fifth Air Force to rescue downed pilots. (Anderson Collection)

il of his Lightning. Jeakle's P-38 spun down, the pilot radioing a terse, "This is Jeakle, going in!" He managed to get out, and then pop his 'chute, only to drift down towards Japanese-held territory.

His canopy caught high in the mangrove trees. When the lieutenant released himself two things happened instantly — the fall wrenched his knee and his survival gear remained high above in the tangled parachute. Hurt, without supplies, and in hostile territory, Jeakle was at risk.

Coincidentally, the night before Z-Day, intelligence officer Captain Krause ran a refresher course on survival skills. Generally pilots held such lectures with mixed regard. Some of the gems of wisdom were silly ("If shot down, form a group and head for the hills," the logical question, of course, With whom and what hills?"), and partially because such information nurtured the possibility of being downed, an unsolicited and unwelcome thought. Jeakle, however, needed that knowledge. Summoning all his strength and courage, the lieutenant began a painful odyssey through the jungles of New Britain.

Neely staggered home on bent propellers. Believing he had caused his leader's death, the lieutenant suffered badly. The 433rd flew the accident's area the next day searching the jungle's endless greenery for signs of a parachute and then south off of Cape Ward Hunt for Jeakle's life raft, all to no avail. Jeakle, meanwhile, slowly worked his way towards the coast, arriving there on 27 December where a patrolling Navy "Dumbo," a Consolidated PBY, saw and rescued him. After ten days in the jungle, a squadron member wrote: "He looks beat." But more to the point, Jeakle survived.[21]

A few days later, Christmas eve, 475th officers inaugurated the Group's "Club 38," fashionably replete with female guests, a small swing band, and liquor. Beginning that afternoon the men celebrated in more austere, but no less jovial surroundings. Holiday cheer, both spiritual and alcoholic, prompted "Silent Night" and songs of "less lofty nature" long into the night. The next morning the 432nd Squadron adjutant's after-action report read: "Slight damage, nil casualties." Later Christmas Day, the cooks outdid themselves, a roasted chicken dinner with trimmings, and for

awhile the jungle receded. The next day the Americans poured ashore at Borgen Bay, Cape Gloucester, New Britain.

Operation Backhander secured MacArthur's eastern flank. Marines landed south of the Itni River's outlet on beaches designated Yellow and Green. The 432nd patrolled with a full sixteen-ship complement but saw no action. At 1420, twenty-five Japanese Navy Aichi Val divebombers, probably from Rabaul, attacked the landing force, escorted by both Army and Navy fighters. The picket destroyer lost the bogies on its plot and the two P-38 squadrons sent to intercept never made contact.

Just as the Vals attacked, they plunged through twenty-four Mitchells of the 345th Group out to strafe Hill 150. Navy gunners opened fire on the entire group shooting down a Val — and two B-25s. It was this mass of bombers, flak, and Vals that the 475th engaged.

Hades Squadron fell upon the enemy at 10,000 feet. Fred Champlin, Franklin Monk, Paul V. Morriss, and Ormond E. Powell shot down one each, while Vincent T. Elliot and Herman W. Zehring scored doubles. McGuire swooped in low, downed three Vals and a probable, now with sixteen kills the front running scorer among Satan's Angels. He would never relinquish that position. This engagement also signaled the beginning of a period of relative quiescence for the group.[22]

With increasingly successful control over New Britain, by 2 January 1944 the 475th flew missions supporting the Saidor invasion on New Guinea, just opposite Cape Gloucester. By 16 December 1943 MacArthur had approved the attack because Saidor would provide advanced airbases and a small boat shelter for the westward advance along the north of New Guinea. Sporadic fighting occurred in the air but victories remained limited to strafed targets.

On 29 February, the U.S. First Calvary Division staged a reconnaissance in force, landing on Los Negros in the Admiralty Islands. Located to the northwest of New Britain, its capture would almost completely seal off Rabaul from the outside world, ". . . like a cork in the bottle," according to MacArthur. The 475th participated with but eight escort missions, little realizing that this seemingly insignificant event harbored enormous consequences for its future.

By early 1944 the Joint Chiefs of Staff still held MacArthur in a state of abeyance. Would they allow him to liberate the Philippines? A conference between Nimitz and his representatives only reproduced previous agendas, twin drives against the enemy with the general's furthest approved target Eastern New Guinea. Dissatisfied, MacArthur placed his lieutenant, Sutherland, on TDY (temporary duty) to Washington, D.C., hoping to press his views.

Over the next weeks the struggle for strategy "waxed warm" as Sutherland took on the Army, the Joint Strategic Survey Committee (advisor/planners to the JCS), and Admiral "Ernie" King. Despite strong language and bruised egos, the disputes hinged on two genuine uncertainties: could Nimitz neutralize and bypass the Central Pacific fortress of Truk, and what speed could MacArthur make against what most planners considered the heaviest concentrations of Japanese troops in the Pacific basin? February answered those questions.

During 31 January and the first week of February 1944, Nimitz's Central Pacific force successfully and quickly subdued portions of the Marshall Islands group. Encouraged, CENPAC (Central Pacific) forces attacked Eniwetok Island. In order to cover that invasion, Rear Admiral Marc A. Mitscher's Fast Carrier Force raided Truk on 17 and 18 of February. In a dramatic demonstration of seaborne airpower, Mitscher's F6F Hellcats swamped the Japanese defenders, shooting fifty aircraft out of the air and destroying even more in strafing attacks. Navy Avengers razed the base with incendiary bombs while divebombers sank ships in the bowl-like harbor. Truk could be broken. Paths through the Pacific came clearer as planners crossed off Truk's name.[23]

MacArthur still brooded over SWPA's fate. Sutherland achieved no commitment to an ongoing offensive once New Guinea fell. Further, if the JCS continued favoring the axis that produced the ". . . more rapid advance towards Japan . . .," Nimitz's hurdling of Truk made CENPAC front runner for the vanguard thrust on the Home Islands. However a fascinating report began to break up MacArthur's gloom.

On 23 February Kenney wired his general a report on a recent reconnaissance of the Admiralties. Named after Britain's Admiralty, the islands had been held successively by the Germans, Australians, and now the Japanese. Strategically they sealed Rabaul off from the northwest and contained a fine deepwater harbor, Seeadler.

According to SEXTANT directives the islands had been slated for missions by 20 April, but recently Kenney noted that reconnaissance sweeps met no opposition and weeds had overgrown major airfields. To further probe Japanese dispositions, Whitehead directed the 17th Reconnaissance Squadron to send its Mitchells to the islands. They flew low over the target for ninety minutes, not only observing but offering Japanese gunners targets impossible to miss. Upon return, the pilots reported not a single enemy sighting and, more gratifyingly, not a single shot fired.

Opinions at headquarters were divided with Kenney pushing a radical speed-up of the planned invasion, Brigadier

General Charles A. Willoughby, MacArthur's intelligence chief, in opposition. Willoughby maintained that the Admiralty Group had 4,000 troops and that number had not just disappeared. He was right. Captured Japanese plans indicated that the island's commander had hidden his resources, ordering no activity in daylight.

MacArthur, however, held a trump card. On 15 April 1942 he had authorized Central Bureau, an American-Australian decrypting service. In 1943 Central Bureau counted over 1,000 people on staff and had a fine reputation for communications traffic analysis. They also received and disseminated Ultra, the high level intelligence derived from the Enigma encoding machine.

In January 1944 Central Bureau received a real find, the Japanese Army's main codes recently captured from the enemy. This in turn allowed the Bureau to crack the Eighteenth Japanese Army's full order of battle. Intelligence is merely dead words on a page if a commander chooses not to act on it. Kenney's report coincided with the Central Bureau's assurance that the Japanese were pulling out of the Admiralties. Convinced, MacArthur ordered the Admiralties invasion.

Frustrated by Washington's lack of support and fearful of the consequences, MacArthur decided to move up the Admiralty invasion date by a month. Due to the rush, and not convinced the Japanese had fully evacuated the targeted site, he ordered a reconnaissance in force composed of a squadron of the First Calvary Division supported by the Navy. They had six days to prepare.

On 29 February U.S. forces went ashore over light opposition. The Japanese, expecting the Americans to land at Seeadler Harbor, had concentrated the bulk of their troops there. The U.S. Army waded ashore on the opposite side of the island at the smaller Hyane Harbor. By the time the Japanese main force could react, reinforcements covered by air and sea support had landed. By 18 March, America owned the Admiralties.

In retrospect, the invasion had been a gamble. Had the Japanese commander reinforced quicker, he could have overwhelmed the initial landing. Later Admiral Daniel "Uncle Dan" Barbey, MacArthur's amphibious specialist, believed that he could not have withdrawn the squadron if it had been attacked. The loss would have staggered the SWPA's future efforts.

The Admiralties' fall, however, had an enormous impact on Pacific War and the history of the 475th. The dramatic swiftness of the campaign surprised Washington. Planners began to reconsider their recent abandonment of the SWPA; that perhaps it remained a timely, economical route to Tokyo. Exploiting this breach, MacArthur modified the Reno IV plan and again pressed it on the Pentagon. Invigorated by his recent success, MacArthur not only moved up his entire timetable, foreseeing the invasion of Luzon by January 1945, but he also reintroduced a familiar concept which dramatically altered the shape of his strategy.

MacArthur had pioneered the tactical bypass earlier in the New Guinea campaign. Heavy fighting in the interior and

conventional landing had since occupied his time and denied
use of "island hopping." But the denial of that concept also
seemed rooted in a lethargy or tiredness that permeated the
SWPA's commander. Part of Washington's reticence grew out
of MacArthur's lengthy schedule for the rest of New Guinea,
made so by plans to invest most major Japanese bases along
the road to Western New Guinea.

The Admiralties operation banished that fog of conven-
tionality with Reno IV recapturing sparks of older, better
days. Central Bureau estimates supported his plan pointing
out that Japanese concentrations thickened at Madang, Hansa
Bay, and Alexishafen. The general proposed a 580-mile leap
across the top of New Guinea, canceling a late April Hansa
Bay invasion, bypassing Wewak, and isolating approximately
40,000 hostile troops in coastal enclaves. His target was
Hollandia on the eastern border of Dutch New Guinea, with
subsequent jumps in the future.

The JCS fell back on its original plan, two co-equal drives
across the Pacific. This authorized MacArthur to finish New
Guinea and, finally, to take back the Philippines via a
November 1944 invasion of Mindanao. Further, Halsey's
South Pacific forces were to be divided between Nimitz and
the general. That parceling out of resources gave MacArthur
the bulk of Halsey's soldiers with the naval units going to
CENPAC, including Marine Corps air units. Thus the Fifth
Air Force would once again spearhead the SWPA's sweep.
The 475th would help lead this drive against Japan.[24]

Despite intermittent missions, action slowed for the 475th.
The Admiralties saw a total of five escort missions by the
group and despite the significance of that invasion, produced
only sluggish Japanese air responses. Most successes came
from strafing attacks. The group accomplished its long
sought aerial dominance and "Combat was hard to find." On
15 February 1944, headquarters alerted Satan's Angels to
prepare to move.[25]

The forthcoming move had been predicted by the men; too
little had happened for too long a time. Stress wore pilots
down but ground personnel faced different problems, not the
least of which was boredom. Despite the killing pace of
campaigns, men kept busy doing purposeful work, but problems arose in the calm wake of November's strikes against
Rabaul.

The veteran ground crews that came out of New Guinea to
form the 475th's cadre were tired. With the constant work
generated by the Wewak, Huon Peninsula, and Rabaul missions, they stayed busy and when missions did not occupy
them, working on the new base facility did. With the slack in
flying schedules and the construction of their Dobodura
complex completed, a deadly boredom settled in after November. Group censors noted increasing levels of discontent
in correspondence, engendered by fatigue, illness, and strain.
Mistakes were an outward manifestation of that combination
but a bitter tone infiltrated letters and gripe sessions, including complaints about those that stayed behind in the U.S.,
"USO Commandos, 4-F's, and comparisons, justifiably or
not, with the European Theater. . . ." Perhaps worse, the
men began to question whether or not their presence in New

Guinea was really necessary. And whether or not they could
fit into society when they did go home.

Respite came in an announcement made just before the
evening movie on 8 January 1944. Those with eighteen
months of overseas service, six of which were served in the
combat zone, would be rotated home. The announcement
proved true. On 2 February the first contingent of one officer
and twenty-nine men separated from the group. Two had
served since the fall of the Philippines, six others were "Java
men," plucked from Japanese capture to soldier on in New
Guinea. On average that group had been in active service,
mostly in the combat zone, for twenty-five months. Now they
were going home.

Morale vastly improved among all the men because even
those that stayed behind saw proof that their tours of duty
were finite, that rotation was real. Replacement personnel,
such as Statistical Clerk Private Kenneth Paarlberg, assigned
to the 433rd, joined a revitalized group. The proposed move
now occupied all their time and energy.[26]

The 475th headed for Cape Gloucester on 20 February
1944. All hands viewed the move with mixed feelings, the
excitement of transferring tempered by the thought of leaving
Dobodura, a home for the last eight months. The officers
gazed sadly at "Club 38," opened on Christmas Eve, 1943,
and happily inhabited for two brief months. The move
allowed little of the club to be transported save the "demi-
mondaines" mural which graced movie curtains at subsequent bases.[27]

Flying to Gloucester, the advance ground echelon was
composed of one officer and twenty enlisted men from each
squadron, for instance, Lieutenant Joseph "Joe" O'Neil, Jr.,
led the 433rd's contingent. Headquarters provided three men
and the group's leader, First Lieutenant Francis J. Davis. They
brought supplies for fifteen days and material for basic
facilities, a mess hall the top priority. The party had latitude
in site selection. Dobodura had created a model for a good
camp and the party sought to reproduce that environment as
closely as possible.

The advance echelon had just begun to settle in when
ADVON ordered them back to New Guinea, destination

*Temporary camp at Finschhafen, Huon Peninsula. Rain, mud, and
mosquitoes. (Anderson Collection)*

Mess on the alert line, cabbage and bully beef. (Anderson Collection)

Finschhafen on the tip of the Huon Peninsula. By 25 February, thoroughly disgusted, the party began to tear down and repack their materials when disaster struck. The local Air Force commander confiscated all their construction supplies, many of which could not be had in that resource-scarce theater. Particularly missed would be piping, especially when the group reached arid Nadzab.

The advanced echelon struggled across the Vitiaz Straits and joined the 431st and 433rd Squadrons which had just arrived at Finschhafen. They were informed that "Finsch" was no holiday paradise. The Japanese bombed the area with vigor if not effect. Tiring conditions made them long for Dobodura. The latrine's proximity to the mess tent encouraged the local insects to fly a shuttle route between the two areas. Personnel modified drastically their eating habits.

> We'd keep one hand over the canteen cup to deprive the bugs access to their aluminum swimming pool and, while holding spoon, fork, or whatever in the other hand, fan the mess trays madly to keep as many bugs as possible out of our "food."

An impression is gained that the food lost to insect intruders was not truly missed.[28]

The 432nd and remnants of headquarters remained at Dobodura awaiting orders and transport. While the men at Finschhafen struggled to make a camp out of frontier conditions, Group H.Q. sought to run a badly fragmented command. The Fifth Air Force Headquarters did not aid this effort. Orders sometimes reached Finschhafen but not Dobodura and vice-versa. The 475th solved this bifurcation in command by daily conferences with officers flying in from the new base in P-38s modified to carry two men, "piggy-back" Lightnings.

On 11 March 1944 the Fifth Air Force sent Movement

The Lae-Nadzab Road, a twenty-eight mile road hacked out of the jungle linking Nadzab with the sea. (Anderson Collection)

Orders 162, 163, and 164, directing all elements of the 475th to settle at "AUTOMOBILE," Nadzab, situated in the Markham River Valley. The 433rd's new Ordnance Officer, First Lieutenant Thomas H. Thompson, had arrived at Finschhafen only seventeen days before. Now it was time to move again. This concluded the group's sojourn. Kenney never revealed the reason for the February-March moves but the Group Historian shrewdly deduced most of them. As the war moved north, the Dobodura and Oro Bay area ceased attracting enemy attacks, lessening the need for the 475th's protection. The move to both New Britain and the Huon Peninsula reduced flying times and fuel consumption while increasing the radius of action, itself directed west because

The 475th on the plains of Nadzab, hot, dry, dusty. (Anderson Collection)

The 475th at Nadzab, lower Markham Valley, March 1944. (Anderson Collection)

The Erap River near Nadzab camp. The river ran so swiftly that swimming in it was dangerous, March 1944. (Anderson Collection)

Halsey's forces had worked over Rabaul and Kavieng on New Ireland from 21 February on. Unnoted but equally critical, the capture of the Admiralties cleared MacArthur's path to the Philippines, the 475th now poised to spearhead that drive.[29]

By 30 March all hands surveyed the flat, Kunai plains that characterized Nadzab. The thirty-square-mile valley had been well developed by the time Satan's Angels roosted in its northeast portion, isolated by the silty Erap River which ran swiftly the length of the base. Over the black, powdery earth PSM (pierced steel matting) formed the runway. Treeless, wood for building frames had to be sought fifteen miles away along the Lae-Nadzab roadway linking the camp to the sea.

The lack of water proved troublesome. The Markham River was dry and the Erap, though cold, carried tons of earthy particles rendering it impotable. The lack of piping "confiscated" by the New Britain air commander made it difficult to transport water, moving the men to dig a well. Seventeen thousand, six hundred and seventy-one cubic feet of soil and stone later, the men gave up. With an almost vicious sense of satisfaction, they filled the 25-foot deep, 15-foot wide hole with garbage. Eventually water came from the

Erap River through pumps. Despite those hardships, work went forward with the permanent outline of the Nadzab camp slowly taking shape. When established, the installation flanked the west side of the Erap. From north to south the camps ran: 433rd, 432nd, and 431st, followed by Headquarters Group.[30]

The men adjusted to their new home. 433rd crew chief Teddy Hanks made the best of the situation. Sergeant Kenneth H. Perry, an old "Java man" who aided the squadron's armament and maintenance sections, loaned Hanks his records and player. A devotee of pop music, Hanks closed each day as the 433rd's disc jockey, playing selections and always concluding with Bing Crosby's vocal rendition of "Brahm's Lullaby." Removing the disc, Hanks then prepositioned the next morning's selection, invariably the lively "Bugle Call Rag." Just as invariably, the sergeant played it at 4:30 am. Thus ended what the Group Historian wryly called the "merry-go-round" or "March moments."[31]

But the pilots grew restive. March saw as little action as February. With the greatest range of all the Fifth's fighters, the 475th drew the distance assignments including twelve February raids against Kavieng, 816 miles round trip, the longest over-water flights in that theater's history to date. Unfortunately, despite the general lack of Japanese opposition, the 475th lost pilots to the most implacable enemy of all — the weather.

FOOTNOTES

1. *Official History*, frame 659; Lynch, et al., *Satan's Angels*, p. 40; Babel Interview; Hanks Letter, pp. 3-5.

2. Hanks indicates that the Prentice-Roberts conversation took place after ". . . a mission to enemy territory." 432nd records indicate that Roberts flew the day before, 25 September, not on the 26th. Possibly Roberts learned of Prentice's decision the

day before he entered it into his diary. Hanks Letter, p. 6.

3. John S. Babel Diary, 4 October 1943 (hereinafter, Babel Diary); Hanks Letter, p. 7.

4. Hanks Letter, p. 7.

5. *Official History*, frames 22, 659; Hess, *Sweep*, p. 141; Brammeier, "Fighter Operations," p. 25; "Roberts," said the *Official History*, "had 15 Kills (14 officially credited)."

6. *Official History*, frame 659; Lynch, et al., *Satan's Angels*, p. 16; Hess, *Sweep*, p. 141; Brammeier, "Fighter Operations," p. 25; Hanks Letter, pp. 8-10; Letter: Department of the Army, Office of the Quartermaster General to Mr. Tip Roberts, 28 August 1950, pp. 1-2.

7. Lynch, et al., *Satan's Angels*, p. 16; Brammeier, "Fighter Operations," p. 15; Hess, *Sweep*, p. 114.

8. *Official History*, frames 688, 695; Lynch, et al., *Satan's Angels*, p. 38; Dennis G. Cooper, "Tales of Gallantry in the Southwest Pacific, 1942- ," *Aerospace Historian* (Summer/June, 1985), p. 108; Babel Diary, 28 November 1943; Maurer, *USAF Credits*, p. 154; Interview: Charles H. MacDonald, 7 August 1987 (hereinafter, MacDonald Interview).

9. Brammeier, "Fighter Operations," p. 51.

10. *Official History*, frame 695; Brammeier, "Fighter Operations," p. 51; Enclosure: N.A., "Charles H. MacDonald" in Letter: John S. Loisel to Author, November 1987 (hereinafter, N.A., "MacDonald").

11. *Official History*, frames 663-66; Lynch, et al., *Satan's Angel*, pp. 37-40; Brammeier, "Fighter Operations," pp. 16-17, 56-57; Maurer, *USAF Credits*, "Victory Credits Alphabetical," *passim*.

12. *Official History*, frame 666; Lynch, et al.,

Satan's Angels, pp. 16, 39; Brammeier, "Fighter Operations," p. 21; Maurer, *USAF Credits*, p. 119.

13. MacDonald Interview, August 1987; Tilley Letter, pp. 8-9; Maloney, *Fighter Tactics*, p. 80.

14. Letter: Raymond M. Giles to Author, October 1987, p. 10.

15. *Official History*, frames 724-25, 967; Babel Interview; MacDonald Interview; Hood Interview.

16. Tilley Letter, p. 3; Survey: Donald G. Weimer, 13 May 1987; MacDonald, "How To Be An Expert Aerial Gunner . . . In One (1) Easy Lesson!," *Official History*, Annex H-2, frames 731-35 (hereinafter, MacDonald, "Aerial Gunner"); Maloney, *Fighter Tactics*, p. 85.

17. MacDonald, "Aerial Gunnery," frames 734-35; Journal: Joseph O'Neil, N.D., p. 72 (hereinafter, O'Neil Journal); Edward H. Sims, Fore. by John C. Meyer, *Fighter Tactics and Strategy, 1914-1970* (NY: Harper & Row, 1972), pp. 158-59.

18. Craven and Cate, *The Army Air Forces*, vol. IV, pp. 449-55; Spector, *Eagle*, pp. 276-80; Edward J. Drea, *Defending the Driniumor: Covering Force Operations in New Guinea, 1944*, Leavenworth Papers no. 9 (Fort Leavenworth, KS: Combat Studies Institute, 1984), p. 9 (hereinafter, Drea, *Driniumor*).

19. *Ibid.*

20. Craven and Cate, *The Army Air Forces*, vol. IV, p. 335; *Official History*, frame 667.

21. *Ibid.*, frame 667; Hanks Letter, "Explanation of Photographs," pp. 2-#7, 3-#14; Babel Diary, 13, 16, 18, 19 December 1943; O'Neil Journal, p. 87. For a picture of Knecht's P-38 after its collision with the

B-24, see Carroll R. Anderson, "The Saga of Satan's Angels," *Air Classics*, vol. 8, No. 1 (November 1971), p. 32 (hereinafter, Anderson, "Saga").

22. Hess, *Sweep*, pp. 146-47; Craven and Cate, *The Army Air Forces*, vol. IV, pp. 340-41; *Official History*, frame 667, p. 654; Straus File: "Individual Combat Report of Captain Thomas B. McGuire, Jr.," 27 December 1943.

23. Craven and Cate, *The Army Air Forces*, vol. IV, pp. 554-55; Jablonski, "Outraged Skies," pp. 117-119; Spector, *Eagle*, pp. 271-72; Costello, *Pacific War*, p. 488.

24. Craven and Cate, *The Army Air Forces*, vol. IV, chap. 17; Spector, *Eagle*, pp. 279-85, chap. 20; Drea, *Driniumor*, pp. 12-63.

25. *Official History*, frame 669.

26. *Ibid.*, frames 669, 674-75; Babel Interview; Survey: Kenneth Paarlberg, May 1987.

27. *Official History*, Annex B, frames 799-803; Lynch, et al., *Satan's Angels*, p. 18. Later, members revisited Dobodura in the 1970s. "Club 38" had become a native church, the foundation well-chipped to provide limestone for that perennial native habit — betel nut chewing.

28. Tilley Letter, p. 2; Survey: Lewis D. Garrett, May 1987; Survey: Archie J. Weidner, May 1987.

29. *Official History*, frames 768, 781-82, 797-804; 432nd Squadron Diary, 29 October 1944; Lynch, et al., *Satan's Angels*, p. 18; Hanks Letter, p. 5; Survey: Thomas H. Thompson, June 1987.

30. *Official History*, frames 789-90, 881, 914.

31. Hanks Letter, p. 7; *Official History*, frame 816.

Chapter Five

Lightnings East:
Hollandia to Biak, February-July 1944

February monsoons scoured the Bismarck Sea area, twenty missions canceled because aircraft could not penetrate to the targets. On 29 February the 432nd flew cover for the Admiralty Islands invasion. By 0915, eighteen of the ships landed at Nadzab, gassed up, and split into two sections. Staggering takeoff times to provide continuous coverage of Los Negros, their area of operation, the first group of eight Lightnings took off at 1100, the second of ten lifted from

Nadzab at 1215. Twenty miles short of landfall the first group saw a solid rainstorm ahead, radioed the news, and reluctantly turned back. They did not know that their retreat to New Guinea was now blocked by a huge front that had slid in behind them on the outbound leg.

The rear group of ten reversed course, fought through the front, and landed safely at Gusap, New Guinea. The eight P-38s that took off earlier sought refuge on New Britain. The

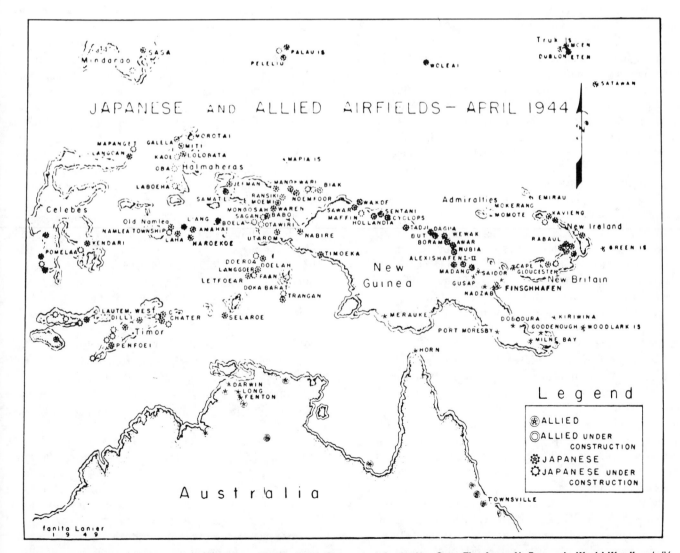

*Japanese and Allied Airfields — April 1944. From Wesley Frank Craven and James Lea Cate, **The Army Air Forces in World War II**, vol. IV (Chicago, IL: University of Chicago Press, 1950), p. 600. Copyrighted 1950 by the University of Chicago. All rights reserved.*

Hades Squadron patrols off the Huon Peninsula, Major Verle Jett leading, March 1944. (Anderson Collection)

storm worsened, the ceiling fluctuating between zero and one hundred feet, and visibility closed to nothing. In the driving rain the aircraft separated, each seeking its own haven. Three of the eight fighters safely landed, two by doubling back to New Guinea and Finschhafen.

The remaining five craft drove for the primitive fields on Cape Gloucester. Lieutenants Edward G. Dickey and Clifford J. Mann successfully managed water landings off Yellow Beach, the site of the original 26 December landings. They floated for an hour until reached by a Higgins boat. Young Perry Dahl made the Gloucester strip, barely; with nil visibility, he crashed into a parked B-24, his Lightning a total write-off. Lieutenant John L. Hannan also put in at the Cape and damaged his nose wheel on landing.

Lieutenant Harold R. Howard, skimming the ocean, made landfall and saw a mountain blocking his path. He banked hard right but too low over the water. The lieutenant's wing sliced, then dug into the water, the cartwheeling Lightning leaving white welts in the sea. Howard died in the crash. The 29 February mission lost the 432nd four craft, one Lightning damaged, and one man killed. The Squadron Historian justifiably called it the 432nd's "most disastrous day. . . ."[1]

March witnessed the end of Wewak, Satan's Angels' perennial target. The Fifth had constantly raided the four fields which now represented Japan's easternmost air power in New Guinea. While the 475th flew long, fruitless, often hazardous missions to New Britain, the shorter range P-40s and P-47s enjoyed good hunting over the Wewak complex in the first two weeks of the month. On the fifteenth the 431st and 433rd escorted B-24s and B-25s to Wewak, the 433rd destroying three enemy interceptors.[2]

On 26 March the 432nd Squadron sent a flight to escort a Navy PBY Catalina. The Catalinas provided rescue service to AAF airplanes brought down on attacks, their gallant efforts rescuing many pilots who ditched at sea. The flight was about to relearn a sharp lesson in tactics.

To cover the lumbering patrol craft, the flight had to reduce speed to 170 miles per hour and in order to spot downed "friendlies," the Lightnings flew at 4,000 feet. The 433rd had traded altitude and speed, the prime assets of the big American fighter, for proximity. At 1715, the Lightnings sighted a mixed bag of 18 to 20 Japanese Army fighters at 15,000 feet. The enemy gaggle slid into the slanting sun, two Oscars and two Tonys peeled off and came in flat from the rear, the sun behind them. Low and slow, the 433rd narrowly escaped the bounce. Splitting into elements, the Lightnings fought for ten minutes to regain speed and fighting height, the paired P-38s scissoring violently to clear each others tails as they labored to 10,000 feet.

Nor was this a onesided battle, the remaining Japanese staying high probably suspecting the four Americans to be decoys. Caught below the recommended 200 m.p.h. minimum combat speed and on the deck, the one-on-one fight produced a draw, two damaged fighters each. Even at that late date, fighting basics still counted. By the end of March, however, Satan's Angels had posted their 300th confirmed kill.[3]

Before March closed, another important transition took place. The venerable H models had seen much combat, were wear and faced reassignment. Two months earlier, on 1 December 1943, a pilot wrote in his diary "drove to 431st to see new P-38Js." The 475th had received new Lightning variants.[4]

Fundamental remodeling could only take place at the factory and the Js represented the sum of those modifications. They ranged from small to large: from optically-flat, bulletproof glass windscreens added for pilot protection in frontal attacks, to circuit breakers substituted for many fuses allowing fliers to reset electrical systems in flight. The most crucial change, however, proved most visible.

The coolers for two turbo-superchargers principally distinguished the J from the H models. In the newer variant, the

The J Model Lightning, chiefly identified by the chin scoops. (Anderson Collection)

carburetor intercoolers moved from the vulnerable leading edges of the wings to cone-type radiators under each engine, giving the Js a deeper profile than its predecessor. With radiators removed from the wings, Lockheed filled the void with a 55-gallon fuel tank per wing, allowing the J to carry internally a total of 410 gallons of gas. With two 165-gallon drop tanks, the Js combat radius grew from the H's 430 to 570 miles. Field modifications had been turning out Lightnings with the new wing fuel cells and by the end of the month, enough had been produced to equip two squadrons. By the flip of a coin, the 431st and 432nd received the long-legged craft. This proved important because the group was going to Hollandia.[5]

With the longer reach provided by the new J Models, the 475th prepared to lead MacArthur's march across Dutch New Guinea. The Hollandia targets were closer than the earlier flights to Kavieng and the Admiralties. But the long-range P-38Js were still important because, unlike those former long trips, no intermediary dromes existed for refueling on the return route. The 530 miles to the target demanded the extended range of the Js.

With Wewak badly battered and facing attacks from the south and the new bases to the east on New Britain, Japanese air power retreated west, concentrating on the triple fields of Hollandia, Cyclops, and Sentani by 15 March 1944. On 19 March eighty-five enemy fighters rested at the fields, increasing to two hundred and seventy-four by 21 March. If MacArthur was to leap to Hollandia, Japanese air assets had to be

destroyed. On the evening of the twenty-ninth the 475th received notice. Tomorrow Hollandia was to be struck.[6]

Four days earlier, MacArthur and Admiral Nimitz met at Brisbane and discussed plans for the forthcoming Hollandia campaign. Despite genuinely convivial spirits, the two men differed over the linchpin to the operation's success, air superiority. Nimitz refused to commit his big carriers to Dutch New Guinea waters fearing Japanese land-based air attacks. Kenney spoke up. Nimitz was not to worry, he would have Japanese air power "rubbed out" by 5 April. Nimitz looked skeptical; MacArthur smiled.[7]

The 30 March raid went off beautifully. The big Liberators went in first, walking hundreds of twenty pound, M-41 parafrags on revetments, facilities, and exposed aircraft. Subsequent waves of B-24s concentrated on flak suppression, flaying anti-aircraft batteries with fragments that wrecked guns and men. With ack-ack silenced, the A-20 Havocs and B-25 gunships came in low. The mediums flew the limits of their range but with flak beaten down, they made efficient, direct attacks that devastated grounded hostile aircraft and then flew out to sea and home.

The 431st and 432nd, equipped with P-38Js, went to the target, the 433rd orbiting south assigned to meet the returning force at Tadji, scraping off any pursuing Japanese. Despite the formidable distance, the Japanese response was weak. The group damaged one Tony.

On the next day a repeat mission triggered a stronger response. The Japanese uncharacteristically attacked the

A Fifth Air Force strike photo showing the damage done to Hollandia, 1944. (Cortner Collection)

The 31 March 1944 attack against Hollandia Drome. The field is dotted with Japanese craft wrecked in the previous day's bombing. (Anderson Collection)

main force before they reached the target. Twenty or thirty interceptors, out of a group of fifty, hit the Fifth's bombing force. Fifteen Zekes, Oscars, and Tonys jumped the 475th high and from the rear. The group broke up but the trailing flight of four ships turned into and disrupted the Japanese attack. Seven enemy fighters fell to the Angels against the loss of Lieutenant Robert P. Donald, who crashed. On the same mission Lieutenant Robert Herman lost an engine over the target and limped home on the longest single-engine flight in the group's history, 460 miles. Although later super-

seded, this instance amply demonstrated the P-38's single-engine capability.[8]

The Hollandia strikes continued. On the date of the second mission twenty-three P-38Js came to the 433rd, now giving them full range. The remainder of the missions ran smoothly.

The last major engagement for aerial control of Hollandia took place on 3 April 1944. Again the heavies and mediums rolled over the triplex with bombs shredding the last vestige of Japanese air power in the region. High above, the 475th took on the enemy defenders. On that day ace Richard I.

The low road over Hollandia. Para-frags (upper center) waft down on parked enemy bombers. (Anderson Collection)

"Dick" Bong flew with the 432nd Squadron. Bong nailed victory number twenty-six, his first as a newly-promoted major and now equaling America's ace-of-aces Eddie Rickenbacker's World War I record. This kill helped pave his way

Captain William S. "Bill" O'Brien, 431st operations officer who led the squadron home on "Black Sunday," 16 April 1944. (Anderson Collection)

to becoming America's top fighter pilot for World War II victories.[9]

Yardbird Lieutenant Joe M. Forster made his combat debut on this mission with the 432nd, shooting down three Oscars in succession as they attempted to disrupt the A-20 Havocs on their attack run. Squadron mate Hank Toll described what happened next: "[Forster] . . . was closing in on a fourth, getting hits. . . . All of a sudden, a shiny silver Lightning flashed past him, hit . . . and blew [it] up." Forster attempted to identify the pilot in order to discuss sharing credit for the kill. When he learned the bright P-38 belonged to Bong, Forster graciously relinquished his claim.

Flight Officer Joe B. Barton did not return from the raid. Separated during the fight, the 432nd never saw him again. But the A-20 boys did. They noticed Barton's Lightning withdrawing, smoke plumes issuing from an engine. Coming under attack by enemy interceptors the Havocs noticed the single, "crippled" Lightning turn and take the Japanese on, only to be bounced by four Tonys who shot it down. The 3 April raid was not without sacrifice.

The 3 April battle netted a good score for the 432nd. In addition to Forster's three kills, Perry J. Dahl and John S. Loisel bagged two each. Henry L. "Slash" Condon, II, John L. "Jack" Hannan, John W. Temple, and squadron C.O. Elliot Summer each scored one. The 431st contributed one and the 433rd two, for a group total of fourteen, fifteen including Bong's victory. In this manner, the 475th helped Kenney keep his promise to "rub out" Japanese air resistance over Hollandia.[10]

Satan's Angels always fought two wars, one against the Japanese and one against the weather. As noted above, the 432nd had already tilted against storms and lost. This time the weather wreaked havoc on the entire Fifth Air Force.

The fifteenth of April dawned much like any other day. The "Met" report for the next day was, in the words of the USAAF official history, "not . . . too favorable." Kenney, however, had until the twenty-second to finish off Hollandia and a surge of renewed Japanese air activity on 11-12 April urged him to keep the pressure on. Besides, if the Fifth depended on perfect visibility and weather they would never have flown a mission. He laid on a strike for the sixteenth — a Sunday.

The force consisted of 58 Liberators, 46 Mitchells, 118 Havocs, with Lightning escorts, including the 475th. Again, as in the case of the 432nd, a huge front slipped in behind the group on a north-south axis, blocking return routes to Nadzab and the auxiliary fields in the lower Markham Valley. What made this truly threatening was Hollandia's long distance from base. By the time the strike force had pulled off their targets, they barely had gas for a straight ride home. Now rolling thunderheads barred the Fifth's path.

Formations broke up and plunged into dense clouds and rain. The Liberators had sufficient fuel granting them a margin of error. Not so the mediums, especially the A-20s who strained their gauges every time they flew to Hollandia targets. The skies from Saidor, the closest Allied field, south to Finschhafen, Dobodura, and east to Gloucester, were pure bedlam. Pilots reported seeing Havocs circling above the clouds, searching for a break, bombers flying reciprocal courses sending them back to Japanese-held Hollandia, of near-collisions, and radio voices saying, "Guess I won't make it. Send something out to get what is left of me." By the next day ADVON knew a tragedy had struck it a blow the Japanese never could, or would.[11]

Satan's Angels penetrated the heart of the monster front. The 431st was led by its Operations Officer, Captain William S. "Bill" O'Brien. An experienced four-victory pilot, O'Brien kept Hades Squadron together, circling the squadron over a bay off Madang making repeated and unsuccessful attempts to penetrate the front. Finally he slid them to the northeast until they struck the coast. If they could follow the thin foaming surf line, it would lead them to Saidor and safety. Throttling back, the Lightnings tucked in very tight, slowly descending until they found a seam of relatively clear air between the sea and the solid overcast above, "white knuckle" flying, one pilot called it. O'Brien skillfully navigated the twisting littoral, announcing and executing course changes slowly, deliberately, allowing the whole squadron to respond. When frequent squalls completely obscured the forward view O'Brien navigated, and the rest of the pilots held station, by looking out the side panels of their cockpits. Suddenly Saidor came into view. The 431st, in perfect formation, landed as quickly as possible. Said 431st pilot Warren J. Cortner, ". . . We put all ours down without a scratch. [We] parked our planes and sat on the wings and witnessed the panic." O'Brien's quick thinking and expert leadership held the 431st's losses to one ship, Lieutenant Milton A. MacDonald, missing.[12]

The 432nd lost two craft in the front. Early in the raid, Lieutenant Robert L. Hubner had developed mechanical

Left to right: Lieutenant Jack Purdy, Captains Oliver MacAfee, and Richard Kimball at Nadzab, April 1944.

problems near Hollandia and had announced he was returning to Nadzab. In an ailing bird, Hubner flew into the front and got lost, his last radio communications calling for directions. Hubner was never seen again. Lieutenant Jack F. Luddington went down in the "soup" and was reported missing. Months later the 475th received a message that Luddington's I.D. bracelet had been found on a dead Japanese soldier near Madang.[13]

Hardest hit was Possum Squadron, the 433rd. The Lightning escorts, encountering no fighter opposition, had sufficient fuel for the flight home. Unfortunately, as the 433rd Squadron left Hollandia, Captain Richard D. Kimball, unaware of the weather over home bases, led his P-38s into an innocent "rat race" in and among the returning bombers. Valuable fuel was consumed as the pilots attempted to hold position, gasoline that would be missed in minutes.

The 433rd flew between 12,000 and 14,000 feet, probing the storm's periphery seeking safe passage. Finding none, they reversed course and made another attempt, this time at zero altitude. Discovering no hole on the deck the squadron retreated and came at the storm again, pulling yokes back in a attempt to go over the front. At 25,000 feet they saw more than half the vertical blanket towering above them. Reluctantly, the "Blue Devils" broke off the attempt and dropped down to 14,000 feet where they plunged into the roiling mass as gas gauges sank lower and lower. The squadron immediately broke up, each man locked in a cloudy cage. Future ace and C.O. of the 433rd, Lieutenant Calvin C. Wire, penetrated the front and splashed down in the ocean off Point Yasnai, short of Saidor. He broke his nose, a cheap price for having survived that ordeal.

Saidor was a madhouse with over thirty craft of every sort converging on the strip, pilots scared and flying on gas fumes. An F-5 and a B-25 Mitchell had collided on the runway, rendering half of the strip useless to incoming craft. A 432nd flight leader skimmed the matting when a Liberator bore

Lieutenant Tommy Tomberg at Hollandia, after his escape during "Black Sunday." (John Tilley photograph)

straight in at him. Slamming the P-38 down he stood on one brake, the Lightning slewing off the runway, the four-engine heavy sweeping by the spot his craft had occupied a moment before. Another Lightning leader had a buddy with no gas. After several airplanes cut his friend out of an approach, he announced on the common frequency that he would ". . . shoot the next bastard who cuts in ahead of my buddy." His friend landed next.

Lieutenant Joe Price lost his craft but saved his life when his broke free of the front and he attempted to land at Saidor. Price flew into that melee with one engine already dead and his fuel gauge rattling empty. With wheels down he lined up on a runway only to be given a red light, the signal to break off and go around. The lieutenant complied, retracting his wheels to clean up the ship. At that moment his second engine dried up, so he bellied in just to the side of the metal strip. Despite warnings to get clear of his craft, Price calmly collected his canteen and maps, stood on the wing, and then fell unconscious into the mud. The lieutenant survived; his Lightning was written off.[14]

Of all the survivors that day, First Lieutenant Robert M. "Tommy" Tomberg had the most amazing escape. A 433rd flight leader, Tomberg flew into the storm's leading edge and immediately ran into trouble, a right-hand spiral that he managed to correct. The lieutenant then reached to switch on his artificial horizon, a mechanism that allowed straight and

level flying without outside visual references. He grasped the knob so hard it broke off in his hand without turning on the horizon's gyroscope. Now the lieutenant faced real peril.

Tomberg's reactions were common among fighter pilots. Overall, they were fair instrument pilots. The Lightning was a robust, stable craft, and instruments, while Spartan by 1980s standards, could have allowed blind flying, at least to the extent of getting through the front. The rush that minimized gunnery training also allotted little time to instrument flying, the pilots preferring dead reckoning and line of sight to dumb dials. Thus Tomberg entered the front with instruments off, now far too late to save the situation.[15]

The lieutenant went into another right-hand spiral, the clouds tinged with green as if veiling the jungle. Tomberg made his decision. Climbing, he popped the canopy and stood up in the cockpit. The P-38 stalled and the lieutenant tumbled back, striking the craft's radio wires before falling between the fuselage booms and beneath the horizontal stabilizer. Tumbling through space, the lieutenant grasped for his parachute's D ring, fumbling until realizing that he was reaching on the wrong side. The opened canopy suspended Tomberg in an eerie, opaque silence. At four hundred feet the mist disappeared revealing jungle and a small native hut drifting beneath and past him.

He landed in a tree, dangled until catching a branch, and then climbed down. After failed attempts to walk out, the downed pilot went back to the hut where, the next morning, friendly natives greeted and fed him. Part of a well established escape route, they passed Tomberg from village to village until he contacted officials. His guide received the standard fee for delivering downed airmen intact — enough money to purchase either two wives or one pig. Tomberg returned to Nadzab six days after bailing out. When he returned to his tent, bunkmate Clarence J. "C.J." Rieman glanced up and asked, "Where the hell you been?"[16]

Three 433rd pilots flew into the front and disappeared. Among the lost were Lieutenants Louis L. Longman and Lewis M. Yarbrough. Lieutenant Austin K. Neely, who earlier had collided with Jake Jeakle over Arawe beachhead, was the third man swallowed by the storm.

In total, nineteen bombers and two reconnaissance Lightnings went missing. The 16th of April missions cost Kenney sixteen men killed, thirty-seven "missing in action." The 475th lost eight Lightnings and six pilots on that April day, known from then on as "Black Sunday."[17]

On 22 April 1944, aptly named Operations Reckless and Persecution hurdled Japanese coastal bases like Wewak and debouched on Hollandia and Aitape. Japanese resistance was light. American air attacks had thoroughly demoralized the defenders, while Admiral Koga, overall commander of the region, had simply disappeared on a flight to Davao, the Philippines, decapitating leadership on the eve of the invasions. Mostly, however, the Japanese expected the Allies to attack closer targets, Wewak the prime candidate. Indeed the entire Eighteenth Imperial Japanese Army deployed for just that contingency. Two days after D-Day, RAAF engineers had already begun to refurbish the Hollandia strips.[18]

The Fifth Air Force strikes Hollandia. Bomb explosions are marked by white smoke. At the bottom of the photograph five luggers have been attacked with at least two hits, the center one is burning. (Anderson Collection)

personnel, 26 new pilots and 120 enlisted men. The veteran ground personnel worked hard on the camp and line facilities, replacement craft needed adjusting. On 20 April an event held near the 475th's fighter strip pointed up another urgent need to train the newcomers. Brigadier General Wurtsmith, boss of the V Fighter Command, presented decorations to pilots and enlisted men. While April saw no rotation, medals reminded all that trained replacements were the prerequisite for a trip home. The fresh batch of pilots and men were a bit taken aback when consistently greeted by, "Good, now I can go home!"[19]

The squadrons filled the slack time produced by minimal missions by reverting back to Amberly days, training and again training. With the camp located in the hills, "groundlings" had front row seats for the intense flying schedule. Aside from the common orientation and "slow timing" flights (breaking in a P-38 at low speeds), the squadron C.O.s shook out the yardbirds. The day usually started with group formation flying which dissolved into string formations. Leaders immediately broke into "rat races," follow-the-leader with a deadly purpose. Still in strings, the squadrons flew evolutions, wing overs, lazy-eights, slow rolls, and other maneuvers, each pilot expected to emulate the patterns. When sufficiently wrung out, the 475th reformed, "buzzed"

Black Sunday's aftermath coincided with a tapering off of operations for the 475th; Hollandia's investment was "a Navy show," covered by carrier air elements. MacDonald used the respite nicely to reform the group. The young unit which had compiled such an outstanding record demanded a name. Word circulated through camp. Four or five months earlier, at Dobodura, Lieutenant John Tilley had already begun to experiment with a squadron insignia for the 431st. Inspired by Hades' call sign, the lieutenant drew a red devil's face on a blue background interspersed with yellow stars representing the Southern Cross constellation, a reminder of the group's Australian birth. The color scheme also caught the colors of the three squadrons: the 431st — red; 432nd — yellow; and 433rd — blue. The halo softened the satanic image, confirming that the 475th were "the good guys." Captain Dennis Cooper, a 475th intelligence officer, suggested the name "Satan's Angels" and it stuck. Group leadership rejected the design as too informal for an official designation, but it stayed on as the 431st's logo. The name, however, everyone liked, and henceforth the 475th bore the proud title of "Satan's Angels."

In a group officers meeting, MacDonald broached the topic of an official designation with "We need a slogan for the group." Officers like Cooper, Frank Nichols, and John S. Loisel agreed that the motto should be in latin and all turned to Lieutenant Louis E. "Legal Eagle" Lynch, 431st intelligence officer and historian of the group. Eventually MacDonald provided the keynote of "joyful battle." Lynch's command of Latin produced "In Proelio Gaudete: Rejoice in Combat!" — fitting words for a distinguished unit.

The transitions continued. April saw a large influx of new

Sergeant Ralph M. Smith, Hollandia, August 1944. (Ralph M. Smith photo)

The 475th over Nadzab, mid-1944.

the camp, and landed, a critique generally winding up the exercise.[20]

Typically an injection of neophyte pilots meant increases in accidents and April was no exception; group records indicate that of the sixteen P-38s lost that month, seven were due to "operational mishaps." Of those seven, only three were classified as repairable. Lightnings lost in combat or weather MacDonald could understand; but he disliked pilots who "broke planes." Further, eight of his fighters went down on Black Sunday and now the remainder were being chewed up by pilot error. MacDonald had orders cut.[21]

The 475th's C.O. authorized a new decoration just for the group, the "Japanese Air Medal." It was to be awarded to any flying personnel for ". . . his conspicuous poor judgment and unyielding resistance to the dictates of common sense, [who] has distinguished himself and has made a substantial contribution to the cause of Japan." The medal sought to curtail injuries and "general wastage" by saddening and instructing pilots to "forever shun" the mistakes that made them possible. The unhappy decoration was to be worn over the right breast pocket from 5 to 9 pm for seven days. Apparently this tactic had the desired effect for MacDonald discontinued its use after the next month produced only three

This Vargas-like beauty urged group members to use their insect repellant at Nadzab. (Ted Hanks Collection)

damaged craft. By then the 475th received orders to move again.[22]

Small communities usually have a well-honed grapevine and Satan's Angels were no different. Ever since the 22 April invasion of Hollandia, the dominant topic of conversation

The jungles at Hollandia, May 1944. (Anderson Collection)

centered on the next move, where and when. Verbal orders sent the camp into action by the 29th, destination — Hollandia drome. By 30 April the men had struck camp and, trucks loaded, trundled down the road to Lae, the same cargo and route traversed just six weeks before. At Lae the water echelon boarded ships for their new home. On 15 May the air echelon left Nadzab. They arrived with virtually nothing with which to set up a camp. Nonetheless, Hollandia was now home.[23]

Lieutenant Joe O'Neil met the air echelon. O'Neil had been tapped to lead the advance party of fifteen men to the new site only four days after the area had been secured. The group's camp lay two miles from Hollandia strip. Evidence of the recent fighting literally permeated the air, the stench of the decomposing enemy dead. With combat still going on, Graves Registration personnel had not yet entered the area. The lieutenant realized the corpses presented a severe health threat. At first O'Neil thought that the sergeant and men should gather and bury the dead. But as a former EM he could not order them to do such a grisly task, so they soaked the bodies in gas and incinerated them. Only at Biak, a few weeks later, did the Air Force use DDT dusted from C-47 transports to kill all insect vectors, buying time to collect and bury the enemy remains. With Japanese stragglers all about, the advanced party had an uneasy stay at the new field. The air echelon's arrival was greeted happily.[24]

Hollandia presented Satan's Angels with the usual grab bag of assets and liabilities. Some noted the coconut trees, a shady relief from the Kunai plains of Nadzab. More importantly a clear, cool stream ran by the camp providing water for drinking and bathing at the day's end. Meanwhile, personnel took in their new surroundings. Over 340 Japanese craft littered the Hollandia area, sharp testimony to the Fifth's anti-airfield skills. A pilot examined an Army Oscar noting the excellent flush riveting and the aluminum skin only half as thick as the Lightning's. The aft portion of the fuselage had been unbolted just beyond the wing's trailing edge. Curious, the pilot attempted to lift it, surprised to find he could hoist it to his shoulders. "No wonder the little devils were so maneuverable," he mused.[25]

Other aspects of Hollandia were not so welcome. When the water echelon passed one of Lae's staging areas on the way to their ship, they noticed a sign that read, "Stay With Us While In Lae." Due to mixed schedules, 30 officers and 570 enlisted men complied with the sign, for a month. Further snafus also saw C-47s bring in building materials while the squadrons at

Japanese supply dump at Hollandia. The aircraft fuselage had been riddled by bullets and bomb fragments. (Anderson Collection)

Wrecked Japanese planes at Hollandia attest to the effectiveness of the Fifth Air Force's attacks. (Anderson Collection)

Hollandia went hungry waiting for food.[26]

Hollandia was a dangerous place. The group had never operated so close to the front lines before. Shots could be heard and Japanese troop remnants, cut off and desperate, presented a constant threat. Driving to the strip each morning brought group jeeps past a high grassy knoll. Sometimes enemy snipers fired on them, the high crack of .25 caliber rifles urging them onward at sixty miles per hour. On 12 May the advanced echelon killed three Japanese in camp with their .45 automatics.[27]

In a sense, Hollandia educated the 475th to realities in other ways. The proximity of the war made them aware of and grateful for the differences between airmen and soldiers. Shortly after arriving at Hollandia an infantry lieutenant wandered into the 431st's camp. Officially American armed forces were "dry," unauthorized to hold or serve liquor. Pilots, however, could have two ounces of alcoholic beverage after combat missions for "medicinal" reasons. Apparently the lieutenant knew this and was rewarded with a drink. War stories were swapped and the pilots asked the inevitable question: "What was it like to shoot someone you could actually see?" (a rare occurrence in air combat). His eyes lit up and widened, taking on a slightly mad glaze. "I don't shoot Japs," he exclaimed, "I BURN 'em. There's nothing like flamethrowers and phosphorus grenades." The flyboys all backed up some and were not unhappy when the lieutenant eventually faded back into the jungle. There was not a single man present who was not mortally grateful he was a pilot.[28]

The strip had been built by the Japanese and terminated in a quarter mile of jungle, beyond which was Lake Sentani. The runway was composed of compacted earth, muddy in the rain and so dusty in dry weather that aircraft took off one at a time. The Army engineers were otherwise engaged in several projects so pierced steel matting had not been laid down.

The 432nd's Henry C. "Hank" Toll rolled down the dirt runway on his takeoff run. As the Lightning gathered speed, his right tire blew out on a piece of "Daisy cutter" (fragmentation bomb). No longer cushioned by rubber, Toll's main gear crumpled, the eight-ton fighter careening right and then through the verge of the strip. A G.I. walked the edge of the

The late Carroll R. "Andy" Anderson, fighter pilot and unofficial group historian, in front of his new Lightning, Hollandia. (Anderson Collection)

runway and watched, terrified, as the runaway Lightning raced towards him. It stopped just short of the man. Toll abandoned ship quickly and ran to the soldier, pushing him away from the ship's guns that now stared him in the face. The lieutenant offered the trooper a cigarette and had to light it for him, he shook so badly.[29]

The recently acquired air bases were "lemons," in the words of one air officer. The presumed anchorage failed to protect shipping adequately and all landward approaches terminated in vast swamps. The ground also proved unsuitable for heavy bomber fields, the key to further expansion in the region. So Biak Island had to be taken and, therefore, the now familiar process began again.

By 22 May American troops conquered Wakde Island, ninety-six miles north up Hollandia's coast. Soon the 475th

432nd pilot and group cartoonist, Lt. Hank Toll standing near his Lightning. (Anderson Collection)

would briefly stage there in support of the forthcoming Biak raids. Meanwhile, missions continued.

Hollandia placed the 475th within range of a plethora of Japanese airfields, all of which had to be neutralized or

Major Warren R. "Louie" Lewis, Possum Squadron C.O. (Anderson Collection)

captured. The day after the air echelon arrived, 16 May, the Liberators raided huge Geelvink Bay, located west of Hollandia, in advance of the Biak Island invasion.

On that mission four veteran Japanese Army pilots took on Satan's Angels. The Oscars fought skillfully for twenty minutes, three falling to the 433rd and only one escaping. The next day the 431st bagged another two. On 19 May the 433rd took off led by C.O. Major Warren R. "Louie" Lewis. An outstanding combat leader, the major had already tallied six victories when a floatplane Zero went down before his guns on the nineteenth. It would be Lewis's last win of the war for he was going home on rotation. In that same flight, McGuire also shot down a confirmed kill for a total of eighteen.[30]

On 27 May U.S. soldiers moved against Biak, coming ashore against no opposition. Only in the late afternoon did serious contact occur inland. The Japanese fought from coral caves and tunnels making the conquest of the island long and bitter.[31]

The Japanese high command clearly brooked no threat to its Filipino outposts and in June its air resources rose to 282 fighters and 246 bombers, all craft scattered throughout Western New Guinea. Hunting, for the 475th, would be the best in months although the veterans put things in perspective with, "But back in November, last year. . . ." First blood went to Hades Squadron on the fourth of June when Captain Paul V. Morriss dove and flamed an Oscar caught napping. This occurred on an escort mission to Manokwari, northwestern Geelvink Bay.

The next day on an escort mission to Babo Drome a 433rd pilot, Lieutenant William H. Kuntz, bailed out of a flaming Lightning six miles from the target. The following morning the squadron returned escorting a B-25 equipped for rescue operations. They searched for seventy minutes but to no avail. As the Mitchell circled at 200 feet, a pair of Oscars flashed down, wings and noses bright with fire. The closest flight dropped tanks and curved in behind the intruders, one wracked by Captain Paul R. Peter's guns until it crashed into the jungle below. The other Oscar escaped into a cloud.[32]

The 8 June mission demonstrated that the sacrifices were not over yet. ADVON eyed the north fully expecting a Japanese attempt to reinforce their crumbling perimeter at Biak Island. Kenney had called down the 17th Reconnaissance Squadron, B-25 gunship pilots well known for their ability to get tough jobs done. It had been three ships of the 17th that had offered themselves as targets as they scouted the Admiralty Islands; that squadron's report seconded MacArthur's decision to invade that group thereby opening paths to the Philippines. Now he had another job for the "Fighting 17th."

On 2 June 1944, Japanese Rear Admiral Baomasa Sokonju's relief fleet weighed anchor bound for Biak, eighteen ships strong. The next day brushes with two Liberators and a U.S. submarine, plus an erroneous sighting report of American carriers, forced Sokonju to split off his heavy units sending on only his destroyers, the former carrying 600 troops of the Japanese 2nd Brigade. On the last leg to Biak, on

June, the U.S. 3rd Attack Group spotted the fast ships and radioed their location. Kenney ordered the 17th, now based at Wakde Island, to strike the convoy; the 432nd and 433rd squadrons were to provide top cover on the mission.

The 17th got the word because the retirement of Japanese capital ships convinced the Fifth that the reinforcement run was either postponed or off. Because of enemy night raids aimed at Wakde, precious bombardment units had been ordered to retire to relative safety at Hollandia. This left only the 17th in position to attack when the 3rd Attack Group's sighting report came in. To worsen matters, the squadron got hit in a nocturnal strike on 6th June losing six of sixteen strafers, leaving ten Mitchells to take on six destroyers.

The general solution to daylight antishipping strikes in all theaters during the war hinged on one imperative, aircraft had to first take out escorts with massed attacks. In doing so they divided defensive fire until their own suppressive power could neutralize anti-aircraft positions. The crews at briefing sensed the numbers were wrong. Two bombers per destroyer did little to thin the expected flak. One pilot commented that, "If we find those damned ships, I'll be cashing in my chips today!"

The pilots of the 432nd Squadron watched the battle-scarred gunships roll down the single, coral runway. An hour later they snubbed out last cigarettes and mounted up. Group C.O. Charles MacDonald led the 432nd, taking off at 1030, his faster fighters easily overtaking the outbound Mitchells. Just south of Biak, the 475th ran into a dark front. Bringing up the rear in the high cover slot, flight leader Captain John K. "Parky" Parkansky watched the two squadrons disappear in the murk. Parkansky led his four-ship flight towards Manokwari, on the northwestern Geelvink Bay, in hopes of finding a break which would allow him to rejoin the squadrons.

Just as his flight cleared the cloudy mass Parkansky spotted the enemy convoy, but no strike force. Radioing MacDonald, the captain reported the ships' positions at thirty to forty miles north of Cape Waios, Dutch for False Hope. Soon the B-25s and P-38s closed on the targets. The gunships broke into elements, each pair taking a destroyer, skimming low into a storm of flak. The Japanese shot the air black and water white around each Mitchell as it drove in at 375 miles per hour.

Squadron Commander Major William Tennille's element had just come within firing range of their .50 caliber nose guns. Wingman Lieutenant Wood had just touched his off when Japanese shells sheared the wing off his Mitchell, sending it into a flat spin at zero altitude, the B-25 shattering into small fragments on impact. Even as Wood's ship self-destructed, Tennille whipped past, eight streams of fire reaching for the destroyer. Shells struck the major's Mitchell, starting fires that grew and merged until it was a burning mass that somehow managed to vault the Japanese "tincan."

Captain John J. "Parky" Parkansky (left) and armorers of Possum Squadron. (Anderson Collection)

An anti-shipping strike off New Hanover, New Britain, February 1944, similar to that of the 17th Reconnaissance Squadron of 8 June 1944. Note earlier hits at top center and the bomb falling between the B-25 and Japanese "tincan." The enemy destroyer was sunk in this attack. (Cortner Collection)

On the far side it turned over and, inverted, plunged into the sea, killing Tennille and his crew. Captain Sumner G. Lind also lost a wing to flak; he who spoke earlier of ". . . cashing in his chips today" fulfilled his own prophecy.

The raid at Cape Waios cost the 17th almost one-third of the squadron, three of ten Mitchells, and nineteen men. All sixty men who flew the mission received the Distinguished Flying Cross, eighteen posthumously. They sank one destroyer and seriously damaged three others. The convoy never reinforced Biak.

It almost trivializes such losses to say it could have been worse, however the 17th's losses would have been higher but for the 475th. The convoy had cover from ten Oscars and Zeroes, yet Satan's Angels granted the limping bombers free passage home. The 475th had spotted the bogies above them, drop tanks tumbling away, and Lightnings climbing directly above the surging destroyers. At 1345 MacDonald took on a black-painted Zeke with a head-on attack, leading the Mitsubishi by thirty degrees deflection. Rounds from MacDonald's *Putt Putt Maru* blew pieces off the craft sending it down among the destroyers below.

Perry Dahl, the youthful member of the 432nd and now a first lieutenant, feinted at four Oscars preventing them from attacking the beleaguered gunships below. Gaining a stern position on one of the Nakajimas, Dahl fired, sending it spinning into the sea. Number six for the 432nd man.

Captain Zack W. Dean latched onto an Oscar, its gyrations throwing him off. Wingman Clifford J. Mann backstopped his leader nicely, catching the evading hostile with a full burst that sent the Oscar down off Waigeo Island.

That third and last victory on the 8 June strike points out an interesting tactical facet. The 475th's elements tended to be much looser than in the European Theater of Operations which rigidly adhered to the wingman-leader formation. Pacific Lightnings flew a much more flexible element especially with their high speed tactics, that cleared tails but also allowed both leader and wingman a chance to score. This tactic smacked of modernity and presently (1987) the Air Force has eliminated the ETO type "Weld Wing" formation for the more flexible element, composed of a primary shooter and an "eyeball" wingman which readily exchanges roles depending on the shot available.[33]

On the northern tip of Vogelkop Peninsula, Japanese air reinforcements were staged east from two major depot dromes, Samate and a nearby coastal island, Jefman. Aerial battles now dominated each raid and even the 475th felt the sting of losses. On 5 June, Lieutenant William S. Hasty was shot down over Babo, a Japanese airfield.

Hasty, a veteran of eight months combat, flew at 14,000 feet in his new Lightning, number 186. At the moment he was hit the lieutenant's concern was not for the guns below but for the unseen enemy in the sun. A Japanese ack-ack shell exploded next to Hasty's machine, metal shards puncturing fuel cells and triggering an explosive fire that blew into the cockpit charring clothes around feet and legs. Yanking the cockpit release handle, he crawled out the left window, kicking free. A 433rd pilot acknowledged the lieutenant's

Left to right: Lieutenant Austin K. Neely, who collided with William Glenn Jeakle over Arawe and later disappeared during "Black Sunday," and Lieutenant William S. Hasty before he was shot down near Babo Drome, 5 June 1944. (Anderson Collection)

escape by radioing, "Possum Red Leader. I see him."

Landing in mud near Babo, Hasty attempted to escape by using his raft to float down a river leading to the sea. At 1430 he was captured by the Japanese. After beating the flier with rifle butts, the enemy trussed him up, blindfolded him, and marched him to the nearby base. At Babo he was interrogated by a Japanese Navy lieutenant who "spoke better English" than the American. On 10 June 1944, after days of questioning, the Japanese loaded Hasty on board a bomber. He could just imagine his Possum Squadron "coming in on a . . . dawn patrol and shooting down the bomber." Bill Hasty felt the ship rumble down the runway. His journey had just begun.[34]

By 7 June Kenney hesitated to send unescorted bombers to Jefman-Samate due to a build-up in fighter strength there. Even though the Japanese 23rd Air Flotilla's strength had been slowly bled off to reinforce the Central Pacific area, especially after Nimitz invaded the Marianas, Jefman-Samate still remained a potent threat to any westward advance. Their distance would be the longest yet for Kenney's Mitchells and it took until the fourteenth of June to install bombbay gas tanks in the 25s. Eventually, the crack 38th and 345th medium groups staged out of Hollandia while the Lightnings of the 8th and 475th Fighter Groups flew from crowded Wakde. The Jefman Island raid, number 1-340, was launched on the morning of 16 June 1944.

The two groups escorted a total of forty-one B-25s, the gunships hitting Jefman at 1255. The successive waves came in line abreast, very low, firing and dropping 100 pound parafrags on parked and taxiing aircraft alike. Fires and smoke from wrecked aircraft and auxiliary equipment blackened the fields; follow-up waves flew on instruments during their attack runs. Sweeping through Jefman, the main force flew straight across the four-mile wide channel and struck Samate in the same manner. Later reconnaissance photos showed at least fourteen enemy aircraft destroyed at the two fields.

Overhead the 475th's three squadrons swept Jefman at 6,000 feet. Some of the P-38s got rerouted avoiding thunder-

Views of Babo taken during an attack twelve days after Hasty's capture. Photographs like this not only accurately assessed raid damage but also gave good indication of Japanese supply status.

heads on the trip out but most rendezvoused on schedule. Group leadership devolved on Mac McGuire after MacDonald's Lightning snafued because of an electrical failure. McGuire spotted bogies and silvery drop tanks fell from his group. The major lined up on a Sonia attack airplane trying to take off, getting hits with a burst, his high speed pulling him off the target prematurely. McGuire's element leader, Lieutenant William C. Gronemeyer, caught the Sonia and finished the job. Climbing for another pass, McGuire spotted a second Sonia, not missing this time. Number two came as he intercepted an Oscar that was attacking the main force. Taking the Nakajima in a bow attack, the major measured out

short bursts, the strikes starting fires. The Oscar swung into a turn and the P-38 closed the distance, a final firing touching off its main tanks.

Paul V. Morriss, now a captain, made ace on this trip by doubling with two kills. Lieutenant Franklin Monk also entered that select circle with a single to make five victories. Captain Bill O'Brien and Lieutenant Enrique Provencio got one each, with Lieutenant Horace B. Reeves shooting down the first of an eventual string of six confirmed kills. Hades Squadron downed nine enemy over Jefman-Samate. The 432nd got three when Lieutenant Robert L. Hadley's twin scores were added to Deputy Group Commander Major

Meryl M. Smith's single. The 433rd raised the group's total to fifteen with three individual scores including one by Lieutenant Joe Price. By the Jefman-Samate raid, old and new pilots had coalesced into a first-rate fighting machine. It would also be the last large scale air combat seen by the group for some time to come.[35]

The twenty-sixth of June brought blazing heat with temperatures over 110 degrees and a humidity to match. In "officer's country" MacDonald and Meryl M. Smith were playing a desultory game of checkers when a figure entered the tents, waited patiently while the C.O. studied the board, and then introduced himself as "Lindbergh." Charles A. Lindbergh had come to the 475th Fighter Group.[36]

FOOTNOTES

1. *Official History*, frame 767; Lynch, et al., *Satan's Angels*, p. 17; 432nd Squadron Diary, 29 February 1944.

2. *Official History*, frames 783-84; 433rd Squadron History, 1-31 March 1944, frames 852, 856-57.

3. *Official History*, frames 854-56; Lynch, et al., *Satan's Angels*, p. 16; the PBYs performed gallant rescue work for the Fifth Air Force including snatching airmen up *inside* Simpson Harbor during the November raids. See, for instance, Toll, *Tropic Lightning*, pp. 6-7; Babel Interview.

4. Babel Diary, 1 December 1943.

5. Weber, "P-38J-M," pp. 5-6; Shennan, *Lockheed P-38*, pp. 10-13, "Technical Details," insert; Brammeier, "Fighter Operations," p. 62; *Official History*, frame 785; HQAAF, *Official Flying Safety Pilot Training Manual for the Lightning P-38* (Cincinnati, OH: NP, 1944), *passim*.

6. *Official History*, frames 783-84; 433rd Squadron History, 1-31 March 1944, frames 852, 856-57.

7. Spector, *Eagle*, pp. 285-56.

8. *Official History*, frames 785-787, 820-21; for information on ordinance see Stockholm International Peace Research Institution (SIPRI), *Anti-Personnel Weapons* (NY: Crane, Russak, and Co., 1978), p. 145. Often M-41s were dropped in clusters of six, MIAI.

9. Maurer, *USAF Credits*, p. 25.

10. *Official History*, pp. 877-78, 894; Toll, *Tropic Lightning*, p. 10; Hess, *Sweep*, p. 161; Maurer, *USAF Credits*, pp. 653-57; Lynch, et al., *Satan's Angels*, pp. 19-20.

11. *Official History*, frames 875-76; Craven and Cate, *The Army Air Forces*, vol. IV, pp. 596-97; Hess, *Sweep*, p. 162.

12. Tilley Letter, p. 13; *Official History*, frame 876; Survey: Warren J. Cortner, November 1987 (hereinafter, Cortner Survey).

13. *Official History*, frames 877, 898, 903-4.

14. *Ibid.*, frame 905; Toll Letter, p. 11; Craven and Cate, *The Army Air Forces*, vol. IV, p. 595; Tilley Letter, pp. 13-14; Steve Birdsall, *Flying Buccaneers* (Garden City, NY: Doubleday and Co., 1977), pp. 164-65, 167 (hereinafter, Birdsall, *Flying Buccaneers*).

15. Tilley Interview, 24 August 1987; Brammeier, "Fighter Operations," p. 65; Interview: Robert M. Tomberg with Author, September 1987 (hereinafter, Tomberg Interview); Birdsall, *Flying Buccaneers*, p. 166.

16. Tomberg Interview; Hanks Letter, p. 9.

17. *Official History*, frames 900, 902, 906; Brammeier, "Fighter Operations," p. 30; Hanks Letter, pp. 1, 9.

18. Craven and Cate, *The Army Air Forces*, vol. IV, pp. 604-05; Spector, *Eagle*, pp. 286-86; Willoughby and Chamberlain, *MacArthur*, pp. 183, 185-86.

19. Tilley Letter, pp. 12-13; Lynch, et al., *Satan's Angels*, p. 20; *Official History*, frames 859, 880, 883; Madison Interview.

20. *Official History*, frame 880.

21. *Ibid.*, frames 878, 894-909, Annex E; *Ibid.*, frame 887, Annex A; Brammeier, "Fighter Operations," pp. 57-59.

22. *Official History*, frames 878-79, 910-12; Brammeier, "Fighter Operations," p. 31.

23. *Official History*, frame 884.

24. O'Neil Journal, p. 90.

25. Lynch, et al., *Satan's Angels*, p. 20; Brammeier, "Fighter Operations," p. 31; Tilley Letter, pp. 4-5.

26. *Official History*, frame 923; Toll Letter, p. 3; Survey, William L. Richards, May 1987.

27. O'Neil Journal, p. 41; Lynch, et al., *Satan's Angels*, p. 20; Brammeier, "Fighter Operations," p. 31.

28. Tilley Letter, p. 3; O'Neil Journal, p. 70.

29. Toll Letter, p. 3; Hess, *Sweep*, p. 163.

30. Craven and Cate, *The Army Air Forces*, vol. IV, pp. 608-610, 615, 625-27; Hess, *Sweep*, pp. 163-64; *Official History*, frame 925; Brammeier, "Fighter Operations," p. 31.

31. Craven and Cate, *The Army Air Forces*, vol. IV, p. 635; Costello, *Pacific War*, p. 514.

32. *Official History*, frames 965-66; Lynch, et al., *Satan's Angels*, p. 23; Maurer, *USAF Credits*, p. 138.

33. *Official History*, frame 966; Spector, *Eagle*, pp. 292-933; Carroll R. Anderson, "Suicide at Cape Waios," *Air Classics*, vol. 6, no. 1 (Oct. 1969), pp. 4-13, 56, 58, 62; Craven and Cate, *The Army Air Forces*, vol. IV, p. 638; Lynch, et al., *Satan's Angels*, p. 23.

34. Carroll R. Anderson Papers: unpublished manuscript, N.D. (hereinafter, Anderson Papers); William L. Hasty Memoirs, 27 March 1977 (hereinafter, Hasty Memoirs).

35. Craven and Cate, *The Army Air Forces*, vol. IV, pp. 639-41; *Official History*, frames 966-67; Hess, *Sweep*, pp. 166-67; Brammeier, "Fighter Operations," p. 31; Carroll R. Anderson, "The Lindbergh Kill," *AirPower*, vol. 11, no. 6 (November, 1981), p. 16 (hereinafter, Anderson, "Lindbergh Kill"); Anderson Papers; Carroll R. Anderson, "Thomas McGuire — Fighter Pilot" (unpublished manuscript, N.D.), pp. 7-9 (hereinafter, Anderson, "Thomas McGuire").

36. Carroll R. Anderson, "We Called Him Mister Lindbergh," *Plane and Pilot* (July 1971), pp. 20-21 (hereinafter, Anderson, "Lindbergh").

Chapter Six

Lindbergh:
Biak to the Philippines, July-August 1944

The Lone Eagle, Charles Augustus Lindbergh. In 1927 Lindbergh's solo trans-Atlantic flight stunned the world and turned him into an overnight hero. Two years before the Depression struck, Lindbergh seemed to epitomize the very essence of an ebullient America that never looked back. His lanky good looks, nicely muted by a shy, almost diffident smile, proved the perfect foil to a deed of enormous courage. The U.S. bowed happily before its new hero, "Lucky Lindy."

With fame and hard work, Lindbergh prospered. His marriage to Anne Morrow, daughter of distinguished statesman and diplomat Dwight W. Morrow, proved long and abiding. His fortunes multiplied, as did his family, when Anne bore their first son on 22 June 1930, her birthday.

Novelist F. Scott Fitzgerald wrote: "Show me a hero and I will write you a tragedy." On the night of 1 March 1932, the Lindberghs' child, lovingly called "Fat Lamb" by Anne and "Buster" by Charles, was kidnapped and murdered. The weeks of anguish which followed embittered Lindbergh — heightened by the intrusions of the press and hideous crank calls that mocked his grieving. Nothing quenched Charles' disappointment — in America and its people. On 7 December 1935 he made a decision, telling Anne to pack and be ready to leave on a day's notice. They would abandon the U.S. Fifteen days later the two set sail for England.

Lindbergh's dalliance with Europe forever changed his life. An earlier acquaintance and distinguished British civil servant, Harold Nicholson, offered Charles and Anne the use of Long Barn Cottage, near Nicholson's castle at Sissinghurst in southeastern England. At that place the Lindberghs rebuilt their lives in the solitude of the Kentish countryside; from that place Lindbergh ventured out into a changing world.

Over the next few years he became acquainted with a number of people but it was through the Army Air Corps' singular attache in Berlin, Major Truman Smith, that Lindbergh went to Nazi Germany. He accepted an invitation from the Nazi Government, initiated and forwarded by Smith, to visit Berlin. Once there, German officialdom threw down the red carpet and dazzled Lindbergh. The Lone Eagle came away from that trip with a changed perspective.

At heart Lindbergh had one serious flaw. An honest man, he believed people returned that honesty. That others lied, the man found hard to accept; that a government lied was beyond his comprehension. His tour had been carefully staged; unseen were the political camps and obvious anti-Semitic demonstrations. Instead Lindbergh saw a dynamic Germany

churning out "defensive weapons," awesome in numbers and quality.

The epicenter of his crises, however, devolved on a simple fact — Lindbergh feared for the U.S. How could the Depression-crippled nation he left behind compete with the material and moral superiority of a resurgent Germany? Lindbergh returned home in the spring of 1939. But he had seen and understood too much to remain silent any longer so the Lone Eagle set in motion events that would eventually see him fly with Satan's Angels.[1]

In the years following his return, Lindbergh slowly alienated himself from the Administration and the American people. He joined one of the strongest noninterventionist groups, the American First Committee, in April 1941, and became a major figure in its campaign to keep the U.S. neutral. The crunch came with a series of radio talks in which Lindbergh warned against supporting the Allies because of a perceived German conquest of Europe. His stature among Americans was seen as a powerful counterweight to F.D.R.'s attempt to support the Allies "short of war."

On 29 April 1941, two days after Roosevelt impugned his loyalty in a speech, Lindbergh resigned his colonelcy in the Air Corps Reserve. Public reaction that once idolized him, was no longer sympathetic.

The Japanese attack on Pearl Harbor sank both ships and isolationist aspirations. It placed Lindbergh in a quandary but in a patriotic spirit he offered to aid the U.S. by returning to the Air Corps. It was too late. The Administration refused his services and then, in a mean spirited mood, forced Lindbergh's many aviation employers to cancel his advisory positions, including Juan Trippes' Pan American Airways. Only one man resisted that move, Henry Ford, and Lindbergh went to work for him on 3 April 1942 as a technical consultant helping Ford convert from auto to bomber production.

Over the next year Washington loosened a bit. Lindbergh's undeniable expertise with aircraft and pilots thawed the bans against him. Indeed, his diary shows an enormously busy schedule of test flights that solved pressing problems of new aircraft. In that process the Lone Eagle flew, and came to know well, almost every combat craft in the U.S. inventory. But Lindbergh hungered for combat and as early as January 1944 had made inquiries as to that possibility. The Marines responded first. Cautiously, a tour of Corsair bases in the Pacific was arranged.

In April a friendly U.S. Navy sanctioned and covered

Lindbergh's trip. He would go to their theater, the Pacific, as a civilian technical assistant. Neither the White House nor even Secretary of the Navy Frank Knox knew of this trip. After kitting up with Navy uniforms from Brooks Brothers (sans any insignia) and taking the usual rounds of shots, Lindbergh left San Diego for the War Zone.[2]

By March he had already regularly contacted the United Aircraft Corporation, producer of the F4U Corsair, and had agreed to act as its liaison in the field. Once situated at Guadalcanal, South Pacific Area, he corrected problems of the "bent-winged bird" and established better communications between United Aircraft and the Marines. There, local Marine officers consented to take Lindbergh on a patrol to Rabaul, the first of fourteen combat missions he would fly with the Corps. With the exception of air-to-air combat, Lindbergh flew patrol, escort, strafing, and divebombing assignments. As would later occur with the Army Air Forces, officers winked at his extraordinary activities by according him "observer status." Lindbergh concluded his business on the Canal. By 15 June he landed at Finschhafen bound for the 475th Fighter Group.[3]

The next day Colonel Robert L. Morrissey briefed Lindbergh on the Lightning. For all his flying experience he had never flown the P-38. A major motivation for the civilian's trip to New Guinea centered around United Aircraft's interest in the feasibility of a new twin-engined fighter. The P-38 was the sole American representative of that genre. He had heard that the 475th was a hot Lightning outfit so Lindbergh sought to learn from the best.[4]

He announced his presence to V Fighter Command at Nadzab. Colonel Merian C. Cooper lunched with Lindbergh and on Sunday evening, 18 June, the civilian dined with Whitehead, talking of New Guinea developments and, doubtless, Lindbergh's plans. This proved later insufficient for proper authorization in the theater. On Tuesday he got in an hour and twenty minutes Lightning time with 35th Squadron, 8th Group. A week later Lindbergh flew to Hollandia and walked in on MacDonald and Smith's checker game.

After obtaining permission to accompany the group on the next day's mission, Lindbergh retreated to V Fighter Command Headquarters only to be retrieved later by MacDonald. The mission, explained the colonel, would launch at dawn. It would be better to rest at the 475th camp and cut down transportation problems. Lindbergh agreed.[5]

Meanwhile the "word" spread quickly. Lindbergh was among Satan's Angels. In the 433rd camp, First Lieutenant Carroll R. "Andy" Anderson tried to summon up enough strength to write a long overdue letter to his wife, Virginia Marie. Suddenly friend C.J. Rieman popped in and announced, "Charles A. Lindbergh is going to fly with us!" Letters were quickly forgotten.[6]

The next day's mission was to Jefman Island, now a familiar target for the 475th. With the possibility of interception much higher than on Guadalcanal flights, MacDonald took no chances. The four-craft patrol included some of the best pilots in the group: MacDonald, with Smith in the number two slot, followed by Lindbergh and his wingman

The men who flew Lindberg's first mission with Satan's Angels. Left to right, Thomas McGuire, Lindbergh, Meryl Smith, and Charles MacDonald, group C.O. (Anderson Collection)

Group Headquarters, left of the road, Hollandia, Dutch New Guinea. The solitary half-tent to the right foreground is the four-hole latrine. (Anderson Collection)

Mac McGuire. By that flight the veterans already had a total of thirty-six victories between them.

Except for flak, Jefman produced no action and so, as had been the recent practice, the quartet of Lightnings shot up barges and luggers on the way home. The Japanese used the terrain to mask their boats from air strikes. Spotting a barge in an indentation formed by two hills leading to the sea, Lindbergh flew up and over the nearest ridge clearing the top by a dozen feet, shooting as he partially straightened, and then banked hard left to clear the opposing hill, all this at 250 miles per hour indicated air speed. The four Lightnings left several craft sinking or burning before turning for home.[7]

Later the group approved of Lindbergh's handling of that

first mission. Intelligence Officer Dennis G. "Coop" Cooper was impressed by his accurate and thorough observations during debriefing. He flew well and low against the targets. They did not realize that Lindbergh's time on Guadalcanal had already honed his combat skills.

A number of his missions in F4Us involved strafing difficult targets. In that process, he learned to fire accurately no matter what his fighter's attitude. "I do not think about the plane's position; that is taken care of subconsciously. All my conscious attention is concentrated on the sight. The tracers are going home, that's all that matters." Further, Lindbergh was a natural marksman. He shot trap and skeet and while on a PT boat speeding at 26 knots, shot a flying fish with his .45 automatic. Before going overseas he practiced air-to-air gunnery at El Toro, California, and Hickam Field, Hawaii, and his time at Guadalcanal allowed him to fire guns in action. Lindbergh's modesty kept him silent about his skills.[8]

Lieutenant John E. "Jack" Purdy of the 433rd looked forward to meeting Lindbergh. Eventually a seven-victory ace, Purdy brooked no formality; already it was "Charlie." Almost as if sensing the stir caused by Lindbergh's appearance, MacDonald called a meeting two days after Lindbergh's arrival. The 475th's C.O. sought to clarify the civilian's status among Satan's Angels. The Lone Eagle would be accorded all officer's privileges and would be addressed as "Mister Lindbergh" as befitting his non-military status.[9]

The Lone Eagle sortied regularly with the 475th and the missions reveal two things only partially seen by the group itself. The first concerned changing roles. Japanese resources dwindled at this the closing of the New Guinea campaigns. Now they faced the terrible mobility of Nimitz's Central Pacific carrier task forces while MacArthur primed for the drive north against the Philippines. Gone were the relentless daylight air attacks. Husbanding resources in the Southwest Pacific, the enemy took to nocturnal raids against targets like newly-invaded Biak. Until MacArthur moved against the Philippines, the 475th provided aerial protection but did little damage to Japanese resources. This was unacceptable to Charles MacDonald.

Satan's Angels' C.O. began ordering strafing missions on the homeward leg of all patrols. Andy Anderson of Possum Squadron explained that the skipper was "a real bear for getting his money's worth on every mission." Thus the recent spate of strafing attacks like the one that concluded Lindbergh's first outing with the 475th.[10]

On the mission slated for 30 June, his second, the Lone Eagle took part in another of the many tactical transformations the group witnessed in recent months. With nil aerial opposition the group carried 1,000-pound bombs to Noemfoor Island. They would continue to carry "freight" for the rest of the war and Lindbergh accompanied them on this second such attack.[11]

The seventeen ships lifted off the mat strip, flying through broken clouds and out to sea by 1125. Over the target they circled, waiting for the A-20s to complete their runs, watching them crater the revetment area down the entire side of the

Captain Dennis G. "Coop" Cooper, group intelligence officer, Dobodura, 1943. (Anderson Collection)

enemy runway. The resultant smoke cleared and the 475th began its attack. Lindbergh, the only one who had recent divebombing experience, rolled off at the edge of a squall, steadied his Lightning, and "pickled off" his weapon at 2,500 feet. He pulled out of the dive before the ten-second delayed bomb touched off.

Later the group's *Official History* recorded all bombs were delivered with "fair accuracy." Lindbergh saw part of the subsequent attacks and noted "three bombs in the target area, two in the jungle, and three in the ocean." Experience, however, would make the 475th as proficient with bombs as they were with bullets.[12]

The second and critical passage made by the group concerned fuel consumption. With additional fuel cells in the J model P-38, Satan's Angels had been making six and one-half and seven-hour flights. On 1 July Lindbergh flew a third mission with the group, an armed reconnaissance to enemy strips at Nabire, Sagan One and Two, Otawiri, and Ransiki, all on the western shore of Geelvink Bay. Already Lindbergh's technical eye noticed something. After six and one-

Lindbergh and McGuire at Hollandia. (Anderson Collection)

First one, then two pilots reported dwindling fuel and broke off for home. MacDonald ordered the squadron back but because Lindbergh had nursed his fuel, he asked for and received permission to continue the hunt with his wingman. After a few more strafing runs, Lindbergh noticed the other Lightning circling overhead. Nervously the pilot told Lindbergh that he had only 175 gallons of fuel left. The civilian told him to reduce engine rpms, lean out his fuel mixture, and throttle back. When they landed, the 431st driver had seventy gallons left, Lindbergh had 260. They had started the mission with equal amounts of gas.

Lindbergh talked with MacDonald. The colonel then asked the group's pilots to assemble at the recreation hall that evening. The hall was that in name only, packed dirt floors staring up at a palm thatched roof, one ping pong table and some decks of cards completing the decor. Under the glare of unshaded bulbs, MacDonald got down to business. "Mr. Lindbergh" wanted to explain how to gain more range from the P-38s. In a pleasant manner Lindbergh explained cruise control techniques he had worked out for the Lightnings: reduce the standard 2,200 rpm to 1,600, set fuel mixtures to "auto-lean," and slightly increase manifold pressures. This, Lindbergh predicted, would stretch the Lightning's radius by four hundred miles, a nine-hour flight. When he concluded his talk half an hour later, the room was silent.[13]

The men mulled over several thoughts in the wake of their guest's presentation. The notion of a nine-hour flight literally did not sit well with them, "bum-busters" thought some. Seven hours in a cramped Lightning cockpit, sitting on a parachute, an emergency raft, and an oar was bad, nine hours was inconceivable. They were right. Later, on 14 October 1944, a 432nd pilot celebrated his twenty-fourth birthday with an eight-hour escort to Balikpapan, Borneo. On touching down, he was so cramped his crew chief had to climb up and help him get out of the cockpit.[14]

The group's chief concern surfaced quickly, that such

half hours flying time, he landed with 210 gallons of fuel remaining in his Lightning's tanks.

Two missions later, on 3 July, the group covered sixteen heavies on a strike against Jefman Island. Lindbergh led Hades Squadron's White Flight as they wove back and forth above the lumbering B-25s. After the attack the Lightnings went barge hunting.

*The 475th's C.O. Charles MacDonald and Charles A. Lindbergh in front of **Putt Putt Maru**. The group's devilish motif decorated the ship's nose. (Anderson Collection)*

procedures would foul sparkplugs and scorch cylinders. Lindbergh methodically gave the answer. The Lightning's technical manual provided all the figures necessary to prove his point; they had been there all along. Nonetheless the 475th remained skeptical. A single factor scotched their reticence.[15]

During their brief encounter, MacDonald had come to respect Lindbergh. Both men pushed hard and had achieved. Both were perfectionists never leaving things half done. And both had inquisitive minds. John Loisel, commanding officer the 432nd, remembered the two men talking for long periods over a multitude of topics beyond aviation. If, as MacDonald had informed his pilots, better aircraft performance meant a shorter war, then increasing the Lightning's range was worth investigating. Lindbergh provided the idea, but it was Mac-Donald's endorsement, backed by the enormous respect accorded him by the group, that saw the experiment to fruition. The next day, the Fourth of July, Lindbergh accompanied the 433rd on a six-hour, forty-minute flight led by Captain "Parky" Parkansky. Upon landing, the lowest fuel level recorded was 160 gallons. In his journal entry Lindbergh felt ". . . that the talk last night was worthwhile." The 475th had lengthened its stride.

On 7 July Lindbergh flew back to Nadzab. The 475th continued its tasks but began to incorporate the lessons taught by the departed aviator. But it was not the end of their association. They would meet again on the road to the Philippines, a road that MacArthur had long been anxious to travel.[16]

met with President Roosevelt at Pearl Harbor. F.D.R. explained that Washington planners felt encouraged to scrap the year-old "Strategic Plan for the Defeat of Japan." This guideline posited the securing of China's southern coast, Formosa, and Luzon as a prerequisite to striking the Home Islands. Now Washington boldly sought direct attacks against Formosa, or Japan itself, thus bypassing Luzon. The ensuing conversation was lively.

Nimitz generally conceded the need for long-range air cover in any attempt at taking Formosa. In a long exegesis MacArthur pointed out the moral imperative: freeing the gallant Filipino people and expunging a defeat of American arms; his defeat, the general might have added. In an earlier message JCS head George C. Marshall reminded MacArthur that "personal feelings and Philippine politics" should not cloud over the war's prime objective, to defeat Japan. To MacArthur they were one and inseparable. F.D.R. reacted to those lofty sentiments by taking an aspirin . . . and ordering another for the morning. Nonetheless the meeting's end saw F.D.R. agree to support the two commanders and push for an invasion of the Philippines.

For the 475th, those were great — but distant — events. Life for them still revolved around coral, seas, and sky. Lindbergh's departure made no dent in the 475th's regimen. On 2 July 1944 the Allies strengthened their grip on routes to the Philippines by attacking Noemfoor, most westerly of the Schouten Island group. Lightnings from the group covered that landing as well as those at Sansapor, the northwestern-most part of New Guinea on the thirtieth of the month. By

The last planes out. Transports loaded with group equipment and men poised to take off for new fields on Biak Island. (Ted Hanks Collection)

MacArthur's clean-up of Eastern New Guinea took fifteen months. With supplies, experience, and proper tactics, he had leaped the top of the Guineas west to Vogelkop and then north to the Moluccas in three months. On 15 September MacArthur looked north from Morotai. He was only three hundred miles from the Philippines; it could have been the moon.

Pacific plans still remained unjelled. Ironically this time the culprit was success. The success that saw MacArthur's seizure of New Guinea also sent Nimitz rampaging through the Pacific islands. On 26 July 1944 MacArthur and Nimitz

then Satan's Angels had moved again.

Biak Island highlighted a continual problem for Southwestern Pacific campaigns. The heart of that dilemma involved Allied dependence on captured Japanese airstrips. Japanese-engineered runways lacked the polish of their American counterparts. The lighter enemy craft could employ runway surfaces that were thinner, their lengths shorter. U.S. fighters had difficulty enough, but steel matting helped convert them to American specifications. The real problem revolved around the heavies, B-24s and -17s. The enemy had

Lieutenant "Sammy" Morrison in front of his tent across a lagoon from Sorido Village, Biak. Sea breezes cooled the area but at low tide the coral baking under a tropical sun raised a stench. (Anderson Collection)

ing struggle for the island was one of the worst of the war. Even as the Seabees and engineers reconditioned strips at Owi Island, just off Biak, and then on Biak itself, Japanese snipers and suicide teams kept the area a combat zone. Some of the enemy held out for months. The 475th again lodged hard on the edge of battle.[17]

On 10 July the air echelon landed on Mokmer Strip, Biak. Two men were missing. Crew chief Sergeant Teddy Hanks, swinging aboard the last C-47 transporting the air echelon to Biak, noticed a 38 limping back to land, snafued. With no mechanics left, Hanks and fellow Sergeant George A. Brown dismounted. Brown had repaired airplanes before the war and was one of the few men that came to the 475th with prior experience. Together they repaired the Lightning, telling the pilot to buzz them on the way out. Happy to oblige, the pilot roared in so low that a terrified earth-mover operator bailed out onto the ground. The entire group completed the move four days later.[18]

Mokmer strip had been chiseled out of a hillside overlooking the beach and sea. The runway was white, compacted coral with good drainage in rain and dusty in the heat. The temporary camp lay at the eastern end of the strip. The later

431st area at Biak. The mess tent is behind the men. (Anderson Collection)

no such massive craft and so heavy bomber runway facilities were hardest to develop. The many moves completed by Satan's Angels stemmed as much from airfields proved inadequate as from the rapid progress of the war. Cape Gloucester, Finschhafen, and Hollandia evicted the 475th. Biak now beckoned.

Located 275 miles west of Hollandia, Biak had been attacked by the 41st Division on 27 May 1944. Local defense commander Colonel Naoyuki Kuzume had learned that Japanese troops on the waterline inevitably died or could not retreat under preinvasion bombardments. He pulled his men back into coral catacombs dotting the landscape. The ensu-

Satan's Angel's B-25 "Fat Cat" named "Fertile Myrtle." This picture was taken at Biak Island, 1944.

"permanent" encampment at Sorido would be a mile and a half from Mokmer, connected by a bumpy road. Both sites spread out over the same crushed coral as the strip, road, and island. Early on, Tokyo Rose acknowledged the 475th's presence as the "Butchers of Rabaul" and promised a nasty welcome. A 432nd pilot later explained, "It's hell trying to dig a foxhole in coral."[19]

Foxholes were no laughing matter. The temporary camp lay but 400 yards from the mopping up operations and in the early weeks firefights could be heard beyond the perimeter. Furthermore, Japanese night bombing raids were frequent if inaccurate, the men theorizing that the center of the airstrip was the safest place during such attacks. Gas masks also made them aware of the war's proximity. Intelligence officers worried, knowing that Colonel Kuzume had received orders to employ poison gas in the island's defense. Nothing came of that order but masks decorated each American's cot for sometime to come.[20]

General camp conditions were decent by earlier standards. While hot, the tradewinds cooled things off in the evening and the ocean always beckoned for a swim. Showers were available, and while the food improved little, one could always scrounge survival, "melt-proof" chocolate bars from the parachute riggers who seemed to have an endless supply. Liquor remained habitually scarce. Yardbird Lieutenant Lloyd C. Lentz, Jr., 431st Squadron, solved the problem in style. His wife sent him Scotch or bourbon in medicinal containers. On scattered Pacific atolls "are empty Listerine bottles in island trash heaps," mute testimony to American ingenuity and the demand for a decent drink.

A welcomed addition arrived in the Satan's Angels' revetment, a B-25 Mitchell. Late of the 345th Bomb Group, it had flown its share of missions and now served to make "Fat Cat" runs to Australia. A silvery ship with a solid metal nose, the Mitchell bore the title "Fertile Myrtle," a name straitlaced Lindbergh found objectionable. On its maiden voyage, officers and men kicked in money for supplies and especially fresh produce, milk, and meat. Much to the disappointment of the EMs, "Myrtle" returned with liquor, most of which went to officers' country. Later flights were more equitably divided. Unfortunately even with fresh provisions, their proper preparation was still occasionally lacking. Private First Class Curtis F. Tinker, Jr., of the 432nd Squadron, recalled that the cooks, upon receiving a shipment of fresh eggs from a "Fat Cat" flight, promptly fried them in Australian mutton tallow.[21]

Air engagements grew increasingly rare as the Japanese girded for the forthcoming struggle for the Philippines. Except for victories in the first four days of July, the group waited out a drought in air fighting. By the end of the month circumstances changed.

On 16 July Lindbergh returned to the group. Earlier Kenney had called him back to Brisbane, the civilian arriving by 21 July. Apparently the problem stemmed from miscommunications, protocol, and a genuine concern for the Lone Eagle's safety. Conversation brought agreement and much like Marine Corps officialdom on the Canal, Lindbergh

received "observer-status" and permission to use his guns in self-defense because, as Kenney told him, ". . . no one back in the States will know whether you use your guns or not." Officially sanctioned, he returned to the 475th.[22]

Lindbergh easily re-entered the flow of group activities. Despite the mandated "Mr. Lindbergh" title, the officers and men accepted the former Air Corps colonel as well as any outsider could expect. They kidded him, carefully measuring Lindbergh's response and never finding him wanting.

Lindbergh and the results of a group "fishing" trip at Biak, 1944. "Bait" was grenades and high explosives. (Anderson Collection)

Good humor, in fact, was necessary because flying combat missions had not made him a combat pilot. After one takeoff, Lindbergh noticed he lagged behind the 433rd despite his best efforts to catch up. A pilot quipped over the radio, "Get your wheels up! You're not flying the Spirit of St. Louis." Lindbergh had forgotten to retract his landing gear. Other incidents had less humor but were met with the same unfailing grace.

Possum Squadron, the 433rd, owned and groomed an idiosyncratic reputation. They did nothing by half measures. Major "Louie" Lewis insisted on sharp flying, often bringing the squadron over a runway in precision order, each fighter trailing ribbons of condensation from wingtips as they peeled off to land. Lindbergh received a rude introduction into the intricacies of squadron styles while flying with the 433rd.

Lewis employed a rapid two-craft takeoff, the entire squadron expected to be emplaced within a single circuit of the field. Sound reasoning backed his method. Long takeoffs and assemblies meant less gas in flight, often spelling the difference between success and failure over the target or life and death on the long trip home. On one such mission Lewis

Lightnings of the 475th at Biak, 1944. Two men beat the heat in the shade of the background P-38. (Anderson Collection)

July. At 0745 the group lifted off to escort the first U.S. strike on Halmahera, one of two major islands in the Molucca Group, air "intel" estimating 150 aircraft scattered over three fields, 75 to 100 probably fighters. With the 433rd Lindbergh flew close cover to the B-25 strafers, the other squadrons flying at intermediate and high altitudes.

Now fully aware of radar's ability, the battle group traced the sea at 2,000 feet staving off their presence on Japanese plotting boards for as long as possible. Halmahera's hazy purple coastline appeared, then cleared to white sand beaches and verdant jungles. High cover rose above the group and the 475th broke into its combat strings that wove protectively above the forty gunships. The sweep into Galela strip, their target, took them past an active volcano, its sulfurous fumes invading cockpits, ashen smoke reducing visibility to a minimum. As the leading wave of B-25s smothered Galela in a wash of tracers and parafrags, Lindbergh and the 433rd rose and circled the drome watching the second line of Mitchells do their work before escorting the third echelon of strafers out to sea. In their wake the Fifth left sixty smoldering Japanese craft. The 431st tangled with some Oscars and despite skillful enemy flying, shot down three, one falling to Mac McGuire. This was his twenty-first, making him the SWPA's leading ace.[24]

Possum Squadron at Biak. Left to right in rear: Lt. Jerome "Jerry" Hammond, native, C.O. Maj. Warren R. "Louie" Lewis, Baldos, a native child, Lts. Al Coburn, Stan Northrup, Charles "Chuck" Joseph, and Pierre Schoener. From left to right: Lt. E. B. Roberts and Sammy Morrison. (Anderson Collection)

looked back to see a lone P-38 on the strip, Lindbergh's. After the squadron completed a number of circuits the Lightning ambled off the runway, made a leisurely ascent, and joined up with the now fretful Possums. Later Lewis explained how the squadron operated and Lindbergh promised to preflight before the 433rd assembled and to "pull streamers" on takeoff. The Lone Eagle was learning.[23]

In support of the Sansapor invasion, a raid had been slated for the next day but bad weather delayed the mission until 27

The next day, 28 July, the big fighters again cleared Mokmer by 0740, target Amboina, a small island off the southwest coast of Ceram. The B-25s of the 345th Bomb Group had already launched and the Lightnings easily caught them at the McCluer Gulf, forming up into airborne legions as they swept past dead or dying enemy fields like Babo, Kokas, and the Sagans. As they passed on, the weather worsened until the Mitchell main force quit and turned for home.

Lieutenants Jack Fisk and Herbert Cochran, left to right, of the 433rd. (Anderson Collection)

MacDonald and Lindbergh, flying with the Possums, led two flights up to 18,000 feet and cleared the thunderheads. Unnoticed, Lieutenant Herbert W. "Herbie" Cochran's Lightning, number 186, was going down after first the right, then the left engine quit. Too low to bailout, Cochran successfully ditched in the sea. So quickly had the lieutenant gone in that later his wingman, Lieutenant Ethelbert B. "E. B." Roberts assumed the downed pilot had snafued and had gone back to Mokmer.

Floating in his emergency raft Cochran paddled about. Suddenly droning engines caught his attention, the 345th had aborted the mission and now flew directly overhead. Only then did he notice the open bomb bay doors. Unseen from above, a tiny figure furiously waved an oar. Cochran thought, "Don't drop those damn things here. You're gonna kill me." Suddenly the air filled with bombs which somehow all missed the lieutenant. Later Cochran paddled ashore and, still wet, was greeted by "What happened to you?" Usually a calm man, he blurted out "What happened? What happened! I darned near got killed, that's what happened!"[25]

Blue and Yellow Flights of the 433rd, sans Cochran, broke free of the storm front and closed on Ceram Island. Moving south towards enemy fields the squadron swung into their loose, weaving formation and upped speed to the preferred 250 m.p.h. Approaching Amahai the cloud deck forced the squadron to just below the billowy white at 10,000 to 13,000 feet. Around 1000 the radio waves evidenced an unseen fight.

Two Mitsubishi 51 Sonias, armed, two-place reconnaissance-attack craft, returned from searching for a comrade missing after escorting a convoy of the 35th Division to Sorong. Part of the 73rd Independent Flying Chutai, the Sonias were piloted by the 73rd's C.O. Captain Saburo Shimada and Sergeant Saneyoshi Yokogi, doubtless happy to be nearing home at Amahai. It was then that the P-38s of "Captive" Squadron, the 9th Squadron of the 49th Group,

dropped down on the Japanese duo. The "49ers" had forged an enviable record in the SWPA despite the fact that only the 9th Squadron flew Lightnings. It was that squadron that now squared off against the two Japanese over Amahai.

The enemy pilots were clearly veterans. While Sonias shared basic characteristics of other Japanese craft — low wing loading and a high power to weight ratio — they were still two-place airplanes with fixed landing gear. And yet beset by the 9th's Lightnings they flew like demons stymieing Captive's best efforts.

MacDonald's flights traced the 9th's growing rage and frustration as the frantically twisting Japanese continued to evade their P-38s' gunfire. They listened anxiously to their radios, following the course of events as best they could:

> "Damn! I'm out of ammunition."
> "The son of a bitch is making monkeys out of us."
> "I'm out of ammunition, too."

MacDonald keyed his mike asking for the location of the fight but the 9th grimly ignored the call; enemy craft were scarce enough without competition from Satan's Angels. A 49er, Lieutenant Wade D. Lewis's cannon shells caught a Sonia in the left wing triggering a fire. As the enemy straightened out to run, Lieutenant J.C. Haslip finally slipped behind the green and brown mottled ship, fired a long burst drawing smoke, the stricken craft diving down into the sea. So died Sergeant Yokogi.

For thirty minutes Captain Shimada fought off Captive Squadron while MacDonald's flights frantically searched for the fight. Banking around a huge thunderhead, black flak drew the 475th to the long running battle three miles off Amahai drome. At 1045 drop tanks fluttered away as MacDonald led the flights into a turning dive from 3,000 feet, triggering a short burst that spangled the Mitsubishi with hits. It began to smoke. Trapped, Shimada decided to fight. Banking furiously, his wingtips streamed condensation as he wracked his craft around in a wicked left-hand turn. MacDonald's wingman and Group Operations Officer, Captain Danforth "Danny" Miller, tried pulling lead on the hostile fighter. Danforth caught it briefly in his sight's reticle and

Lieutenant Joseph E. "Fish Killer" Miller in 1944.

then lost the Sonia's track, his tracers falling off eighty feet behind. By then Shimada had completed his turn and dove on the next attacking Lightning lining up on the second element leader, Charles Lindbergh.

For all his experience the civilian had never seen, let alone fought, an enemy craft. Now he and Shimada flew at each other head-on at 500 m.p.h. Lindbergh instinctively sighted on the Mitsubishi's radial engine and held down the buttons, his fighter bucking, gunpowder fumes filling his cockpit. The civilian's bullets and shells, six seconds worth, slammed into the front of the Sonia, its propeller perceptibly slowing but still Shimada refused to break off. A moment before impact, Lindbergh pulled hard on the yoke vaulting Shimada's ship by mere feet. As the stricken Mitsubishi poured smoke, it half rolled and took its last dive. Lieutenant Joseph E. "Fishkiller" Miller, Lindbergh's number two, snapped out rounds that took the Sonia in the wing, ripping off pieces. Shimada's gallant fight ended in a spray of foam that briefly marked his passing. Years later MacDonald expressed admiration for that pilot who single-handedly outflew a squadron of P-38s only to be killed by Charles Lindbergh.

A grinning "Fishkiller" Miller, so named for his missed bombing strike that brought thousands of stunned fish to the surface, carried the word back to his comrades. Lindbergh scored his first kill! "I was there, and the old man got a Sonia fair and square. . . . It really was something. I blew some pieces off the wing, but it was Mr. Lindbergh's victory." Congratulations flew through the camp.[26]

Three days later, on 1 August, Lindbergh ventured out on a hazardous mission that almost proved his last. In a sense the affair happened because of boredom. Air activity had diminished and the pilots hungered for victories. Hades Squadron's Diary entry for July 1944 reflected a general frustration with the lack of combat. A mission on the twenty-seventh brought hostile contact and the squadron took on two Japanese fighters. Air discipline broke down and ". . . a general melee followed in which there occurred more danger from midair collision of friendly attacking aircraft than from enemy action." It was from this hunger for victories that the Palau raid was born.

The evening of 30 July brought no hint of future events. MacDonald and Lindbergh played checkers, Meryl Smith tossed cards at a hat, while Major A.R. "Sam" Fernandez, Group Adjutant Officer, brewed powdered coffee for an honored break called "smoke" or "smoko." The field telephone sounded. Danny Miller announced the next day's mission, escorting a B-25 raid back to Amboina on Ceram Island. Dropping the receiver in its holster, MacDonald glanced up at the wall map, focusing on a small group of islands 600 miles from Biak, the Palaus.

The colonel turned to Lindbergh. "You know," he mused, ". . . with what you've taught us about fuel economy, we could go to Palau and stay at least an hour." Lindbergh enthusiastically agreed. "Smitty" Smith broke in, reminding them of the morning's mission. Everyone forgot the suggestion, everyone but MacDonald.

The raid was postponed the next morning for an hour when F-5 "recco" Lightning reported Ceram sealed in clouds. Half an hour later word came down, the mission had been scrubbed. MacDonald turned to Lindbergh, Smith, and Miller, "Do you want to go to Palau?" They agreed. At 0927 their Lightnings raised coral dust as they lifted free of Mokmer.

The northerly Palaus had been slated as a future invasion target but more than that, meteorological reports gave an atypical green light for passage to and from the target. Recent intelligence sightings estimated over 150 enemy craft secreted at various dromes, targets enough for all. And in a sense MacDonald also complimented Lindbergh by inviting him along. The four would make a 1,200-mile, over-water flight to an untested target. This would not be the usual "milkrun" mission reserved for beginners.

On the sweep north the civilian dove on a reef, clearing guns as he checked the boresighting on his borrowed Lightning. MacDonald, navigating skillfully with only a compass heading and a wristwatch, climbed to 8,000 feet and lit a cigarette, prepared for the long haul ahead. Despite frontal disturbances the flight crossed the southern portion of the islands, Peleliu, approximately two and one-half hours later. Climbing to 15,000 feet the marauding Lightnings skirted the eastern fringe of the islands as they moved north.

MacDonald was trying to pick off hostile craft in isolation but when none crossed his path the colonel decided "to ring the doorbell." Slanting down into a fast, shallow dive, the four ships drew ack-ack fire over Koror Town half-way up the island chain. Circling back to the coast they flew north to Babelthuap, the largest of the Palaus. Again crossing the surf divide they moved inland, now at combat speed, weaving through scattered clouds returning south. The Americans dived to the deck hunting the enemy. Skimming a lagoon they spotted several small boats and promptly strafed them. Suddenly Meryl Smith radioed, "Bandits two o'clock high!"

Lindbergh's untrained eyes failed to see the pair of Zero floatplanes, "Rufes," that patrolled the far end of the convoy. Thus he later expressed some surprise when the lead element's drop tanks tumbled away. Following suit, he felt a slight bump as they cleared his ship. Instinctively hands reached out turning mixture full rich, brightening the gunsight light to compensate for the sun's glare, a glance showing 2,600 rpms and forty-five inches of manifold pressure.

Swinging starboard, the four Lightnings swept after one of the Mitsubishis low on the water. Lindbergh saw its partner to the left but held station, fully aware that the Palaus' overwhelming air defenses now knew that intruders threatened. MacDonald moved in behind the floatplane as it headed for the clouds, cut across its wild left bank and fired. The Rufe caught fire and a second later broke up on the sea's surface.

Now freed from guarding the attacking element, Lindbergh radioed that he was going after the lone survivor. The last time he saw Smith, the major flew wing position but as the civilian made his final stalk an indistinct motion caught his eye to the left. Instinctively he turned to the threat and snap fired at too great a distance. It was Smith. Fortunately Lindbergh missed and dutifully lined up behind the major as

LEYTE – SAMAR, P. I.

The Leyte and Samar Islands of the Philippine Archipelago. From Wesley Frank Craven and James Lea Cate, **The Army Air Forces in World War II**, vol. V (Chicago, IL: University of Chicago Press, 1950), p. 343. Copyrighted 1950 by the University of Chicago. All rights reserved.

the 475th pilot took the Rufe under fire.

MacDonald watched from above. Suddenly he noticed four, not three, craft above the water: the Mitsubishi, Smith's and Lindbergh's Lightnings, and a Japanese Hamp that simply materialized from above and behind. Before the C.O. could warn Lindbergh, Smith opened fire, bright motes of tracer bullets searching out, then catching the Rufe. It hit the water at a shallow angle, skipped, and then blew up as Smitty hit the fighter a second time. Firewalling his P-38, Mac-Donald warned Lindbergh, "Zero on your tail!"

Apparently Lindbergh either did not hear or misunderstood the warning because he never mentioned the event in his otherwise meticulously-kept journal. MacDonald dropped hard astern the Hamp. The Japanese, seeing him, pulled up into a sustained vertical climb that carried him to safety in some clouds. The time spent in combat, coupled with the hostile fighter, served notice that things would only worsen. The 475th's C.O. gathered the flight and withdrawing, spotted an enemy divebomber. With Smith and Lindbergh as high guard, he dove and sent the craft down in flames. After thirty minutes over the Palaus MacDonald extracted the quartet of P-38s, taking advantage of cloud cover by flying east before resuming a course south to Biak.

Colonel MacDonald and Danny Miller led a mile ahead as the flight headed out to sea. Suddenly Lindbergh announced "Zero at six o'clock! Diving on us." A Zero plunged through a scattering of clouds curving towards Smith. Lindbergh responded too quickly, banking to intercept the bandit before the Japanese pilot had fully committed himself to pursuing the major. Instantly the Mitsubishi broke off its initial attack and cut inside Lindbergh's turn, coming out on the American's tail.

The situation could not have been worse. The flight had retreated at a low altitude and the enemy had accrued a speed advantage through his dive. Lindbergh could not outclimb or outsprint the Zeke and help looked distant, MacDonald and Miller a mile ahead, Smith, still believing himself the target, climbing hard for the clouds.

MacDonald had already turned back but the Mitsubishi flew for the kill. Lindbergh rammed rpm forward and throttles to the firewall; the Lightning surging forward but the enemy craft still grew larger in his mirror, now within gun range. Realizing the futility of trying to outrun the Zero and too low to dive, the civilian continued turning, denying a no-deflection shot to his pursuer while he hunched low in the seat and its armor plating. Lindbergh remembered his family with startling clarity as the Zero's nose and wings sparkled with gunfire.

MacDonald saw he was too late. Still far out of range he saw the Zero fire, delicate tendrils of tracers reaching out and enfolding Lindbergh's fighter. Apparently America had no monopoly on bad gunnery. Lindbergh's P-38 never faltered. Instead it began a high speed turn, responding to Mac-Donald's call "Break right! Break right!" Slowly the Lone Eagle led his pursuer in front of MacDonald's element, the colonel tightening his turn, ship groaning, buffeting, the tiny lighted "pipper" in the sight sliding through the Japanese craft until proper lead had been established. *Putt Putt Maru*'s gun package erupted bullets and shells; the Zero pulled hard for altitude. Smith flashed in for a quick shot, then Danny Miller, banking at the vertical, caught the climbing enemy with a full burst that drew plumes of black smoke. Critically low on fuel the flight left the crippled fighter and flew for home, landing at Mokmer at 1600.

Upon their arrival V Fighter Command summoned Mac-Donald on 2 August 1944, a day after Lindbergh almost died over the Palaus. Word of the mission had spread. Colonel Bob Morrissey, the civilian's contact at headquarters, phoned a day after MacDonald arrived. Unhappily he informed Lindbergh that the 475th's C.O. had been reprimanded and grounded for sixty days.

Most assumed MacDonald drew a reprimand for risking Lindbergh on a dangerous mission. While true MacDonald shouldered direct responsibility for Lindbergh's safety, one could argue that the free and easy liberties granted the civilian in both Marine and Army areas of operation lent an air of permissiveness to his stay. The extent of Lindbergh's aerial involvement came clear two days before when he shot down a hostile craft, and yet no official prohibition surfaced then. The reasoning behind MacDonald's punishment further weakened in the following days. Lindbergh continued to fly combat. From 3 to 13 August he flew five operational missions that saw fighters, flak, and strafing runs. Not until the latter date did Kenney ground Lindbergh, by then on the verge of returning stateside.

Lindbergh, himself, suggested another reason for the V Fighter Command's peevishness:

> It seems that the bombers have been requesting fighter cover on their Palau raids for some time past and they have been turned down by Fighter Command on the grounds that the distance was too great and the weather too bad. Since our flight somewhat refutes this claim. Fighter Command feels that it has placed them in an embarrassing position, which they do not appreciate.

MacDonald had stumbled into a political tangle not of his own making and paid the price.

In recognition of his outstanding record, both as a pilot and a leader, Kenney softened the blow by simultaneously granting the 475th's C.O. a two-month stateside leave, a chance to go home to his wife and a son MacDonald had never seen. His comrades rejoiced at the well deserved rest but it carried unspoken assumptions. He would probably miss the culmination of MacArthur's campaign, the invasion of the Philippines, and it would mar an otherwise distinguished record.[27]

Just before departing for the U.S. Lindbergh flew a mission touched by tragedy. On the morning of 4 August (the same day MacDonald began the first leg of his trip home), Lindbergh accompanied the 431st on a bomber escort mission back to Amboina Island. Through a mix-up in signals the civilian lost contact with Hades Squadron so he tacked on as a number four man to a flight of Lightnings. The target lay almost completely shrouded in overcast, stratus pierced by spires of huge cumulus clouds.

Over Piroe Bay Lindbergh saw two bogies to the starboard. External fuel cells dropped away but as his flight wheeled to intercept, more than a dozen Lightnings converged on the enemy and a melee began. Captain Bill O'Brien, whose cool-headed leadership brought the 431st through Black Sunday, spotted a Zero and dove for the kill. The enemy pilot spotted the approaching P-38 and pulled hard on the stick, attempting a loop either to come out on O'Brien's tail or, with half a roll at the top, to reverse his course and escape.

One or both pilots misjudged their actions. As the Zero went up, over, and straightened out, O'Brien flew head-on into the still inverted enemy fighter. Over a mile away Lindbergh saw a flash of light that meant only one thing, a midair collision. As the falling ball of flame burned out, thin black smoke rained fragments no larger than a Lightning's tail surface. Despite a search by the 431st the next day, O'Brien never returned and it was on that sad note that the civilian took leave of the group eight days later. Mr. Lindbergh was going home.[28]

FOOTNOTES

1. Leonard Mosley, *Lindbergh* (NY: Dell Publishing Co., 1976), chap. 16-18 (hereinafter, Mosley, *Lindbergh*).

2. *Ibid.*, Frontspiece, Foreword, chaps. 12, 13, 22-24; Charles A. Lindbergh, *The Wartime Journals of Charles A. Lindbergh* (NY: Harcourt Brace Jovanovich, 1970), pp. 755, 769, 773-75 (hereinafter, Lindbergh, *Journals*); Arnold, *Global Mission*, pp. 187-89, 359.

3. Lindbergh, *Journals*, pp. 769, 776, 782, 818, 814-51; Brammeier, "Fighter Operations," p. 32; Mosley, *Lindbergh*, pp. 402-03.

4. Lindbergh, *Journals*, pp. 762, 770, 852.

5. *Ibid.*, pp. 852-56; Dennis Glenn Cooper, "Remembering Lindbergh in the South Pacific," unpublished manuscript, N.D., p. 1 (hereinafter, Cooper, "Remembering Lindbergh").

6. Anderson, "Lindbergh," p. 21.

7. Lindbergh, *Journals*, pp. 857-858; Maurer, *USAF Credits*, pp. 119, 128, 175.

8. Lindbergh, *Journals*, pp. 777-78, 782-83, 788-797, 816-17, 820-23, 827, 836, 839, 842-43, 844-45. See page 841 for shooting at all angles; Cooper, "Remembering Lindbergh," p. 3.

9. Lindbergh, *Journals*, pp. 856, 859; Anderson, "Lindbergh," p. 22; O'Neil Journal, p. 92; Anderson, *Saga*, pp. 36, 64.

10. Anderson, "Lindbergh," p. 22.

11. *Official History*, frame 969; Anderson, "Saga," p. 32.

12. *Official History*, frame 969; Lindbergh, *Journals*, pp. 860-61; 431st Squadron History, July 1944, p. 2.

13. Lindbergh, *Journals*, pp. 855-66, 868-69; Anderson, "Lindbergh," p. 23; O'Neil Journal, p. 92.

14. Toll Letter, p. 4; Anderson, "Lindbergh," p. 22; 431st Squadron History, July 1944, p. 1.

15. Anderson, "Lindbergh," p. 23; For fuel consumption on P-38Js see HQAAF, Office of Flying Safety, *Pilot Training Manual For The P-38 Lightning* (N.L.:N.D.), pp. 40-41.

16. Interview: John S. Loisel, August 1987; Lindbergh, *Journals*, pp. 865-66.

17. Spector, *Eagle*, pp. 291-92; Craven and Cate, *The Army Air Forces*, vol. V, pp. 290-91.

18. Hanks Letter, pp. 4, 8; *Official History*, frame 1005.

19. O'Neil Journal, p. 96; Anderson, "Lindbergh Kill," p. 12; Anderson, "Lindbergh," p. 24; Toll Letter, p. 4.

20. Lynch, et al., *Satan's Angels*, p. 23; Toll Letter, p. 4; Anderson, "Lindbergh Kill," p. 12; O'Neil Journal, p. 96.

21. Tilley Letter, p. 4; Anderson, "Lindbergh Kill," pp. 12, 21; Hanks Letter, p. 6; Lindbergh, *Journals*, p. 853; Survey, Curtis F. Tinker, 20 May 1987; Survey, Glenn M. Maxwell, May 1987; Survey, Lloyd Lentz Jr., December 1987.

22. Lindbergh, *Journals*, pp. 870-71; Anderson, "Lindbergh Kill," p. 11; Anderson "Lindbergh," pp. 23-24; *Official History* frames 8821-22.

23. Anderson, "Lindbergh," p. 24; Anderson "Lindbergh Kill," pp. 11-12; O'Neil Journal, pp. 93-94.

24. Lindbergh, *Journals*, pp. 886-87; Charles MacDonald, "Lindbergh in Battle," *Colliers* (6 February 1946), p. 13 (hereinafter MacDonald, "Lindbergh in Battle"); *Official History*, frame 1005; 431st Squadron History, frames 1068-69.

25. Lindbergh, *Journals*, p. 887; MacDonald, "Lindbergh in Battle," p. 76; Anderson, "The Lindbergh Kill," pp. 14-17.

26. Lindbergh, *Journals*, pp. 887-89; Anderson, "Lindbergh," pp. 24; Anderson, "The Lindbergh Kill," pp. 10-23; MacDonald, "Lindbergh in Battle," pp. 11-12, 75-76.

27. Lindbergh, *Journals*, pp. 887-94; MacDonald, "Lindbergh in Battle, Conclusion," *Colliers* (23 February 1946), pp. 28, 30; Anderson, "The Lindbergh Kill," pp. 10-12, 14-18, 20-23; Anderson, "Lindbergh," p. 24.

28. Lindbergh, *Journals*, pp. 895-96; Toll, *Tropic Lightning*, p. 13; Tilley Interview.

Chapter Seven

"I Have Returned": Leyte to Lingayan, August-December 1944

Things change, even in combat. On 15 August Satan's Angels celebrated their first anniversary as a unit. A comparison of that month's statistics to those of a year earlier acts as a microcosmic indicator of the Pacific War itself. To the old timers August 1943 meant Wewak. Lieutenant Ferdinand C. "Ferdie" Hanson, a 432nd veteran, relived those missions in terse words, ". . . shoot, shoot, fly out[,] circle, climb . . ., dive, shoot [again]." In that first month of existence the neophyte 475th clashed with 118 enemy craft on 8 out of 16 missions, shooting down 48 of them at a cost of 3 Americans.

In the following year the Fifth had killed "Wild Eagles" in the air and nest. August 1944's statistics provided a stark contrast to its predecessor. Hostile encounters occurred only on the 1st, 4th, and 5th of the month, 14 Japanese craft seen and 4 brought down. The Group's sole casualty was the gallant Bill O'Brien.

On that same day the 475th consolidated its two camps at Biak with some personnel evacuating Mokmer and moving to Sorido. The move went well because the Engineering Section had wisely substituted tents for the earlier frame and canvas structures. No longer did camps remain half-done for lack of scarce building materials. Instead, setting up could begin as soon as the ground or coral had been leveled and compacted. With tenting the 475th became truly airmobile.

The last echelon, inexplicably detained at Hollandia since 5 July, finally rejoined the group by 22 August. Unkind rumors circulated that they had stayed overly long waiting for the arrival of the Women's Army Corps, the famed WACs. The group's records do not indicate the echelon's success or failure concerning the WACs, but at least now the 475th was at full strength.[1]

On 13 August the group issued its first newspaper, *Satan's Angels Courier*. Mimeographed and stapled, this project emanated from the group's enlisted men seeking to bring ". . . a touch of humor, items of natural interest, and expressions of appreciation" to outstanding officers and men in the group. The second edition featured articles on the Army's new correspondence courses for high school equivalency, trade school, and college diplomas. Other pieces highlighted camp gossip, public opinion, sports, squadron news, and humor. One article pointed up another fundamental change, the 475th now had a new C.O.

Major Meryl M. Smith had backstopped MacDonald for a number of months as Deputy Group Commander. Of medium height, sporting a neat, dark mustache, Smitty ably led the

Typical camp scene at Sorido, the use of tents greatly increased the 475th's air mobility, making them less dependent on building materials, almost always scarce in the SWPA. (Anderson Collection)

group both in the air and on the ground. On the eve of the Leyte invasion, notification came down from Headquarters, Fifth Air Force, that several thirty-month men were being rotated home. Several of them were with the water echelon enroute to the invasion site. Smith flew their rotation papers to a port of call, Humbolt Bay, and personally delivered them, not wanting those men to face unnecessary danger before going home. Rightly the article noted that Smith already had the ". . . respect, confidence, and loyalty . . ." of all hands. Others were due to head home as well; Master Sergeant Gwynne W. White of the 431st and Captain Elbert Dossett of Group Headquarters left for the states. Also among those departing was Master Sergeant Bruno M. Genarlsky, Line Chief of the 431st. An old hand, Genarlsky had transferred from the 9th Squadron, 49th Group, to the newly forming 475th at Amberly. Lieutenant Chester C. Parshall arrived at Hollandia as part of the replacement crew and joined the ranks of Hades Squadron. Thus August merged into September with unaccustomed serenity. It was just the eye of the storm.[2]

By September the U.S. had not yet decided on a Luzon invasion. F.D.R. pushed for MacArthur's Philippine venture but faced hard, skilled resistance from a formidable colleague. Admiral "Ernie" King, Chief of Naval Operations,

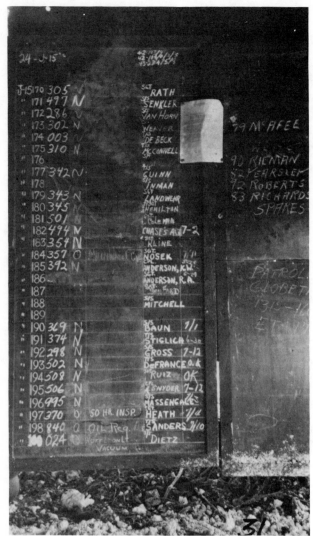

The beginning and the end of each mission — the aircraft status board in the Operations Tent, this one on Biak Island in July 1944. Columns, left to right, "N" = in commission; "O" = out of commission; space is for the reason fighter is out of commission, number 197 was undergoing its fifty-hour inspection; name of crew chief. The aircraft numbers without manufacturer's numbers are lost fighters whose replacements had not yet arrived. (Ted Hanks Collection)

and seemingly weak Japanese responses, Halsey proposed a complete bypass of Mindanao to be replaced by an invasion of the centrally-located Leyte Island by 20 October. MacArthur concurred.

The lack of hostile concentrations and the proposed speed-up of invasion timetables melded with other factors. King's pet, the Formosa operation, needed far more manpower than was yet available, with personnel and supplies unavailable until freed by victory in Europe! Nor did the Japanese passively sit and wait. East China coastal airbases, critical to the Formosa invasion, had been overrun in a massive Japanese sweep called *ICHIGO* by the end of 1944. By 3 October, smarting under those events, King could do nothing but give his reluctant consent to the investment of the Philippines. MacArthur would return home after all.[3]

Those dramatic shifts had little impact on Satan's Angels during September. A colorful sign outside the group's "ops-intel" (operations-intelligence) section displayed three Lightnings, one from each squadron, soaring above the falling remains of two Japanese fighters. Superimposed on the painting were running totals of kills. The month of September produced five columns of "0's," no victories, symmetrical in appearance but entirely unsatisfactory to the 475th.

Despite the disappointing returns, those autumnal days saw the group carry out important missions. On 2 September they escorted the big Liberators to the Davao area on the southeastern part of Mindanao. Only two bandits were seen and both fled. Upon returning, Satan's Angels became the first American fighter group to penetrate Philippine airspace since 1942.

The 475th continued its fighter bomber role on several missions. During those sorties, group Lightnings sustained some damage from drop tanks that gouged engine cowls,

disagreed; Formosa, not Luzon, held the key to Japan's defeat. But the sweep of Pacific events dramatically altered his perspective by that month's end.

By 31 August Admiral William "Bull" Halsey had ordered three American carrier task forces deep into Philippine waters. His fighters and bombers raged through the islands of the Bonins, Palaus, and, by 9 September 1944, Mindanao in the southern Philippines. Resistance there was light in the wake of the Army's 13th Air Force operations, so much so that Halsey's chief of staff Rear Admiral Robert Carey wrote Sutherland that Kenney's pilots had ". . . just about spoiled the war for our carriers. . . ."

By the third week in September Task Force 38 attacked Luzon, the heart of Japanese air power in the Philippines, and then concluded its voyage by hammering Visaya. For the loss of 114 U.S. airplanes, Halsey's task forces destroyed 1,000 enemy aircraft and 150 ships. Encouraged by the destruction

Mechanics go over a Lightning on its 100-hour check. "Andy" Anderson rides a captured enemy bicycle. (Anderson Collection)

Mechanics and armorers work on a group of P-38s at Biak. Note makeshift stands. Supply conditions improved only in the Philippines. (Anderson Collection)

gondolas, and trailing wing edges. More seriously, bombs now occupied hard points, external attachment spots under the wings, normally used for drop tanks. On 30 September strong headwinds literally ran the group out of gas, forcing a diversion to a secondary target closer to home. The pilots were not entirely sold on their new role. Total missions flown amounted to forty-one, the lowest in the group's history.[4]

The September lull had one salutary effect on the group, more men, pilots now numbering 125. Some veterans departed. Major Sam Fernandez, Group Adjutant, returned to the states after almost a three-year absence, as did Major N.E. Wexler, Group Surgeon. The line crews fixed "broken" fighters and received new P-38s. At the beginning of the month group maintenance reported 63 Lightnings. By 1 October the number climbed to 72 craft. In those ways September stood as an important preamble to the days that followed.

With a less harried schedule, men pursued the diversions available. Abundant "cat's eye" cowries, conches, and other marine shells triggered a wave of jewelry making. "Fishing" with grenades and explosive charges continued. Pilots like the 431st's Louis D. "Frenchy" DuMontier, remembered the happy times when Lindbergh joined in that sport and over time and distance DuMontier wished him well. Nightly newscasts came from Lieutenant Martin L. Miller and movies were shown about three times a week. A variety show produced by Black Quartermaster Corps troops proved popular, the "Quartermaster Caravan" drawing applause throughout its three-hour show.

Brigadier General Wurtsmith, Commanding General of V Fighter Command, brought the month to a close. On 23 September he arrived at Sorido Camp to present decorations

September 1944, replacements come to Biak. Veterans wondered how they would do in combat because stateside training had become "safer" with the war winding down. Once informed by veterans that they had to fly hard to survive, the "yardbirds" performed well. (Anderson Collection)

to the men and officers of the group. Smith, now a Lieutenant Colonel, received an oak leaf cluster to his Distinguished Flying Cross (DFC). Captain Francis J. "Frannie" Lent, veteran headquarters pilot, also received a cluster to his Silver Star. Mac McGuire got his Silver Star, as did Lieutenant Vincent T. Elliot. Sixty-seven pilots received awards, ample demonstration of the group's expertise.

Wurtsmith's informal comments, however, interested the

Some of the "Line." 433rd enlisted men who labored long and hard to keep the Lightnings in combat. (Anderson Collection)

group most. He intimated that the doldrums would end soon, "that the group would be given an opportunity in the not-distant future to prove its merit against the enemy." The general proved true to his words. Actual notification of the move came on 15 September, that the 475th on "HORLICKS," Biak, would be sent to "STATION SE-CRET." By 25 September final move orders arrived. On 5 October the water echelon struck camp and began combat loading onto transports. "STATION SECRET" was the long anticipated invasion of the Philippines.[5]

The Philippine Archipelago contains over 7,100 islands dispersed over 114,830 square miles. The largest islands had been slated for investment but Mindanao, the southernmost, had been crossed off in the wake of Halsey's September air attacks. Now Leyte, one of the two biggest islands in the centrally-located Visayan Group, got the nod as the primary target. Located on the eastern edge of the Philippines, the invasion site's chief advantage lay in its closer proximity to the main prize of the campaign, northerly Luzon. With the Leyte lodgment set for 20 October, MacArthur planned the Luzon attack to follow in two months.

With King's agreement to the Philippine invasion, the massive U.S. military machine began to grind out the logistics necessary for the event. MacArthur would command General Walter Krueger's Sixth Army, the spearhead force. A close MacArthur confederate, Vice Admiral Thomas C.

Kincaid, provided the Army's transportation and local protection with his Seventh Fleet, while Bull Halsey's Third Fleet acted as the overall covering force. As the invasion force captured enemy fields, the Fifth and Thirteenth Air Forces would quickly occupy them. So the planners estimated. How the enemy would respond remained a mystery.

The Japanese had sustained almost continuous blows through 1944 and as they watched their defensive perimeters shrink, they fell back consolidating holdings. Two American offensives in the Pacific placed the enemy squarely in a crossfire. This dilemma worsened in the face of extreme American mobility, carrier task forces that struck at will, and the "silent service," U.S. submarines that by the end of 1944 had sunk 600 Japanese vessels for a staggering total of 2.7 million tons of shipping lost. Those factors went far in explaining enemy thoughts on the eve of the Philippine campaign.

The Japanese countered with four plans, all overoptimistically prefaced with *Sho* or "Victory." *Sho-Two* through -*Four* concentrated on direct American attacks on the Home Islands and nearby territories like the Kuriles or the Ryukyus. Many enemy planners, however, had guessed a move on the Philippines — had expected an attack in that region since the capture of the Marianas in August of that year. Now aware of America's propensity for intense pre-invasion bombardment and interdiction, the Japanese de-

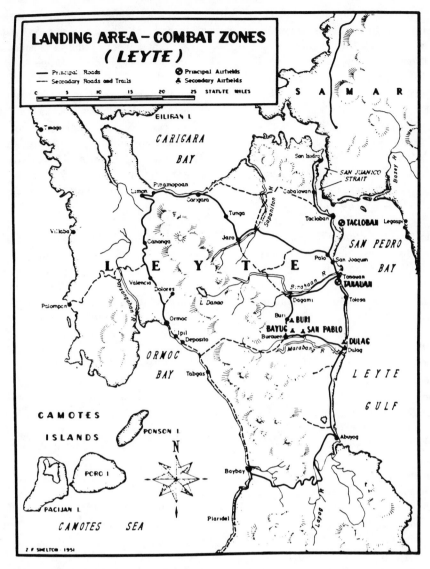

The Landing Areas and Combat Zones of Leyte. From Wesley Frank Craven and James Lea Cate, **The Army Air Forces in World War II***, vol. V (Chicago, IL: University of Chicago Press, 1950), p. 357. Copyrighted 1950 by the University of Chicago. All rights reserved.*

cided, as seen at Biak, to give up the beaches and mass their resources for a defense in depth. *Sho-One* saw a drawn out attrition campaign in the Philippines. When the moment came, a coordinated army, navy, air arm counterattack would finish off an already bleeding enemy. So read *Sho-One*.

On 10 October Halsey raided again, his carrier air power hitting the Ryukyus, Okinawa, Formosa, and Luzon, giving no hint of the intended invasion point. The admiral's pilots found the aerial combat Satan's Angels so avidly sought and for ten days running flew, fought, and died within the inner circle of Japan's defenses. By 20 October Halsey's Third Fleet had shot 500 enemy craft from the skies and destroyed large quantities of shipping, for the cost of 100 U.S. airplanes and two damaged cruisers.

The Japanese greatly exaggerated their small victories during the American incursion. Even the thinning of Vice

Admiral Jisaburo Ozawa's carrier pilots seemed a fair exchange for the alleged defeat handed the Westerners. To the uncritical eyes of the Imperial Japanese Army, the reduction of American carriers meant far less air interdiction if *Sho* was activated. They therefore revised the plan. Any enemy invasion would now be fully resisted at any point of contact. Japanese naval officers said nothing to even imply that the reported damage to the U.S. fleet might be slightly exaggerated.

At 2400 hours, midnight, 20 October 1944, the massive American fleet entered Leyte Gulf steaming towards the northeastern portion of the island. Two beaches masking two Filipino towns, Tacloban to the north and Dulag fifteen miles south, formed the primary landing sites. In the predawn dark, MacArthur paced the cruiser *Nashville*'s bridge, faintly seeing Tacloban. No records trace his thoughts, perhaps of father

Arthur MacArthur's bravery in the Philippine jungles that led to a Medal of Honor, perhaps to his first tour as a "shavetail" second lieutenant stationed in that *barrio* forty-one years before. Sleep evaded him that night but by the afternoon, his troopers had successfully moved inland. Along the way they captured a former Japanese strip at Dulag, a field the 475th would come to know well.[6]

With the majority of the 475th departed for the Philippine invasion force on 5 October, operations slowed. Four dive-bombing missions took place on the first three days of the month. On 14 October Satan's Angels flew a very long range mission to Balikpapan, Borneo, the hub of Japan's oil production in the Pacific. Approximately a 1,600-mile round trip, the 432nd, led by Lieutenant Colonel Meryl Smith, took Lindbergh's cruise control system to its limits. Staging out of Morotai, the sixteen Lightnings rendezvoused with B-24s and set course for Borneo. Over the target zone, Japanese interceptors rose in numbers aggressively seeking combat.

Smith took out one fighter that got too close, raising his total to seven. Lieutenant Joe Forster soon found action as well. Forster already had three victories, all collected on the 475th's first raid on Hollandia. On the fourteenth the lieutenant spotted an Army Oscar diving on the squadron strings. From the rear of the formation he instinctively coordinated hands, feet, and eyes, bringing the Lightning's big nose through the fleeting target before shooting. The Japanese craft waded into the cone of fire, staggering before falling off. A bit surprised, Forster had carried off a classic ninety-degree deflection shot.

Suddenly the Lightning shuddered, the lieutenant seeing his left engine stream oil and smoke. A glance behind showed another Oscar, high and behind, closing for the kill. Pivoting his stricken mount, Forster turned into the Nakajima, making it break off the attack, earning him time to reverse and dive away. The coast flashed by as the P-38 slid out over the ocean leaving the Oscar behind.

Alone, the enormity of his problem sank home — eight hundred miles of water to traverse on a single engine. Good training, common sense, and Charles Lindbergh saved his life. Quickly Forster reduced drag by feathering the left propeller. The lieutenant then decided that any sustained climb to altitude would needlessly deplete his fuel supply; it was the low road for this passage home. He then began to scan a bit of paper taped to the center of his control yoke.

Even before his departure, Lindbergh's settings for maximum cruise ranges had been condensed and typed onto a plaque for every fighter in the group. On it were the manifold pressure and corresponding rpm setting for different altitudes. Forster sought out what every pilot hoped he would never use, single-engine cruise at zero altitude. Carefully the lieutenant adjusted his controls. The weather remained clear, his navigation accurate. Four hours and eight hundred, thirty-five miles later Forster set down on Morotai having completed the longest single-engine flight in the 475th's history to that time. His shiny new Lightning never flew again.[7]

Colonel MacDonald returned to the group from his enforced leave on 13 October. By then new units had taken over

the vacated camp. For the previous six days the squadrons had loaded onto the Liberty ship, *SS Louis E. Weule*, known to all as "Lewie Woolie," the 431st later boarding the *SS Cushman* and a new ship, the *SS Joseph Lane*. For the next seventeen days they would sail the waters of the region, killing time and taking aboard materials. Cards and dice, fishing lines and hooks, and the group tradition of "smokos" all helped pass the time. Shortly after weighing anchor, the group also watched with "some misgivings" as the *Lewie Woolie* took aboard 722 tons of bombs, fuses, and fins, plus high octane gas. The memory of those inert explosives would return in the days to come. Sixteen hundred miles later the 300-ship convoy entered the Leyte Gulf on A-Day plus four, 24 October 1944.[8]

MacArthur had slight misgivings about the air cover over Leyte. Complimenting Kenney's efforts, the general felt uneasy about committing his land forces to the care of Navy aviation in such a crucial operation as the Philippine investment. After the war Major General Charles A. Willoughby, his Chief of Intelligence, would entitle the chapter chronicling that campaign "Leyte: MacArthur Beyond His Air Cover." The distant operation, however, demanded such arrangements. The pull of those islands proved powerful and MacArthur felt consoled that the Fifth would be emplaced and operational within days after the initial landings. Had he known Japanese plans, the general might have been less sanguine.[9]

Sho-One relegated heavy responsibilities to Japanese air elements in the Philippines, to ". . . make Leyte the decisive air battlefield as well as the decisive ground and naval battlefield. . . ." America's targeting of Leyte drew in the enemy Fourth Air Army, responsible for that region and composed of the 2nd and 7th Air Divisions, the 12th Air Brigade, and the 30th Fighter Group. The entire force received orders to commence operations on the night of 23 October. Three major raids were planned for the next day, just as the convoy containing the *Lewie Woolie* and the *Cushman* hoved to off of Tacloban.[10]

The relative peace of the previous two weeks and three days had lulled the 475th's personnel and the return to chaos shocked them. Even before dawn thinned to day, the horizon was punctuated by the flash and boom of naval weapons. The

Leyte between raids. The 475th waits to offload. (Anderson Collection)

Navy sent lines of landing craft to a secondary invasion beach between Tacloban and Dulag, its dark blue Helldivers and F6Fs diving on the Japanese defenders. The first enemy raid of the twenty-fourth commenced, the men watching a twin-engine bomber skim the wave tops vainly trying to lose a Hellcat. In the distance another airplane etched a dark curve before flaming red as it crashed into an LST (Landing, Ship, Tank, also known as "Long Slow Target"), all this against a background of smoke and flame rimming the landing site.

By full light the *Woolie*, with the 475th aboard, lay well off Tacloban on the outer fringe of the convoy. Mess kitchen began to serve the first of two daily meals when the ship's five-inch guns, followed by 20 millimeters, blasted over the heads of the men. The Japanese Fourth Air Army's raids had begun.

The sheer pandemonium of an antishipping raid almost defies description; sporadic shots that ignite firing from the entire mass of maneuvering ships, the sky filling with black, greasy bursts of the 5-inch general purpose guns, accented by the firecracker explosions of quad-40 millimeters and the wraith-like tracer trails from hundreds of smaller 20 millimeter and .50 caliber guns. The noise was deafening. Defensive weapons aside, ships rumbled under flank speed, klaxons blared while above the roar of combat rated aircraft engines at high speed created a wave of sound that deafened. And through it all the bleak feeling of helplessness as the 475th's personnel watched the panorama unfold.

As the initial shock lessened, the men watching from the rails, despite repeated warnings to take cover, began to discern specific facets of combat. Ship's officers shouted commands, gun crews smoothly coordinated their activities. Spent anti-aircraft fragments fell from above as Navy gunners fired on both Japanese marauders and friendly combat air patrols with a fine lack of distinction. A nearby LST disappeared in a horrendous explosion, victim of a Japanese suicider. Supply Officer Lieutenant Joe O'Neil remembered the high explosives and aviation fuel stored in the *Woolie's* number one hold and then blocked the thought out of his mind as his eyes locked onto the horizon. The enemy main force was coming in.

Shrouded in flak twenty Nakajima Kate torpedo planes came at the convoy, breaking into singles as they chose targets. Two swung low over the sea and dove for the *Woolie*. One flashed over the bow so close that the Americans could see the shininess of its newly painted red roundel. Tracers tracked the Kate, short rounds raising white spumes beneath it as the bomber went into a banking turn. Another ship across from the 475th fired a three-inch gun twice, the enemy craft inverting and going in with a wash of spray.

At mast height the second Nakajima began its run against the *Woolie*. The ship's gunners brought the incoming aircraft under fire at 600 yards, the secondary arms joining in as the enemy closed on the ship. Suddenly it banked left and a three-inch gun barked twice, the second round exploding at the Kate's right wing root. As the craft went into a shallow glide, a Hellcat braved the flak and finished the torpedo plane with a single burst.

Moments later a Kawasaki Ki-48 Lily twin-engine bomber crossed the ship's stern passing twenty-five feet above the water. As it flew overhead, the *Woolie's* gunners picked it up. Fiery lines arched back and to port, a 20 millimeter established lead, splashing strikes down the length of the Lily. It destroyed itself as it tumbled through the sea. The raid was over.

At noon the *Woolie* and *Cushman* moved south towards the Dulag. Crowded conditions at Tacloban made the 475th odd man out so under cover of smoke screens the two ships plodded towards their new base. On the way they were stunned to see female "crewmen" wave at them from a passing Norwegian freighter. As they passed not a few wondered how hard it would be to change vessels.

As the 475th's Liberty ships drew near Dulag in late afternoon another Japanese strike occurred and was repeated that night. Repetition blunts even the most terrifying experiences. What now interested the men of the 475th was the complete absence of all protective naval vessels except for the old *USS Pennsylvania*, raised from the mud of Pearl Harbor. At 0430, 25 October, curiosity became terror when the unguarded ships received the alert for imminent enemy attack, surface action.

A 431st radio operator, Staff Sergeant N.H. "Nick" Campese, stood watch when the *SS Lane's* captain mustered the 475th personnel on deck. Lining them up, he reported that in case of an enemy breakthrough, they would all jump overboard and swim for safety. Campese noticed destroyer escorts ranging about making smoke that immediately blew away. He also remembered the sharks that infested the surrounding waters. It was a very long night.[11]

That enormously complex naval struggle called the Battle of Leyte Gulf has been chronicled enough and better elsewhere. The Japanese *Sho-One* plan had anticipated an all out struggle for the Philippines, now aimed at the American point of entry, Leyte. Admiral of the Combined Fleet Soemu Toyoda started the operation by 23 October but *Sho-One* was complicated in the extreme.

The Japanese envisioned a decoy-pincer entrapment. Vice Admiral Jisaburo Ozawa would lure Halsey's protective Third Fleet north of Leyte with his "Main Body," a group of carriers now impotent, their pilots and airplanes lost to Halsey's Hellcats during the September raids. Simultaneously the remainder of Toyoda's assets, battleships and heavy cruisers, were divided into two fleets commanded by Vice Admirals Takeo Kurita and Shoji Nishimura. Both battle groups sought to needle through the myriad islands and attack the hopefully undefended invasion force in Leyte Gulf. Kurita's northern force would enter the top of the Gulf through the Straits of San Bernardino while Nishimura would close the trap from the southerly Surigao Straits. Kurita's northern group, however, underwent American submarine and air attacks from the twenty-third through the twenty-fourth of October, forcing him to retreat at 1500 on the latter date.

At the same time Halsey had located the bait carriers. He had planned to form a guardian force of heavy units, called

Task Force 34, to close San Bernardino but hearing that Kurita was retreating at flank speed decided that Task Force 34 would be a needless diversion of strength. Thus Halsey began to hunt Ozawa's flattops leaving the San Bernardino Straits unmasked.

On that same day, 24 October, Vice Admiral Thomas C. Kincaid's Seventh Fleet heard that the now phantom Task Force 34 would shield northern approaches to the Gulf. Assuming it was in place, Kincaid concentrated his capital ships and destroyers near the mouth of Surigao Straits waiting for Nishimura's arrival. Through the night of the twenty-fourth and the next morning, the Seventh Fleet ripped the Japanese southern force, Nishimura's survivors retreating before dawn. By then Kincaid had decided to confirm Task Force 34's presence, radioing: "Is TF34 Guarding San Bernardino Strait?" At 0700, 25 October, the admiral received a chilling reply, "Negative, TF34 With Me Pursuing Enemy Carrier Force." Twenty minutes later Kincaid received a second radio message. Japanese surface forces were attacking the invasion fleet. Kurita, too, had returned.

All that stood between the Japanese and the American invasion force was "Taffy Three," a handful of destroyers, destroyer escorts, and "jeep carriers," merchantman hulls overlaid with flight decks carrying a few aircraft. Playing a harassing game, the American ships stayed just out of killing range and attacked with airplanes carrying small bombs or none at all, bluffing enemy ships with "dry runs." Other craft made repeated strafing attacks with only their machine-guns.

Ironically, smoke screens proved one of the most effective deterrents. Destroyers had been equipped with smoke generators and used them to cover recent landings. An EM earlier complained, "Hell, I've waited two years to see the Philippines and when I get there they lay a screen so I can't see a damn thing." Now destroyers made smoke that enfolded Taffy Three, saving ships and buying time. It would be from that same ephemeral barrier that the tincans delivered their torpedo attacks that further delayed the enemy.

At ten o'clock in the morning a tired Kurita noticed increasing air attacks. Exposed by a rising sun, his fleet was a long way from home. Two and one-half hours later he reluctantly broke off the attack. Taffy Three scarcely believed it. A signalman aboard the *Fanshaw Bay* exclaimed, "G-dammit, boys, they're gettin' away!" The Japanese fleet sank two "baby flattops," including the *Gambier Bay*, two destroyers, and a destroyer escort, but Taffy Three had thwarted Kurita's efforts. He had failed to smash the invasion fleet and in that failure, sealed Japan's fate.[12]

Off Dulag, thirty miles south of Taffy Three's sacrificial struggle, Satan's Angels heard the boom of big guns and knew a battle was taking place. The *Woolie* and *Cushman* received their share of damage, delivered by Japanese air raids. An attack at breakfast time saw the inevitable — the *Woolie* was peppered by friendly anti-aircraft fire. A 20 millimeter shell exploded on the deck, wounding five 475th officers, including the group's Flight Surgeon, Captain Amos S. Wainer. Wainer, who had just relieved the 475th's original medical officer Major Nathan H. Weyler in August, was evacuated

with serious wounds. By the end of October Captain George R. Smith took Wainer's place.[13]

At one o'clock that afternoon, between a break in the constant air strikes, an Army Corps of Engineers major boarded the *Woolie*. The situation at Dulag was desperate. With escort carriers under attack, damaged, or sunk, Navy pilots had only two choices: ditch or seek refuge at the recently cleared fields at Tacloban or Dulag. With no naval crews ashore, the Seventh Fleet turned to the Army Air Force for aid. Within minutes 204 maintenance and support personnel had assembled from the *Woolie* and the *Cushman*. An hour later they were at Dulag, Satan's Angels' Major Thomas U. Lineham the commanding officer.

Lieutenants Alexander MacGregor, Headquarters, and Daniel R. "Dan" Krall, 432nd Squadron, directed mechanical repairs. They borrowed tools and got parts by cannibalizing wrecked Navy craft. The job was not made easier when the men found out just how much different Navy airplanes were from the familiar Lightning. Nonetheless, in the next two days they patched up forty F6F fighters, TBF and TBM torpedo bombers, and sent them back into combat.

Two 475th officers were charged with repairing Navy guns. Lieutenants Thomas H. "Tom" Thompson came out of the 433rd with a knowledge of armaments and water-pump repairs. He was ably aided by a 432nd man, Lieutenant Darrell W. Moran. Their crew labored, hard sharpening the Navy's cutting edge. Their after-action report noted the poor condition of the .50 caliber weapons. The Navy pilots had burned out barrels strafing Kurita's fleet. While Taffy Three fought to save Leyte landings, the officers and men of Satan's Angels tended her mechanical children at Dulag strip.[14]

The 475th contingent bunked with the 808th Army Engineers at the northeast end of the runway, the sounds of war never distant enough. On the next morning they went to the beachhead expecting to guide in another group, but the men never arrived. The 475th guides were about to leave when an enemy aircraft dropped a single bomb on an ammunition dump. The ensuing explosion detonated tons of shells and small-arms munitions, killing and wounding many Americans. The depot continued to blast itself out of existence until 0400 the next morning, 27 October.

No men of the 475th were hurt but all remembered the explosives still on board the *Woolie*. Given the continued air attacks, now even more dangerous because of Japanese *Shimpu*, or Kamikaze suicide tactics, the urge to leave the ship grew stronger each day. The feeling of disquiet grew as offloading began on 26 October.

Rising expectations of feeling land turned to frustration as priority went to equipment and materials, the men watching enviously from the deck. Even the offloading of bombs and fuel from number one hold failed to ease anxieties as Satan's Angels warily scanned the distant horizons for danger. Their fears were not unfounded. Postwar records revealed that the Japanese, aware of the lack of American fighter cover due to the sinking of escort carriers the previous day, had ordered allout attacks against the landing forces, twelve attacks

Damaged P-38 in the Philippines. (Anderson Collection)

aimed at the Tacloban convoy alone, all between noon and 1600.

Later in the morning a lone raider slipped through combat air patrols and picket ships, chose the 431st's *Cushman* as its target, and loosed a bomb. It hit short by only eighty yards and to the side, a huge white column marking the miss. The enemy bomber retreated without drawing a single round from the surprised convoy. The usual lunchtime attack came when another Japanese aircraft bombed, missed a tincan, and withdrew unchallenged. The last attack came at 2100. Part of a specially formed night bombing unit, three twin-engine Mitsubishi Bettys swept very low across the water. One barely cleared the *Woolie's* stern, appearing as a black, roaring mass to the men on deck, so close that gunners fired at point blank range. The Betty crashed, spreading flames on the water that lingered and then died. There were no more attacks that night.

Next morning, 27 October, saw more raids but just before noon the high pitched whine of turbocharged Allisons brought the men on deck. Above, P-38s of the 49th Group, the first U.S. fighters to operate from Filipino fields since 1942, cut through skies south of the *Woolie*. They answered a 25 October request from Admiral Kincaid for land-based air

cover after Kurita sank his jeep carriers. Working around the clock, Army Engineers and Air Force crews laid down steel matting at Tacloban, the last section secured just as thirty-four Lightnings of the 49er's 9th Squadron flew over the *Woolie*, landing at that field a few minutes later.

As if signaled they too were needed, 475th EMs and officers went ashore. Towed to the beach on barges they grabbed vehicles and, led by an Army lieutenant, drove to the site of the permanent camp located a quarter mile from Dulag strip. Led by Captain Francis J. Lent, acting Group Operations Officer and ace, and Lieutenant Joseph G. Phillips, the men began the now familiar task of setting up home. A new tent city arose while holes deemed a military necessity, slit trenches and latrines, were dug. After the monotony of limited ship's fare served twice a day, the unusually welcomed smell of "10 in 1 rations" scented the air, liberally supplemented by local bananas and coconuts.[15]

A number of factors slowed the 475th as it prepared for combat. The *Woolie* continued to laboriously unload bombs, slowing the group's equipment and supplies to a dribble. The *Cushman* delivered Hades Squadron's necessities more quickly and they rapidly became operational.

At this time the group received their first L model Light-

*MacDonald's L Model Lightning in the Philippines. He named his plane **Putt Putt Maru** after the sound made by the seemingly innocent Japanese ships that plied the waters around Pearl Harbor before 7 December 1941.*

nings, the new variants responding to needed improvements learned in combat. Chiefly it sported hydraulically boosted ailerons for much improved roll rates, and of greater import, dive flaps that finally tamed that machine's greatest nemesis, compressibility. Now the Lightning could enter steeper dives and, in skilled hands, flaps could be applied allowing pilots to follow the Japanese in a turn. Bigger Allison engines gave the requisite power, all of which made for a heavier airplane.[16]

Not all pilots applauded the newcomer. Some veterans like John Babel and John Hood felt the lighter H and even J models flew with a nimble deadliness missing in the new mark of P-38. As with all new craft, "bugs" had to be worked out. But while the L might not have been superior to earlier Lightnings, it was probably no worse.

On 2 December 1944 Operations Officer Captain Jack A. Fisk, 433rd Squadron, sent a "Combat Evaluation Report" to V Fighter Command. In it he commented on the new L model. In a fight on 15 November, a flight patrol composed of three Ls and a J Lightning jumped nine Oscars. In their second pass, the older J variant ". . . was unable to follow a fast half roll and split S, which in the L-1 seemed an easy action with aileron boosts and dive flaps." With timing askew, the J driver completed the maneuver late and got separated below the flight. The Nakajimas closed on him until the remaining Ls drove off his assailants. Later informal tests indicated that the older P-38s could not stay with the Ls in half and full rolls or in a steep dive. The new craft seemed to have had some virtues after all, but the transition to L model Lightnings would take time.[17]

Vicious Japanese raids also slowed preparations. This danger escalated because mobile GCI (Ground Control Intercept) units had not yet been set up. GCIs were primitive, portable radars used to plot airborne craft and provide early warning of inbound hostiles. Satan's Angels found how important the mobile radars were when shortly after arriving at Dulag, they witnessed a dogfight near their strip. Suddenly six Japanese fighters, skimming the tree tops, roared in without warning and shot up the field next to theirs. All hands took an unusual interest in deepening their slit trenches as soon as the incident ended. Later Sergeant Nick Campese was personally offended when, while taking a G.I. bath in his helmet, a strafing Zero forced him, stark naked, to retreat behind a very "skinny coconut tree," the retreating fighter so low that the wet Campese clearly discerned the pilot's face. Air raids continued to punctuate the early days on Leyte.[18]

On 1 November Mac McGuire and his 431st Squadron ferried 17 Lightnings to Tacloban for the 49th Group. Upon approach, the controller asked them to begin a local patrol. McGuire caught a big-cowled Tojo fighter and sent it down, the group's first kill in the Philippines and McGuire's twenty-fifth. That night he reported the day's action and concluded by announcing the imminent arrival of the 475th air component. Fifty-eight technicians from the 432nd were needed to service that squadron's craft as they arrived. As they gathered themselves and equipment for transport to Tacloban the rains came.

While short in duration, the downpour flooded the camp.

The two unrepairable: Dulag and mud, 1944.

In its quiet aftermath men heard things not recognizable from before; streams and waterfalls now dotted the landscape, merging to flow into every slight depression of land. Group members measured sixteen inches of rain in their slit trenches. By the end of November, Dulag would receive nineteen more inches of precipitation. Mud replaced dust.

The 432nd arrived at Tacloban on 2 November. Japanese pressure was intense and conditions showed it. Upon approach, the tower directed half of Clover Squadron to land, the other half to patrol, protecting their comrades. This was no idle gesture. A 432nd pilot sat on the wing of his Lightning waiting for his load of gas when, without warning, two Japanese fighters came over the palm tops, guns hammering the strip. The field's border held several wrecked Navy aircraft, remnants of Taffy Three's defense just days before. The lieutenant leaped behind a torpedo bomber's bulk waiting for the attack to end. He emerged and absently read a recently chalked legend on the side of the ship, "DANGER, ARMED TORPEDO."[19]

By 4 November Dulag was scrubbed as a permanent camp because of its general unsuitability, the personnel going to Buri Strip about five miles west. Inured to the inconvenience, the men moved out of the half-finished site and began to construct the new camp. Buri had the same hardships as Dulag, plus it was nearer the combat zone. A line of 90

431st Squadron P-38 over the Philippines, 1945. (Anderson Collection)

millimeter guns lay between the camp and strip. A nocturnal fire mission was an experience few slept through. Therefore when instructions came down on 6 November to move back to Dulag, most were ready and willing. Back at Dulag, work rapidly progressed on the camp when word again arrived that the group should return to Buri. This proved a bit much. MacDonald stormed over to V Fighter Command and on returning confirmed that Dulag was, indeed, their base.

Now on the leading edge of MacArthur's offensive, Satan's Angels saw ample evidence of the war. As at Buri, Army artillery lined the area between Dulag camp and the strip. One 475th headquarters officer described his introduction to the 155-millimeter "Long Tom" heavy artillery:

We bedded down late . . . and about midnight the cannons started firing. . . . When they let go, they belched out a noise and flash that was indescribable. Even at a distance of one hundred yards the muzzle blast was so strong it would lift your entire body two inches off your cot.

The pilots thought the guns equally awesome. A 432nd man lined up his Lightning ready to start a dawn patrol. Just as he began to power down the strip, the whole side of the runway lit up in a sheet of fire as the cannons fired a rousing salute to the new day.[20]

With runway construction slated for completion by the fifteenth, work continued on the camp. In the meanwhile

The group's strip at Leyte, Philippine Islands. Marston steel matting shows up well in this photograph. (Anderson Collection)

Hades Squadron based at Buri and Clover Squadron at Bayug, also west of Dulag, with the 433rd remaining at Biak because most of their Lightnings had been taken to beef-up forces left to defend that island. In the meanwhile the 433rd waited for replacement craft. Missions continued on and still it rained.

Mud became a symbol of the days at Dulag. The simple Japanese fields failed to live up to Allied Intelligence's reports. Tacloban, the best of the lot, had been touted as a "sandy surface . . . all weather" facility. Later fighter squadron personnel commented that the report was "the supreme overstatement of 1944." The other strips were worse. For instance, Buri was "the mudhole to end all mudholes." Only 2,500 feet long with a 500-foot overrun area, it was partially covered in steel matting, both ends blocked by palms. Nothing could prevent the viscous stuff from clotting up runways; V Fighter Commander Whitehead summed up Filipino facilities with "Mud is still mud no matter how much you push it with a bulldozer."[21]

It also afflicted aircraft. Despite increasing efforts by chiefs and the "line," mud multiplied their problems. Lightnings were bogged down and had to be rooted out. No matter how careful, pilots unavoidably tracked the brown clay into their cockpits. When dried, it was ground under foot so that every roll instantly produced miniature dust storms in the cockpit. Later 432nd pilot Lieutenant Jack M. Shelton mused, "Trying to fly an airplane with mud and water up to the knees was not easy!" When 431 Squadron departed from Buri for Dulag on 13 November, it left four P-38s behind, victims of mud-clogged radiators.

Enemy air raids also reduced the 475th's inventory. By the seventh, the enemy had taken out two P-38s at Tacloban and one at Bayug. On that morning another attack hit Dulag, Japanese fighters and bombers coming in low before dropping bombs and bullets. In their wake four more Lightnings sat grounded by damage. When all those factors were coupled with severe shortages of spares induced by rain-delayed transportation, the two squadrons began November with a minimum number of aircraft. The 431st had to borrow seven Lightnings from the 35th Fighter Group, while the 432nd could field only thirteen of nineteen fighters.[22]

On 8 November the 432nd had just launched their morning patrol when yet another Japanese strafer swept in low at 500 feet. Lieutenant Joe Forster picked up the incoming bogie when American anti-aircraft fire announced its arrival, seconded by the three blinking flashes of an "Air Raid-Red" warning. Forster wrenched his Lockheed into a turn, glanced behind clearing his stern, and then chased the Oscar. He closed on the craft and fired several short bursts, sending it down near the Catmon Mountains. Along with another victory a few days before, Forster counted six kills, one over ace. This action closed down operations until the tenth because the wind and rain returned. Disappointed, the 475th could not know it presaged the last, great period of combat in the unit's history.[23]

Despite horrendous naval losses incurred by the Battle of Leyte Gulf, the Japanese stubbornly sought to end American threats to that island. When Leyte was invaded only the 16th Division, numbering 20,000 troops, barred the enemy's path. At great cost the Imperial Japanese Army rushed reinforcement convoys through the islands of the archipelago.

By 15 November two more full divisions, including the veteran 1st, were reinforced by the elements of the 30th and 102nd divisions and pushed into embattled Leyte. Further arrivals would boost Japanese combatants to 50,000 men by early December.

In order to run convoys and support land operations, the Japanese stripped air units from Formosa and the Home Islands themselves, evidence enough of the determination to triumph or die on Philippine soil. Not since the first contest with the U.S. over the Solomon Islands, two years before, did the Japanese lavish so many aircraft on a single campaign. Despite Allied bombings of staging areas — Cebu, Masbate, Mindinao, Los Negros, Palawan, and Panay — enemy numbers and effective dispersal techniques kept the American air arms at bay.[24]

Chiefly, U.S. air power ebbed low during the early days of the Philippine Campaign. The Navy's local defense forces, the escort carriers, had sustained too much damage at Kurita's hand and now fought for their lives against the Kamikazes. The task forces had replenished but were assigned to the forthcoming investment of Iwo Jima. This left only the Fifth Air Force. The lack of suitable fields, in quality and quantity, plus the rains, had severely limited its participation at Leyte. By early November the crack Imperial 1st Division from Manchuria was already ashore. The Japanese had to be stopped. Thus, V Fighter Command again flung its few, best men against high odds.

The 475th focused often on the Ormoc Bay, almost directly opposite its Dulag base, twenty-five miles west. There the Japanese offloaded reinforcements that drew American strikes attempting to stop those operations. By 9 November the enemy's 26th Division attempted to land at Ormoc, screened by the same typhoon that had grounded the 475th. Four B-25s of the 335th Bomb Group took on the convoy late that day in a low-level attack. One gunship lost its starboard vertical stabilizer to a flak hit, did a snap roll, slewed to the left, snap rolled again, steadied itself, and then completed its run against an enemy destroyer. None of the ships were sunk but torpedo damage prevented the unloading of equipment.[25]

Running hard the next morning the convoy was struck by 38th Bomb Group Mitchells. GCI spotted intercepting Japanese fighters and alerted the 475th. Just prior to the scramble an enemy craft had bombed Dulag with small fragmentation bombs. Each was armed (made explodable) by a small propeller which invariably bent, ceasing the arming process. When the alert sounded, disposal teams had not yet cleared the runway of the bomblets. Fourteen 432nd Lightnings scrambled off Dulag strip right over them, soaring west at top speed by 0600. MacDonald intercepted two bogies over Ponson and downed an Oscar, the pilot bailing out. MacDonald's craft had not been fueled the night before and knowing this, he and his wingman broke for home leaving Lieutenant Perry Dahl as tactical leader.

The violence of a low-level attack against hostile shipping. Target is obscured behind the rising bomb explosion, center left, and dark explosions of earlier hits. (Anderson Collection)

A few minutes later a tight "vic" of a dozen Kawasaki Tonys showed up high and left beneath a layer of altocumulus clouds. With no sign of alarm within the enemy ranks, Dahl signaled a left climbing turn designed to bring the squadron out high and behind the unobservant Japanese. Slanting dives led the hunters through the enemy formation and in the ensuing fight Clover Squadron dispatched eleven Tonys.

Lieutenants Richard D. Kiick and Hank Toll each doubled while Lieutenants Laurence C. LeBaron, Dean W. Olson, Charles J. "Rat" Ratajski, Lawrence D. "Larry" Roberts, Robert B. Schuh, Donald D. "Willie" Willis, and Perry Dahl scored one a piece. During the fight, Dahl dropped on the

"V" at a very high speed, took out the leader, and then squared off against a second Kawasaki. Turning with the enemy, Dahl told his wingman, Lieutenant Grady M. Laseter, to come down and finish the preoccupied enemy. Laseter complied but when breaking into the circle, misjudged, slashing through Dahl's twin booms at a diagonal angle that also carried him past the right wing. Laseter died in the accident. Seconds before plummeting down Dahl glanced back through his mirror and saw his tails fall off, turned right in time to watch his engine fall away and thought to himself, "This is not my day." Exposed fuel cells blazed flames over the cockpit while the airplane spun. After releasing his

Part of the Clover Squadron gang, from left to right: Lieutenants William F. Savale, Edgar W. Williams, Jack M. Sheiton, and Robert B. Shuh. Note squadron insignia on the P-38's nose. (Anderson Collection)

canopy, Dahl struggled to free himself from his P-38, receiving burns on the face and right arm. Standing to jump, the lieutenant's Lightning blew up underneath him.[26]

Amidst the debris, the little pilot had the presence of mind to free fall for five to six thousand feet, avoiding most of the dogfighting above. After opening the parachute, he took in many sights: a dead or mortally wounded Japanese pilot parachuting past him, the enemy convoy under skip-bombing attacks, and, as he neared the water, a sky full of tracer bullets and flak that he somehow passed through unscathed. Dahl made a textbook release from his chute and found himself in the middle of the Japanese convoy.

He inflated his Mae West and one-man dinghy feeling terribly conspicuous until noticing the enemy was more interested in beating off air attacks. Relieved, the lieutenant sat back and watched the war. A Mitchell came into view, flames from its bomb bay-housed Tokyo tanks washing the B-25's belly. It ditched right next to Dahl who thought "Good news! Got some company!" Unhappily, the bomber sank before anyone emerged.

The lieutenant floated alone all day and night. The next morning a Zero strafed him, puncturing the raft in a single spot, but he was able to cover the hole with his body. At the same time sharks appeared, bumping the bottom of the boat. He drifted on the currents, in and out of consciousness. On the second day afloat the airman saw Japanese ships approaching. Dahl played dead as an escort vessel moved close and an enemy sailor scrambled down a rope ladder to investigate. At that moment the Army Air Force attacked and the ship's main battery fired directly overhead. Dahl leaped up and came face to face with the enemy sailor. The American fell backward into the water just as the vessel, now under attack, moved on. As it passed, a gun on the fantail sprayed Dahl with 7 millimeter fire, a slug creasing his skull. Surfacing, he climbed aboard the raft, making landfall on western Leyte by that evening. The young lieutenant was still a long way from home.[27]

As Dahl floated in Ormoc Bay, the Japanese continued to reinforce Leyte. Clover Squadron rose on the eleventh and scored five, including two for MacDonald, his fifteenth and sixteenth. On 12 November the 431st flew out of Dulag and now bolstered by replacement craft, stormed through Japanese fighters for seven definites. McGuire and wingman Lieutenant W.T. Hudnell, Jr., Captain Robert F. "Pappy" Cline, and Major Jack B. Rittmayer, late of the 13th Air Force, spotted four J2M Jack fighters escorting a Lily bomber. The 475th was getting used to encountering the latest makes of Japanese aircraft as the enemy threw everything into the breach. The Mitsubishi-built Jacks split into elements, McGuire and Hudnell taking the left pair, Cline and Rittmayer the right. The Jacks rose and the Americans attacked head-on, McGuire missing, using his dive flaps to swing in behind the Japanese fighter, a few bursts setting it afire. The major then fired a deflection shot that forced an enemy fighter off Hudnell's tail. Reunited, they turned on a Jack chasing Rittmayer, the lieutenant pulling in behind and shooting up the enemy. Out of control, it drove into the ground. McGuire

Luzon-Mindoro. From Wesley Frank Craven and James Lea Cate, **The Army Air Forces in World War II**, vol. V (Chicago, IL: University of Chicago Press, 1950), p. 444. Copyrighted 1950 by the University of Chicago. All rights reserved.

chased down the last Jack, hitting its tail with such force it fell apart, sending the craft spinning down. The 432nd finished the day with five more confirmed kills. Rains closed in that evening and operations were again suspended.[28]

The inferior satellite fields of Buri and Bayug began to deteriorate under the incessant rains. Marston matting sank beneath the mud's surface, revetments melted, and the roads to the strips became morasses. One day beyond the scheduled date of completion, the fifteenth, MacDonald ordered the stranded 431st and 432nd to assemble at Dulag as soon as they could extricate themselves from Buri and Bayug. As engineers graded, packed, and rolled out matting, headquarters personnel rushed to do the thousand things necessary for efficient combat operations.

Captain Danforth Miller assumed control of air traffic as Base "Exec," Captain Reginald G. "Ray" Hawley, Group Intelligence Officer and successor to Captains Bennett "Bim" Oliver, William H. "I.Q." Smith, and Dennis G. "Coop" Cooper, prepared relevant information for forthcoming raids. Captain William J. Pruss, one of the first of the 475th ashore at Leyte, was responsible for Dulag maintenance and refueling activities, while Major Tom Lineham led the communication section of nine enlisted men in the intricate task of linking the scattered group electronically.

On 18 November Hades Squadron made watery landings at Dulag and collected three kills that same day. The 433rd, now refurbished with new Lightnings, came down from crowded Tacloban and scored two definites the day they arrived, the nineteenth. Three days later Clover Squadron completed the 475th's reunion and got a single score upon arrival at Dulag. The real hunt was about to begin.

The twenty-fourth dawned as a red letter day. Satan's Angels shuttled small patrols of four to six ships out of Dulag all day long, constantly seeking out Japanese marauders around the compass. Lightnings gingerly landed on the undulating strip, tape over gun muzzles blown off, tired pilots barely aware of armament men who threw open nose bays to replenish .50 caliber and 20 millimeter belts, while others pumped gas into empty tanks.

At day's end the 431st had dispatched ten enemy craft, the 32nd four, and the 433rd seven, the second highest daily score in the unit's history. By the end of the month nine more Japanese airplanes had gone down under the group's fire. With a total of 69 victories the 475th had achieved the second highest monthly score since the Rabaul raids a year and a month before. High daily score occurred on 15 October 1943 with thirty-six definites; high monthly score was October 1943 listing ninety-three kills.

While veteran pilots continued making inroads into the Japanese, November's totals also showed that the rest of the group had learned its deadly trade. Wingmen, "new guys," and those just unlucky enough to not yet be in a shooting position got their chance and did not miss. Thirty-seven pilots shot down their first or second enemy aircraft; names like Cline, Kimball, and Berry entered the lengthening list of 475th "shooters." Thus November ended with the group ensconced in the Philippines and already scoring heavily against the Japanese.[29]

December continued the struggle for Leyte. The Japanese counter-offensive envisioned major movements to the south by a reinforced 26th Division. Aside from engaging General Walter Krueger's 6th Army, the enemy sought to neutralize Kenney's V Fighter Command by capturing its major fields, Burauen, San Pablo, Buri, and Bayug (both just vacated by the 475th), and Dulag itself. "If the construction of air bases on Leyte is permitted to continue, the communications between the Southern areas and the homeland will be cut and this will be a serious situation." So reasoned General Tomoyuki Yamashita, the "Tiger of Malaya" and Japanese Army Commander in the Philippines.

The complex *WA* Operation, badly hindered by continuous air interdiction and even worse communications, staggered along in a series of "start-stop" orders. It fragmented into units proceeding to battle without coordination. Among those units were the 3rd and 4th Raiding Regiments of the Fourth Air Army. Airborne troops, theoretically they were to spearhead the airfield assaults to be followed up by elements of the 16th and 26th Divisions. They mounted Mitsubishi Ki-57-II "Topsy" transports at Angeles Field, Luzon, on the morning of 6 December 1944, one day short of the Pacific War's third anniversary. By late afternoon they approached their targets.[30]

A few days before, 433rd Supply Officer Lieutenant Joe O'Neil had been notified that he had priority for rotation home and that his papers were being worked up. O'Neil, member of the advance parties at New Britain and Hollandia, was elated. He walked to the mess tent in the failing daylight of the sixth at peace with the world. Suddenly, from the western end of the runway, the roar of aircraft engines filled the air. Looking up, O'Neil watched as paratroopers, fifteen to twenty to a "stick," tumbled from the twin-engined Topsys from 2,000 feet up. "Almost three years overseas," he despaired, "orders to go home, and now this!" Running back to the tent, O'Neil grabbed his .45 caliber pistol and an M2

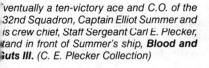

Eventually a ten-victory ace and C.O. of the 32nd Squadron, Captain Elliot Summer and his crew chief, Staff Sergeant Carl E. Plecker, stand in front of Summer's ship, **Blood and Guts III.** (C. E. Plecker Collection)

Lieutenant Perry J. Dahl — and Ormoc the monkey — after his successful evasion and escape from the Japanese-held Leyte. He weighed sixty-four pounds. (Al Nelson photo)

carbine, throwing a helmet on his head. The lieutenant turned just as American anti-aircraft fire began.

To the left of O'Neil, over in Hades Squadron country, a 431st pilot also looked up, "frightened indeed, but [also] awed and fascinated." Clutching his .45 service automatic, he jumped into a water-filled foxhole. Later the pilot reminisced: "Hell's fire! I'm going to end up in the damned ground war after all!" Determined to fight it out, he, too, started at the sound of firing.

Even in the dark the two Japanese transports assigned to Dulag, flying low and slow, became unmissable targets. Gunners on board ships anchored off Dulag and in anti-aircraft batteries on shore sent up thousands of tracer-lit streams of fire that crossed and recrossed the skies so thickly "that a person could have walked on them." Added to the standard anti-aircraft weaponry were hundreds of Americans who blazed away with what they had. The two Topsys simply disintegrated over Dulag coming down near the strip. Anti-aircraft rounds burst among the drifting paratroopers now 200 feet above the ground, showering both enemy and friend with spent fragments. The official Air Force history noted

that only five enemy landed alive. They were quickly killed. Other fields had a tougher time of it. San Pablo, for instance, eventually overcame 124 Japanese before being secured. The last remnants of the drop died four days later as they fired at General Whitehead's headquarters. "The Battle of the Airstrips," ended on 10 December.[31]

On 7 December the U.S. Army's 77th Division landed four miles south of Ormoc Bay, on the west coast of Leyte, in an attempt to flank an already-engaged enemy. Purely by chance the invasion fleet ran headlong into another Japanese reinforcement convoy and chaos ruled the day with both sides simultaneously attempting to land troops and sink each other. In the hills above the contested area P.J. Dahl, separated from the group for almost a month now, watched the battle through captured Japanese binoculars. "This," he thought, "is almost like the movies."

The first of Satan's Angels' eighty-one sorties that day rolled down the strip at 0620 and headed west. In order to provide continuous coverage over the invasion area, the group fought in elements and flights. It would be an all day affair.

By late morning MacDonald and Deputy C.O. Lieutenant Meryl M. Smith patrolled the task force when they spotted the chubby outlines of three Japanese "Jacks." Rolling into a dive the pair noticed bombs hanging from their targets, MacDonald flaming the lead craft from the rear while Smith downed one of the two fleeing Jacks. As Smith finished off his man, MacDonald tangled with the sole survivor, a real scrapper. Their aircraft tore through space with neither gaining an edge. Smith took the enemy craft as it concentrated on MacDonald and shot it into flames. His twin kills numbered eight and nine.

Returning to base, the two men refueled, rearmed, and arrived back at Ormoc by early afternoon. In another swirling fight with enemy Jacks, MacDonald scored twice. Smith, however, had been severely hit, both engines smoking, the Lightning diving down at 8,000 feet. The lieutenant colonel entered overcast and was never seen again. Smith's presence would be sorely missed in the future.

Major Richard Bong flew with Hades Squadron and increased his total to thirty-eight while Tom McGuire's overall score went to thirty with a double. By day's end the 431st claimed twelve definites, the 432nd seven, with Joe Forster's twin victories leading the way, the 433rd two by tall Captain Chase Brenizer, Jr., and short Lieutenant Samuel M. "Sammy" Morrison. In all, twenty-one enemy craft destroyed marked the third anniversary of Pearl Harbor.[32]

A frightening lesson had been learned over Ormoc. A group pilot closed on a bomb-laden Zero flying on the deck. As he fired the Mitsubishi rose, made a few, ineffective swings, and then plunged into an American ship below. The 432nd's Operations Officer, double ace Captain Elliot Summer, suggested to V Fighter Command that pilots refrain from engaging enemy aircraft in near proximity to Allied vessels. If they were too close, airmen should allow the enemy to clear shipping, "with a small hope of living another day," before destroying the craft.[33]

On the tenth of December, P.J. Dahl returned.

After colliding with his wingman on the 10 November mission and narrowly escaping capture or death at the hands of an enemy escort ship, Dahl finally drifted ashore on western Leyte. Scrambling inland, he left the trail and hid behind a plant with huge leaves appropriately named "Elephant Ears," a form of the native Taro plant. He also stepped into a war. Firing immediately broke out between a Japanese patrol and a Filipino guerrilla band. As the fighting raged up and down the trail, Dahl, suffering from shock and exposure felt faint. Then a figure stopped in front of the lieutenant's shelter.

On the verge of blacking out, he pulled his service .45, aimed at the back of the man's head, and pulled the trigger. The round was a special cartridge filled with birdshot for bringing down small game. The water had rotted the paper stopper and the pellets had long since departed. The result was an anemic "plop," the gun discharging wet wadding that hit the target in the back of his head. He turned and only then did Dahl realize that he was a Filipino guerrilla — a friend.

The guerrilla helped Dahl to a hidden camp where he was nursed to health, aided by his youth and a mixture of sulfa in boiled coconut oil that healed his burns. It was during the lieutenant's period of recovery that he was given a monkey Dahl appropriately named Ormoc. Once better the lieutenant, constantly watched by his teenage bodyguard "Franky," raided the enemy with the guerrillas. They attacked survivors of U.S. antishipping strikes as they came ashore, ambushed Japanese patrols, and carried out general reconnaissance for the Americans.

The U.S. 77th Division's 7 December invasion dispersed the Japanese throughout the guerrilla's area of operations and the ensuing days brought disaster. Three of Dahl's companions were killed in ambushes. "Franky," running with Dahl through the underbrush, stumbled onto a Japanese sentry in the dark and died on the point of a bayonet. Dahl escaped into the underbrush. After four or five failed attempts to get through to U.S. lines, the small man and Ormoc wandered through the jungle, lost, unarmed, and starving. Ormoc would hunt bananas in the trees and Dahl would share its finds, eking out sustenance for one more day. In desperation the lieutenant took to foraging in enemy camps at night, eating scatterings of rice. Sneaking up on one such camp he encountered Alamo Scouts, an advance reconnaissance team who eventually got Dahl out by PBY. Thirty days after the lieutenant's midair collision, he and Ormoc returned to Dulag. Dahl weighed sixty-four pounds, but he had come home.[34]

Air activity until 25 December ran sporadically, and with 463 group victories, many wondered if the group could top the 500 mark by 1945. On the eleventh, a four-fighter escort of the Possum Squadron hit a gaggle of Japanese fighters fifteen miles north of Cebu. In the fight, five enemy craft fell, the 433rd temporarily losing Lieutenant John E. Purdy who ran out of gas on the way home. Squadron mates lamented his loss; his two kills scored that day lifted him into the ranks of the aces. Purdy eventually returned unhurt and rightly

Even Santa celebrated the Christmas, 1944, breaking of the 500 victory mark over Clark Field, Luzon. (Anderson Collection)

claimed his honored status.[35]

On 15 December Mindoro was invaded and the 475th scored five on the seventeenth, repeating the trick on the next day. For five more days Satan's Angels remained scoreless. Two days before Christmas even a raid by the 494th Bombardment Group on the Japanese stronghold at Manila, Luzon, refused to provoke a response. Photo reconnaissance, however, continued to bring back ample evidence that enemy strength was still building at Manila's Clark Field complex. On Christmas Day, they rose in force.

On 25 December high-winged Liberators went back to Luzon searching out Mabalcat airfield, a major facility at Clark. Hades and Clover Squadrons rode shotgun over the B-24s while Possum Squadron swept Dasol Bay hoping to ambush any Japanese aircraft flushed out of Mabalcat.

Now fully aware that Luzon would be the next invasion site, the Japanese defended the Clark fields with a tenacity that reminded the veterans of the November raids at Rabaul. In MacDonald's words, they were ". . . aggressive and extremely clever at acrobatics." As the bombers ranged over their targets, seventy to eighty hostile interceptors scythed in on the lumbering heavies. At 21,000 feet the 431st flew 9,000 feet above their charges when twenty-seven Japanese fighters dove on them. After the first pass, instead of their usual half roll and split S escape, the enemy turned into the Americans in a head-on attack. In a prolonged fifty-minute battle the 431st dropped eighteen enemy aircraft, tying the 432nd's 22 September 1944 record won over Finschhafen. This battle also distinguished that squadron as the first to break the 200 victory mark.

McGuire accounted for three, raising his total to thirty-four. MacDonald equaled McGuire's total that day with two Jacks and a Zeke. Faulty guns quit in a high speed turn which forced the colonel out of the match but the fight soon earned him his second Distinguished Service Cross. Doubles came to Lieutenants Louis D. "Frenchy" DuMontier, Floyd M. Fulkerson, Thomas M. Oxford, and John Pietz, Jr. Several pilots scored singles. Hade's Squadron lost three men in the swirling battle, Robert A. Koeck, Enrique Provencio, and Floyd H. Fulkerson, the only one who returned after being rescued by guerrillas, later flown home in an L-5.

The 432nd dove on twenty to thirty enemy aircraft sighted at 15,000 feet and the sky filled with dogfights. Clover Squadron fought for sixty minutes before empty tanks forced them home. High honors in the 432nd went to Captain Henry Condon, II, and Lieutenant Harrold D. Owen with two each, Condon's pair promoting him to ace. There were several others with one each.

The 433rd had run out of luck. Only a single Zeke 52 attacked them, Lieutenant Glenn M. Maxwell finishing it off. But that singular kill added to the group's total and sometime during the Christmas Day fight, the 475th scored its 500th victory. In an undated radiogram, Wurtsmith congratulated the group. Such an achievement, the general concluded, could only have been accomplished ". . . by [the] unquestionable skill, loyalty, and courage of your entire organization." The group modestly agreed.

The 475th celebrated both the Advent and their new record. In squadron mess halls, noncoms and EMs rejoiced well and noisily, just reward for their unstinting service. For the officers the evening was more constrained. The fatigue of the day had caught and captured those who had flown, and many were on the board for morning missions. Despite the party's early breakup, each man knew a milestone had been passed and that history had been made that Christmas Day.[36]

Combat for the month ended the next day over the Clark complex. Dick Bong had been "retired" stateside with forty kills. McGuire held the field and fully intended to surpass Bong as quickly as possible. On 26 December he shot four Japanese craft from Manila's sky, sending his tally to thirty-eight, the second highest in the U.S. Army Air Forces, second behind the departed Bong. From then on it was three splayed fingers and a grin. The magic number was forty-one.[37]

With rotation well established, the ebb and flow of men

achieved a regularity unknown a year before. McGuire went to V Fighter Command Headquarters as Operations Officer, with tall Captain Robert F. "Pappy" Cline now capably leading Hades Squadron. The group's rotation quota steadied at one officer and between fifteen to twenty noncoms and EMs a month. Replacements, however, were plentiful.[38]

The camp, forever known as "The Swamp," continued to grow. The most serious problem revolved around leaking tent canvases. Incessant rain had washed away waterproofing and by month's end ninety tents had to be turned in for replacement or repair. Vehicles also suffered in the wet. Ninety-five percent of the 475th's none-too-spritely transports required repairs. The problem was exacerbated by previous wear, some trucks and jeeps having followed the group since Amberly.

The Philippines also offered amenities. Building supplies abounded and diligent "scrounging" produced some elaborate tents raised off the ground on beds of scrap metal, bamboo, and other miscellaneous materials. The group now actually enjoyed a functional Post Exchange (PX) which brought small comforts that made the difference between hardship and content — cigarettes, fruit juices, crackers, candy bars, and America's pride, rations of beer. Christmas packages arrived, some a bit worse for wear but welcome nonethelesss. Despite continued air raids, Special Services began again movies, the first shown on 19 December from a covered booth onto a battered screen. The troops enjoyed their first film in weeks, two months of Leyte forgotten in silvery figures only occasionally obscured by passing showers.[39]

Rain also fell on Japan. By December 1944 Lieutenant Bill Hasty, shot down over Babo in June, had completed a long journey. Questioned and beaten, the American had been passed from camp to camp. After Babo he went to Borneo, then to Yokohama, Japan. Camp Ofuna was a special interrogation center; the prisoners were *horio*, captives unreported to the International Red Cross and thus unaccounted for. Marine Corps ace Gregory "Pappy" Boyington shared the camp with Hasty. At Yokohama Lieutenant Hasty spent months in solitary confinement because of an uncooperative attitude. In early November he was shifted north of Yokohama to Headquarters Tokyo Camp near Omori, centrally located on the shore of Tokyo Bay.

It was there that Hasty saw evidence that Japan was losing the war. Vice Admiral Marc A. Mischer's Task Force 58 raided Tokyo Bay in mid-February 1945, his snubnosed aircraft peeling off over Hasty's camp to begin their attack runs. On the 27 May he was moved again, back to the southern part of the bay, the "Brickyard Camp," Yokohama. The lieutenant continued to fight his war, eking out a victory each time he awoke in the morning.[40]

FOOTNOTES

1. *Official History*, frames 1008, 1010-11, 1088-89; Lynch, et al., *Satan's Angels*, p. 23.
2. *Official History*, frames 1109-14, 1195-96;

Satan's Angels Courier, 13, 20 August 1944, pp. 1, 3; Survey: Gwynne W. White, May 1987; Survey: Elbert Dossett, May 1987; Survey: Bruno M. Genarlsky, May

1987; Survey: Chester C. Parshall, May 1987.
3. M. Hamlin Cannon, *Leyte: The Return to the Philippines*, United States Army in

World War II series (Washington, D.C.: Office of the Chief of Military History, 1954), pp. 1-9 (hereinafter, Cannon, *Leyte*); Craven and Cate, *The Army Air Forces*, vol. V, pp. 275-89; Spector, *Eagle*, pp. 365-71, 417-19; Willoughby and Chamberlain, *MacArthur*, pp. 232-37.

4. *Official History*, frame 1157. See also, 433rd Fighter Squadron, "Combat Evaluation Report," 18 September 1944; 431st Squadron, "Combat Evaluation Report," 2 September 1944, frames 1153-54.

5. *Official History*, frames 1124-30, 1152-70, 1174-77; Interview: Louis D. DuMontier, July 1987 (hereinafter, Dumontier Interview); O'Neil Journal, p. 101.

6. Spector, *Eagle*, pp. 419, 421-27; Cannon, *Leyte*, pp. 10-11, 22-34; Willoughby and Chamberlain, *MacArthur*, pp. 238-44.

7. *Official History*, frames 1189-90; Toll Letter, pp. 29-31; Anderson, "Lindbergh Kill," p. 24; Hess, *Sweep*, pp. 178-79.

8. *Official History*, frames 1189-97.

9. Willoughby and Chamberlain, *MacArthur*, chap. 10; Craven and Cate, *The Army Air Forces*, vol. V, p. 343; Cannon, *Leyte*, p. 3.

10. Craven and Cate, *The Army Air Forces*, vol. V, p. 346; Cannon, *Leyte*, pp. 45-46.

11. *Official History*, frames 1191-1200; O'Neil Journal, pp. 101-02; Craven and Cate, *The Army Air Forces*, vol. V, p. 397; Letter: N.H. Campese to Author, 1 December 1987 (hereinafter, Campese Letter).

12. Spector, *Eagle*, pp. 428-40; Craven and Cate, *The Army Air Forces*, vol. V, pp. 355-66.

13. Survey: Amos S. Wainer, May 1987.

14. *Official History*, frames 1201-02; Lynch, et al., *Satan's Angels*, pp. 26, 64, 83; Craven and Cate, *The Army Air Forces*, vol. V, pp. 363-64; Campese Letter.

15. *Official History*, frames 1202-05; Letter: Jack M. Shelton to Author, November

1987, p. 2 (hereinafter, Shelton Letter).

16. Foss and Blay, "From Propellers to Jets," pp. 9-16; Shennan, *Lockheed P-38*, pp. 12-13; insert, "Technical Details."

17. *Official History*, Jack A. Fisk, "Combat Evaluation Report," 2 December 1944, frame 1281; Toll, *Tropic Lightning*, p. 62; 475th Fighter Group Interview, August 1987.

18. *Official History*, frames 1202-06; Craven and Cate, *The Army Air Forces*, vol. V, pp. 368; Lynch, et al., *Satan's Angels*, p. 26; Campese Letter.

19. *Official History*, frames 1255-58; Craven and Cate, *The Army Air Forces*, vol. V, p. 386; Toll Letter, p. 5.

20. O'Neil Journal, p. 104; Toll Letter, p. 6.

21. *Official History*, frames 1259-62; Craven and Cate, *The Army Air Forces*, vol. V, p. 373; Tilley Letter, p. 4; Lynch, et al., *Satan's Angels*, p. 27; Survey: Overton W. Long, May 1987; Letter: Louis D. DuMontier to Author, November 1987 (hereinafter, DuMontier Letter).

22. *Official History*, frame 1263; Tilley Letter, p. 4; Shelton Letter, p. 2.

23. *Official History*, frame 1264; Hess, *Sweep*, p. 88.

24. Craven and Cate, *The Army Air Forces*, vol. V, pp. 371-74.

25. Craven and Cate, *The Army Air Forces*, vol. V, pp. 326-79; Spector, *Eagle*, pp. 511-12.

26. *Official History*, frames 1264-65; Toll, *Tropic Lightning*, p. 39; Maurer, *USAF Credits*, p. 656.

27. Interview: Perry J. Dahl, N.D. (hereinafter, Dahl Interview).

28. *Official History*, frames 1365-66; Hess, *Sweep*, pp. 190-91.

29. *Official History*, frames 1270-71, 1289-91; Lynch, et al., *Satan's Angels*, p. 28; Hess, *Sweep*, p. 93.

30. Craven and Cate, *The Army Air Forces*,

vol. V, pp. 379-81; Spector, *Eagle*, pp. 515-16.

31. Craven and Cate, *The Army Air Force*, vol. V, pp. 380-81; Cannon, *Leyte*, chap. 17; O'Neil Journal, pp. 104-5; Tilley letter, pp. 4-5; *Official History*, frames 1320-21; Survey: Ralph Smith, May 1987.

32. Lynch, et al., *Satan's Angels*, p. 28; *Official History*, frames 1321-22; Hess, *Sweep*, pp. 195-97; Maurer, *USAF Credits*, pp. 654-47; Dahl Interview.

33. *Official History*, frame 1343, Annex C-1, Captain Elliot Summer, "Combat Evaluation Report," 28 December 1944.

34. Dahl Interview.

35. *Official History*, frame 1323; Maurer, *USAF Credits*, p. 155.

36. *Official History*, frames 1324-27, 1373; *Ibid.*, frame 1344, Annex C-2, Captain Elliott Summer, "Combat Evaluation Report," 6 January 1945; *Ibid.*, frame 1375, Annex K, Brigadier General Paul B. Wurtsmith to COFITGR, N.D.; N.A., "MacDonald"; Dumontier Letter, p. 1; Craven and Cate, *The Army Air Forces*, vol. V, pp. 393-401, 406; Hess, *Sweep*, pp. 204-05; Lynch, et al., *Satan's Angels*, p. 28; Maurer, *USAF Credits*, pp. 653-57; Anderson Files: "Fifth Air Force News Release," 25 December 1944.

37. *Official History*, frame 1327; Craven and Cate, *The Army Air Forces*, vol. V, p. 406; 475th Fighter Group Interview, August 1987.

38. *Official History*, frames 1329-30.

39. *Official History*, frames 1333-34; DuMontier Letter.

40. Hasty Interview, October 1987; Hasty Memoirs; Craven and Cate, *The Army Air Forces*, vol. V, p. 588; Gregory "Pappy" Boyington, *Baa Baa Black Sheep* (NY: Bantam Books, 1958), pp. 232, 248, 251, 289-90.

475th Art Gallery

(The following drawings were done by Robert A. "Heavy" Hall and Henry C. "Hank" Toll at the time of the Pacific action and contain their original captions.)

The following scenes were painted by Robert A. "Heavy" Hall, in 1944, an intelligence officer with the 431st Squadron. Hall, not surprisingly, became a graphic artist after the war.

A few hours after painting this water color of Leyte's untenable **MUDDY BURI STRIP** these three unexplainably valuable P-38s were destroyed in the Japs' only parachute drop in the Philippines. Only a few yards away, entrenched in the mud this frightening, black 8 December 1944 night were several unarmed men of the 431st Fighter Squadron and me. . . . Totally unprepared for this experience except for my tiny officer's pistol and paint brush.

We **PAINT** and **PLAY** . . . while others are deep into preparation for our next move into enemy territory. Unknowingly, here just off 5th A.F.HQ in Hollandia, New Guinea, I paint the very two ships destined to carry me and most of the 475th Fighter Group into Philippine action.

Flashing backwards to . . . **EVENING WATCH** shipboard on our arrival off Leyte, D + 4 . . . to view the most intense naval and air warfare possible. We were angered beyond reason and impatient to get to, and destroy the bastardly enemy pilots, as we watched Kamikaze Jap suicide planes dive on our warships. How sick be the enemy in his feeling of probable defeat.

Clover Squadron pilot Hank Toll's artistic bent led him to communicating with his wife, Edith, through cartoons sent through "V-mail" letters. She received a photographic copy off 35mm film. His efforts nicely portray the full spectrum of wartime activities and emotions.

Hank Toll

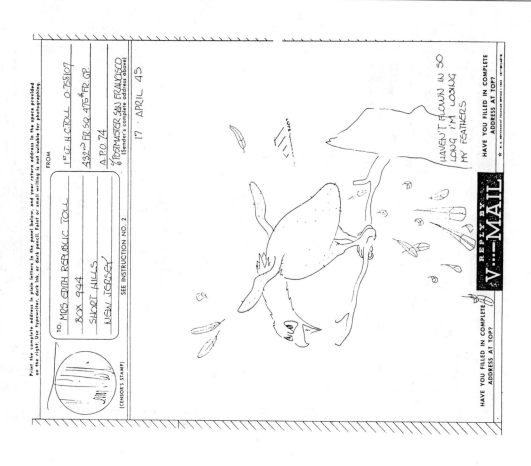

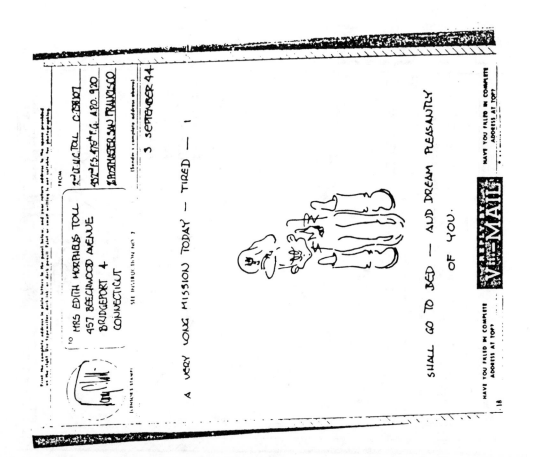

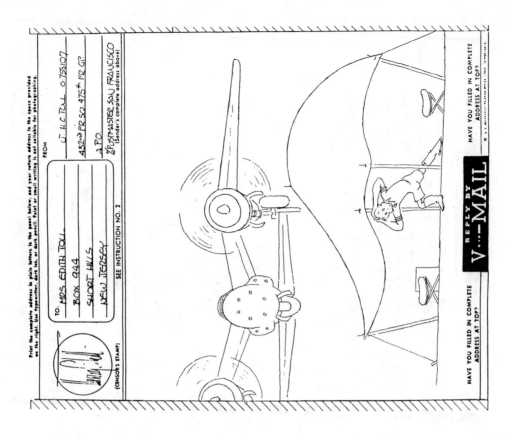

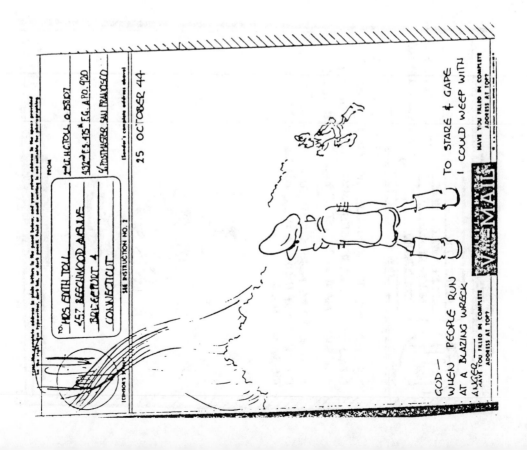

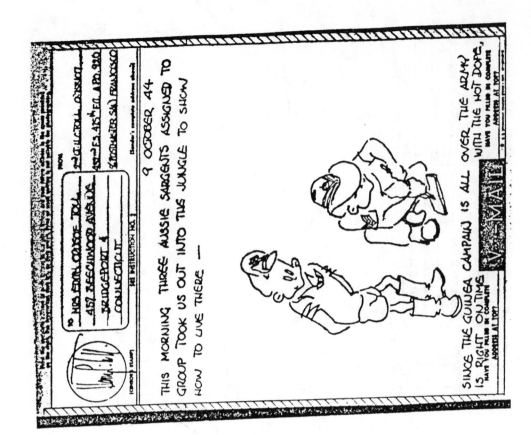

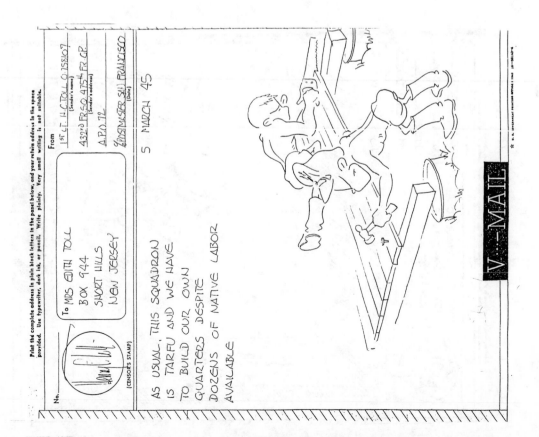

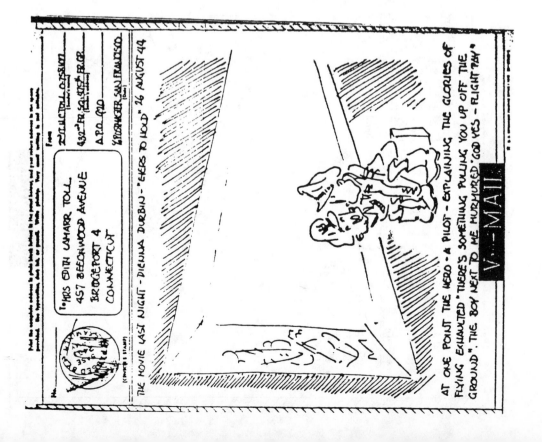

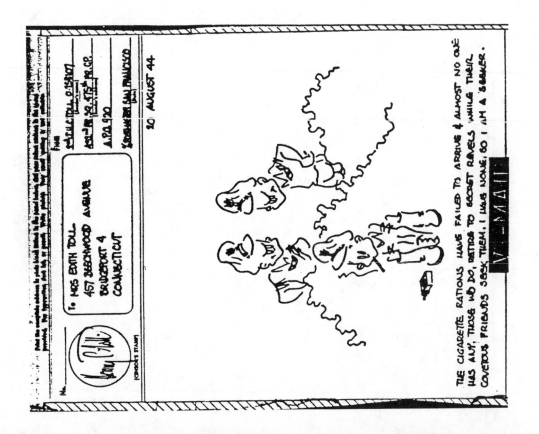

HITTIN' TH' ROAD AGAIN — THIS TIME TO A.P.O. 70 — DAMN

SIZE ISN'T EVERYTHING — MY MISTRESS WEIGHS 20,000 POUNDS, MY WIFE WEIGHS 100, YET MY MISTRESS IS SO MUCH EASIER TO HANDLE

Chapter Eight

Home: December 1944-September 1945

The last year of the war broke with orders to move again. Alerted first on 29 December, detailed instructions arrived on 7 and 12 January. Advanced parties proceeded to Elmore Strip near San Jose, Mindoro, by the former date and staked out a new camp. This time, however, long delays prevented any movement, the 475th relocating only in February.[1]

On New Year's Day the 475th fought its last major battle of the Philippine's air campaign. That campaign also proved the last attenuated struggle for air superiority in the 475th's wartime history. October the year before saw less than 100 sorties, November leaped to 1,150, with December climbing high to slightly less than 1,500. To be sure, armed clashes continued, but never at the same sustained tempo as before.

Again Satan's Angels escorted B-24s to Clark Field, Luzon. Mechanical attrition from December's war was apparent, the group fielding the 433rd and composite flights of the 431st and 432nd combined. Looking down from 19,000 feet the Possums spotted fifteen bandits below. Five Lightnings entered a spiral dive that brought them to the enemy's six o'clock position, dead astern at 15,000 feet. The 433rd's C.O., Major Campbell P.M. Wilson, Lieutenants E.B. Roberts and Jerome R. Hammond dispatched one fighter each. Clover Squadron's Captain Paul W. "Luke" Lucas shot down his sixth and last aircraft of the war, as did Lieutenant Christopher "Chris" Herman of Hades Squadron. MacDonald destroyed a twin-engined Dinah and a Tojo for victories twenty-five and twenty-six, one short of his wartime high score. The group escaped without casualties.[2]

The diminuation of Japanese air power cleared the way for the assault on Japan's stronghold in the Philippines, Luzon. The invasion of southwestern Mindoro on U-Day, 15 December 1944, had gone smoothly with only five Japanese killed and two captured. Immediate "prepping" of enemy fields began in anticipation of air support for the forthcoming Luzon invasion. It was to one of those strips, Elmore, that the 475th had sent its advance party on 29 December.

While Mindoro evolved into a forward station for land-based air power, the Fifth and Thirteenth Air Forces continued to pummel Japanese fields on Luzon. The seventh of January saw a maximum effort raid slather Clark Field with over 8,000 parafrags dropped from 132 medium bombers. "Wild Eagles" were obliterated by waves of bombs; Japanese aerial opposition almost ceased to exist before the invasion began. In the meanwhile, air battles over Mindoro raged long and hard, prime hunting grounds for avid fighter pilots, pilots like McGuire.[3]

A photograph of McGuire reveals something of the man. It was the "Iron Major," a confident smile beneath his dark mustache, his old 500-hour flight hat cocked back on his head, probably still smelling faintly of the Limburger cheese smeared there during the less than sedate farewell party for the 433rd's former C.O. "Louie" Lewis. Slim, about five feet seven and one-half inches tall and 145 pounds, the man always looked larger than life. Thus his death assumed mythic proportions.

The death of any man is complex because an infinite number of variables have to coalesce at precisely the right moment. In retrospect some of the factors that led to McGuire's demise seem obvious, some obscure, but enough is now known to at least create a framework that helps to explain the passing of the man who was, at the time, America's number one operational fighter pilot. It happened on 7 January 1945.

At least part of the reason that the 475th's top pilot died on that January morning arose out of the man's past. McGuire was a tired man by mission 1-668. He had been in constant combat since his arrival in the SWPA, first with the "Forty-Niners," the 49th Fighter Group, and then with the newly formed 475th by August 1943. Mac's tenure with Satan's Angels alone measured sixteen months of fighting.

Time eroded his strength, exacerbated by poor diet, the physical rigors of combat flying, and disease. During August and the first of September 1944, dengue fever and then malaria kept him hospitalized. McGuire immediately went back to operational flying upon release and a warning to rest. He kept up a killing pace in the group's last great campaign over the Philippines. On 27 December Kenney placed temporary restrictions on him, partially because Mac looked very tired, partly to insure that Dick Bong, on his way home, would arrive there as America's ace of aces.

Mac's appearance only mirrored a growing war-weariness called combat fatigue. In a 1987 interview, ex-433rd pilot John S. Babel, agreed that combat fatigue was insidious, beginning with a tiredness unbanished by sleep and leading to impaired judgment. In McGuire's case, his decline was magnified by the race to beat Dick Bong's forty-kill record. Slightly more than two months before McGuire's death, Hades Squadron pilot Lieutenant Chris Herman prophet-

Mac McGuire and Dick Bong at Biak. By this time the two pilots had shot down seventy-six Japanese airplanes between them. (C. C. Parshall Collection)

Lieutenant H. N. "Pete" Madison, 431st Squadron. His arm rests on the Hades insignia. (Anderson Collection)

MacMcGuire's P-38, "Pudgy V," with thirty-eight kills and room for four more.

ically noted:

> Our CO [McGuire] knocked off two more for a total of 26. . . . The CO got nicked too — part of a Nip plane he shot up tore off the top of his canopy and creased his noggin; later he got an engine shot out [when] strafing a troop convoy [in Ormoc Bay]. So maybe he's tamed down a bit for a while! He's still hot after Bong's record tho [sic]. . . . Mac will break it or his neck trying, I guess!

With Bong on his way stateside by 29 December, the major had an unimpeded run for the prize, America's best fighter pilot. In a sense it was a dual meet, his slated rotation in February pressuring him to add to the thirty-eight Japanese flags painted on his P-38 Pudgy V. Together, the factors pulled him into the waiting darkness.

Despite his driving aggressiveness, McGuire led the 431st well. While not the most personable of men, the major was fair. Of greater pride to his squadron, McGuire was an excellent air leader. In a letter former 433rd pilot Carroll R. "Andy" Anderson wrote: "Mac never lost a wingman in combat." But fatigue enforced by competition began to alter his perspective.

On an earlier fighter sweep from Biak, McGuire led Hades Squadron over the harbor at Manokwari, Vogelkop. Spotting a small freighter he ordered the Lightnings down in a strafing run. When queried about releasing belly tanks, the major replied in the negative. The freighter would take nothing to finish and the patrol could continue. His men complied.

A P-38 encumbered with 165-gallon drop tanks was a fearsomely heavy thing that in combat had two disadvantages. A single tracer bullet hit in those gas-laden containers could turn an airplane into a fireball. Young Lieutenant H.N. "Pete" Madison graphically discovered the second liability.

Rolling in on the freighter, Madison focused on its bridge, now covered in tiny, winking flashes from his API rounds. The ship grew larger in the lieutenant's bullet-proof windshield when he decided to pull out of his dive. As the pilot hauled back on the steering yoke the Lightning shuddered and groaned as the tanks' full weight fought the pullout. Furthermore, Madison was still on cruise control settings, engines nowhere near requisite power. Instead of its characteristic zooming climb, his ship sank lower and lower, the Japanese freighter now blotting out his forward vision. As the P-38 barely cleared the bridge, a mast surged into view and Madison braced for a crash.

Lt. Hal Grey near his plane. Note the steel matting. (Anderson Collection)

The noise and impact stunned the lieutenant as the right engine grazed the mast, the propeller breaking free and smashing the cockpit, Plexiglas shards badly cutting his head. Slamming into the mast flipped the Lightning over as it cleared the ship. Despite the pain, Madison chopped power on his good engine, righted the craft, and set out for home.

Squadron mate Lieutenant Harold W. "Hal" Gray escorted Madison out of the target zone and at 300 feet above the ocean they flew towards Hollandia. Running low on gas, the wounded Lightning made a belly landing on recently captured Wakde Island. Seeing no one tumble out of the smoking craft, Lieutenant James A. "Jim" Moreing landed and ran to the stunned Madison whom he found calmly filling out a Form Five, "Report on Aircraft Condition." He had been lucky. But this would not be the last time McGuire would order an attack with tanks attached.

Personally, McGuire began to take chances. Mac's prime rule was never turn with the enemy but in recent months he had done just that. A number of reasons led him on. Foremost, McGuire was an absolute master of his craft, his unbroken string of victories ascertaining his marksmanship and flying prowess. The new L variant Lightning reinforced this sense of competence with its aileron boost making for even faster turns. Conversely, the newer marks of Japanese fighters had broken with the lower horsepower, low wing loading tradition of the early Zeroes and Oscars. While still better turning than the Lockheeds, the Tojos, Franks, and Jacks had lost some of the nimbleness that had characterized Japanese designs. Capitalizing on this, Mac McGuire had begun reducing speed and turning with the enemy, sometimes for a full circle.

This alone would not have been enough to entice the major into such maneuvers but recently the general quality of Japanese airmen had declined. The war of attrition had finally caught up with the Japanese by the end of 1944. This is not to say that all enemy pilots fell into the beginner category. Veterans like Sakai survived but in small numbers that shrank

with time. Turning with the Japanese was a calculated risk but it had worked so far. Thus several circumstances were present when the last factor fell into place. Kenney called for Mac and told him Bong was safe and a hero in the U.S. More importantly the major was now operational again. That evening, 6 January, McGuire encountered three 431st pilots and asked, "How about going on a four-plane sweep tomorrow?"

The men that volunteered to accompany McGuire on his last mission were veterans. Captain Edwin R. Weaver, Mac's wingman, had flown in North Africa against the Nazis earning two victories there. He had flown on McGuire's wing several times and knew his habits. Leader of the second element was Major Jack B. Rittmayer, recently transferred from the Thirteenth Air Force and breaking into stride with four kills in December. His number two was young Lieutenant Douglas S. Thropp, Jr., who had flown a respectable 133.5 combat hours and had one victory credit.

The quartet took off from Dulag heading west to sweep the Los Negros Island strips — Fabrica drome, situated on the northern end of the island, and Manapla beyond it to the west, before heading for the Mindoro invasion beaches. Deliberate or not, this coverage of Japanese fields as a prelude to entering the main area of combat roughly paralleled a new Navy policy aimed at beating down the increasing threat of Japan's kamikazes.

"Daddy" Flight climbed to 10,000 feet and exercising cruise control techniques learned from Lindbergh, kept 170 m.p.h. on the "clock." West of Leyte the clouds thickened to ten-tenths, no visibility, so the flight slanted down to 7,000 feet and then ten miles from Fabrica, to 1,700 feet where they finally found clear air. At 0700, "Daddy" Flight circled Fabrica at 1,400 feet but no challengers rose.

After five minutes McGuire broke off and flew west toward the next strip. Rittmayer reported engine trouble and as he and Thropp came through some clouds, noticed the lead element "several miles" ahead. McGuire then ordered Thropp into the number three position, now element leader. He was then told to close but as he did so, Rittmayer fell behind and was still trailing when Weaver announced, "Daddy Leader! This is Daddy Two! Bandit, twelve o'clock low!"

The Ki-43 Oscar was piloted by Warrant Officer Akira Sugimoto of the 54th *Sentai*, or Squadron. He tiredly flew east to home base at Fabrica after a long and unsuccessful patrol seeking American convoys bound for Mindoro, and now north to the Lingayun Gulf in Luzon itself. As the veteran let down through the clouds that had plagued his hunt all morning, he was joined by another Japanese; Sugimoto noted, perhaps with a little envy, the new arrival was flying the new Nakajima Ki-84 *Hayate* or Gale, codenamed "Frank" by the Allies.

Sergeant Mizunori Fukuda had also not found any convoys but his youthful twenty-one years and the fresh excitement of combat dampened any disappointment. Flying east to his 71st *Sentai's* base at Manapla, the sergeant spotted an Oscar flying just below the cloud base and in the same direction. Approaching cautiously, Fukuda slid his mottled green Frank into position next to Sugimoto, both briefly enjoying the universal pilots' pleasure of formation flying. Over Manapla, Fukuda broke for home as the Oscar continued on towards Fabrica — and Mac McGuire.

At the instant of Weaver's warning two things set the stage for the action that followed. The captain spotted Sugimoto low and ahead at 1,000 yards, the fighters closing fast at about 350 to 400 miles per hour. At that moment Daddy Flight was still split up with Thropp, complying with Mac's order to join up, about 500 feet behind the lead element and Rittmayer's ailing Lockheed trailing still further back.

Before either side could react, they flashed past, Sugimoto reefing his Oscar into a violent, climbing right-hand turn aimed at bringing him behind McGuire's lead element. Simultaneously Mac and Weaver dove left sharply to attack the Japanese. As the warrant officer sliced into a pursuit curve, he came upon the trailing Thropp who had come across intending to intercept the enemy fighter. Turning in behind Thropp, Sugimoto touched off a burst at 300 feet, tracer bullets probing for the P-38 and apparently missing. Straightening briefly, Thropp toggled his drop tank switches, ready to jettison his external fuel cells. It was then that McGuire ordered, "Daddy Flight! Save your tanks!"

McGuire's order is still a point of debate. Doubtless many factors came to bear on the major causing his decision. He was determined to beat Bong. The 475th unofficial historian "Andy" Anderson noted that *Pudgy V*, Mac's regular ship languishing in a Dulag repair bay, had four blank spaces reserved for McGuire's anticipated victories. Disposing of the tanks would force a premature return to Leyte and lose chance at more kills over the lucrative Mindoro hunting grounds. Major Charles L. Brammeier, in a USAF Air Command and Staff College paper, agreed with Anderson that Mac's race to beat Bong ". . . clouded his judgment." But Brammeier also conjectured an overconfidence born of declining enemy skills and the four-to-one odds against Sugimoto.

All those considerations, though, must be seen within the matrix of combat fatigue, as catalysts to an already potent malaise. As noted above, this was not the first time McGuire went into combat with drop tanks on. Only this time the opposition was not a freighter but a hostile fighter in competent hands. Nor was this the first time McGuire attempted to turn with the Japanese, but never had he tried to do so with full drop tanks.

As Thropp's loggy P-38 tried to shake the Oscar, Rittmayer caught up with the flight just in time to fire at Thropp's assailant. Sugimoto tightened his right-hand turn, avoiding Rittmayer's fire, which placed him immediately behind and above McGuire and Weaver who had just completed their original turn initiated at Sugimoto's first sighting. Weaver, slightly trailing McGuire, glanced back and saw the Oscar lining up, fire leaping from its nose and wings in short, practiced bursts. Keying his mike Weaver called, "Daddy Leader! This is Weaver! He's on me now!"

McGuire reacted instinctively. With his borrowed Lightning grossly overloaded with drop tanks, at low speed, and

Major Thomas B. McGuire, Jr., second highest scoring American ace of World War II. (Anderson Collection)

without sufficient altitude, the major reefed into an evertightening turn trying to establish lead and shoot Sugimoto off his wingman's tail.

Months earlier another 431st pilot spotted a B-25 and with drop tanks still slung below his fighter, attempted a similar turn to move in behind it. As his turn sharpened the heavy Lightning suddenly buffeted sharply as the wings lost their grip on the air rushing past. The pilot just barely released back pressure in time to avoid a stall.

McGuire could not do this. The high speed stall probably came too suddenly. Under attack, Weaver saw that his leader ". . . increased his turn tremendously. His plane snap rolled to the left and stopped in an inverted position with the nose down about thirty degrees." A few seconds later Weaver saw the ground leap with the explosion and fire that marked the passing of Thomas Buchanan McGuire, Jr.

Thropp and Rittmayer saw the explosion as they closed on Sugimoto who had broken off his attack and now climbed for the overcast. Thropp pursued, lining up his sight's pipper on the Oscar and firing just as it entered the clouds. Sugimoto had been hit by both Rittmayer and Thropp. Shaking the Americans, the Japanese sought a landing spot, putting down in a flat area. Later, Filipino guerrillas shot him to death.

Other eyes watched the engagement. Sergeant Fukuda was on final approach when he spied the air battle east of his field. Cleaning up his ship and applying full throttle, he sped to the aid of his momentary flying partner. At top speed he came at the three Lightnings head-on. Fukuda attacked Thropp's fighter from the 10 o'clock high position, 13 millimeter tracers rending the P-38's left engine, filling the space between the twin booms before walking through the Lockheed's right fuselage just forward of the rudder.

In pursuit of McGuire's attacker the Americans appear to have been confused, understandable under the circumstances. Stunned by Mac's death, the Frank's appearance surprised them and for years afterward the survivors believed that Sugimoto had returned. After-action reports also indicate that while Thropp led, no one knew who flew his wing as

Captain Henry L. Condon, II, later C.O. of Clover Squadron, at Biak, September 1944. (Ralph M. Smith photo)

Flying Sergeant Minzunori Fukuda, Imperial Japanese Army Air Force. Fukuda intercepted "Daddy" flight moments after McGuire had crashed. In the ensuing fight, the sergeant shot down and killed Major Jack B. Rittmayer.

the lieutenant's number two. Weaver fired rounds at the Frank and missed. Thropp, his left engine smoking, made a slow turn starboard. Rittmayer and Weaver went into a hard-banking 180 degree turn but Fukuda, almost out of gas and determined to ram if necessary, completed his circle, back-tracking towards the American pair. Only as Fukuda bore down on the Lightnings did they release drop tanks. By then it was too late.

Thropp, in his ailing bird, swung through, fired, missed. Weaver also turned right, climbing and shooting with no effect. By then the Japanese Frank touched off bullets that wrecked Rittmayer's Lightning at the left wing, the side of the pilot's gondola, and then, in a shower of Plexiglas, the cockpit. Swerving, the P-38 went straight in, "a huge explosion" covering the ground less than two miles from where Mac McGuire had died just minutes before.

Thropp closed on Fukuda's stern but lost his target in a sharp left turn. Weaver, below the Frank, also fired and missed, rewarded for his pains by another enemy attack from the left rear. Now clear of the cumbersome drop tanks, Weaver outran Fukuda who then turned on Thropp. The lieutenant also escaped into the clouds.

The 7 January mission closed the book on one of the USAAF's best combat fighter pilots. Unaware of the un-folding tragedy, the day McGuire died Headquarters, V Fighter Command authorized him to receive the Distin-guished Service Cross. On 7 March 1946 a grateful American people posthumously awarded McGuire the Medal of Honor for his efforts over Clark Field, Philippine Islands, on the 25th and 26th December 1944, and for the fatal mission 1-668, 7 January 1945. Rightly, the citation ended with traditional words: "Major McGuire set an inspiring example in keeping with the highest traditions of the military ser-vice."[4]

* * *

The work went on at Dulag. Air fighting radically tapered off after the first. The 433rd's last victory of the war came to Lieutenant LeRoy H. Ross on the twenty-fourth. Again the group took on the dangerous task of strafing. It cost them dearly. On 2 January Clover Squadron lost its C.O. Captain Henry L. "Slash" Condon, II, who had learned about the birth of his son after landing from a sweep at Dobodura in 1943. On the fifteenth, Captain Paul W. "Luke" Lucas took five other 432nd Lightnings on a strafing run against an enemy strip on Los Negros. As he sped across an open field towards a revetment-protected bomber, hidden foxholes opened up subjecting him to withering fire. He bellied in but was not observed to move. Later that day a return flight saw his Lightning burnt out. Lieutenant Jack Purdy, a 433rd ace, was one of the lucky ones. On a bombing mission to Luzon he strafed ack-ack positions and then was hit, forcing a crash-landing. With the aid of Filipino guerrillas Purdy returned to the group.[5]

That month also saw future portents in experiments car-ried out by Group Technical Inspector Captain Danforth P. Miller, Jr. Using the D-820 shackle, Miller mounted two

Fukuda, sitting center, and his flying students, before being sent into combat. With the exception of Fukuda, all were killed in the Philippines or defending the home islands. Note the Type 97 "Nate," a former Army fighter and then advanced trainer.

2,000-pound bombs on the inboard wing sections and then proved a Lightning could fly with that weight. Eventually the group would range as far as 280 miles to drop those behemoths. Satan's Angels was in the freight carrying business again.[6]

The 475th had begun divebombing as early as August 1943. While tentative at the start, the group slowly sharpened their skills at this new and to some, distasteful, task. Until the Ipo Dam attacks in the Philippines, bombing strengths commonly ranged from flights to squadrons, rarely more. Tactics varied accordingly to anticipated enemy defenses. Against light anti-aircraft the P-38s dove individually, one after another. Against heavy flak the squadrons approached with the flights in their normal weaving pattern. The four-craft formations went in together, pilots dropping off the leader as other flights attacked in succession from different directions. It was not pinpoint bombing but against general targets Satan's Angels got the job done.[7]

Eventually a satisfactory method bomb-release technique evolved. One obstacle was solved by the late J and L variants' use of dive flaps located outboard of the nacelles just aft of the main spar. Now the 475th could pitch into steeper dives than before with increased accuracy and without fear of compressibility.[8]

Lieutenant "Frenchy" DuMontier of the 431st Squadron recounted the technique employed. The problem concerned the lack of forward vision presented by the P-38's long nose. This was solved by a 60 degree dive with the target centered between the two upper guns. At the proper height the pilots began the pullout, waited until the nose just obscured the target, and then toggled off the bomb. For all its simplicity the system took out targets.[9]

January passed with mixed results. The month had taken a heavy toll of some of the group's best. Others rose to take their place. Captain Elliot Summer replaced the late Condon, II, as C.O. of the 432nd. Tall Major John S. Loisel, just returned from temporary duty at the Army's Command and General Staff School, Fort Leavenworth, Kansas, became Group Operations Officer. All would be needed because earlier in the month, on 9 January 1945, Allied forces stormed Luzon. The road to Manila lay open.[10]

Vivid dreams of Manila's luxuries shattered when radiogram F-1389-E, Headquarters Fifth Air Force, directed the group northward to Elmore Field, southwestern Mindoro, by 3 February 1945. On the day they began operations, the 6th of February, notification arrived informing the 475th that its stay was temporary. The news came as a relief.

The camp had been set on a dry, treeless, grass plain southeast of the Bugsango River. It was Mindoro's dry season and the winds raised up constant dust storms, the stuff covering everything. The transient nature of the camp also lessened the quality of life with tents set directly on the ground, maintenance facilities nonexistent, and food reduced to field rations served picnic-like by the harassed cooking staff of the 433rd. Mindoro was generally hated and became known as the "Dust Bowl" in the group's collective memory.[11]

February saw a drastic reduction in air combat. On the thirteenth MacDonald led four of the 432nd's Lightnings on an escort of B-25s searching the South China Sea for a Japanese convoy. Two hundred miles off the China coast the flight saw an enemy Topsy transport at 10,000 feet. The 475th C.O. dropped astern, fired, getting strikes that set the craft burning, breaking to pieces as it fell. It was his twenty-seventh victory. He had one more than America's World War I ace of aces, Eddie Rickenbacker's twenty-six, confirming his status as the SWPA's leading active fighter pilot. It was also MacDonald's last victory of the war.[12]

Still the war drew out the performance of duties. Along with standard divebombing raids, the group began to diversify its roles. February saw the 475th begin a frequent, future assignment, direct troop support. On 25 February two Lightnings of the 433rd responded to a request for strafing attacks against hostile troop concentrations. Apparently the group had some experience, or at least instruction, in close-support missions. On patrol over Cebu they were contacted by a nearby ground-air support controller and were directed northeast of Cebu City. White panels marked friendly lines and the controller, perched on a jeep overlooking the target area, directed the Possum pilots' approach. Two passes later the groundling thanked the pilots, calling their attacks "perfect."[13]

The group resumed long-distance raiding with sweeps over Formosa on 11, 16, and 19 February. Despite the potentials, each trip proved a dry run. On the same day the 432nd strafed Cebu, the twenty-fifth, the 475th began again extreme long-range flights. The night before, Captain John Tilley, believing he had a free day coming, invited his crew chief over for a drink from an accumulation of "combat ration" liquor. The evening passed pleasantly. At 0400 the captain was shaken awake and informed he was to lead a mission to Camranh Bay, French Indochina (presently the Socialist Republic of Vietnam). Still a bit winded by the previous night's camaraderie, Tilley received the briefing: Indochina and back to cover a Navy B-24, a PB4Y, as it attempted to locate Japanese radar stations. After taking off with ten other 431st Lightnings, the captain pulled deep on pure oxygen trying to clear his head, enormously grateful for the Mitchell guide ship that navigated the way.

Once on station, Hades Squadron tried to locate their charge. Tilley finally made contact with the PB4Y and was informed that it had accomplished its mission. He asked if the snooper craft needed an escort home. Told no, Tilley ordered the squadron to break away and follow the coast to Camranh Bay.

The 431st roared over the harbor. Two Rufe floatplanes rose against the intruders, Lieutenants James H. Barnes and Thomas E. Martin each shooting one down. The squadron destroyed four more at their moorings, sank two small motor

Sergeant George W. Rath, who knew Charles Huff, stands in front of the Lightning he crewed, Major Warren Lewis' number 170. (Ted Hanks Collection)

transports, and then fired up a petroleum storage facility. Leaving the smoking harbor the captain followed a reciprocal course derived from the outbound trip, estimated for drift, and was pleased to see Mindoro eventually rise from the sea. Typical of eight-hour trips, few of the pilots walked straight for a few minutes until kinked muscles relaxed. The group would reach out again, and soon.[14]

Five times during the month the 475th carried a fiery, new weapon, napalm. One hundred and sixty-five-gallon drop-tanks were filled with a mixture of 94 percent gasoline and 6 percent napalm powder. Without napalm the semi-gaseous gasoline would explode in a violent but quickly dissipated fireball. The additive created a "rubbery, sticky, highly inflammable pseudoplastic" which spread and fixed the burning gas over an area approximately 100 by 300 feet. Ignition came from two phosphorous grenades, one in the nose, the other in the tail, fitted with unidirectional fuses.

Napalm attacks were terrifying, the flames trapping and incinerating everything they touched. Jellied gas also killed indirectly by burning off all available oxygen, suffocating those that escaped the direct effect of the fire. This made the weapon particularly deadly against the Japanese who favored underground ambush points and strongholds. On 26 February the group carried out its first large scale napalm attack against Palawan Island, sixty-six tanks dropped against ground targets.[15]

The *Official History* of the 475th closed February with the group's losses for the month, one pilot missing. It also briefly noted that: "Three experienced and able line men were lost when a runaway plane crashed into them. . . ." One of those men was Staff Sergeant Charles C. Huff of the 433rd Squadron.

In a sense Huff embodied the best of the enlisted men; those who never earned glory on the line but who served it every day. Leaving a well paying job as a foreman in a Pittsburgh steel mill, Huff had enlisted through a sense of duty. One of the new men, he joined the 433rd at Amberly.

Line chiefs noticed Huff doing K.P. ("kitchen police"), latrine duty, and other drudge work and assumed he was a "goof-off" consigned to punitive chores.

But Sergeant George W. Rath, who knew the new man, later explained that Huff simply never complained. Sergeant Teddy Hanks, Danny Roberts' chief, spoke to Huff, offering him a slot in his flight. The new man replied, "Now let me tell you something, Sergeant Hank [sic] . . . every job has to be done by someone. If I am picked to do a job, then someone will not have to [do it]. You don't need to feel sorry for me." As time passed Huff was promoted and continued to conscientiously carry out his duties. By the time the group moved to Elmore Field, Mindoro, Huff was a staff sergeant and a crew chief.

At 0920 on 22 February Huff and his assistant, Sergeant Edward J. Hamilton, refueled a Lightning parked in the dispersal area. They pumped gas from a refueling truck situated in front of the craft, Hamilton hunkered on the left wing, Huff on the ground on the opposite side of the P-38.

Suddenly a P-47 Thunderbolt, experiencing engine trouble, swept low over Elmore. Possibly approaching from downwind, the pilot may have mistaken the dirt taxiway for the Marston matting of the runway. Under the best of conditions they could be difficult to distinguish and with fogged or dirty windshields it was nearly impossible. Perhaps the pilot simply could not fly the seven-ton fighter any further. The Thunderbolt put down on the short taxiway and slammed into the fuel truck. A flaming blast swept the area.

Hamilton apparently saw the rampaging 47 from atop the wing because he leaped down, running a short distance until stopped by the roots of recently bulldozed trees cleared for parking spaces. The fire caught him there. Taken to the field hospital Hamilton lingered until the next morning when he died. Crews found the remains of Huff near the burnt out Lightning's nose gear. Earlier Sergeant Charles C. Huff had said, "It was my duty to do my part," now a fitting epitaph for a man of simple patriotism and high principles.[16]

By February's end even Mindoro began to feel like a backwater. Combat had raged on Luzon since the second week in January, while the Navy raided Tokyo and the Marines landed on Iwo Jima by the nineteenth. Personnel fretted as they looked north through the constant haze of dust. On the twenty-seventh, Major Thomas W. "Tom" Cheney, head of Group Supply as S-4, received a radiogram that sent the 475th into practiced action. Satan's Angels were going to Luzon.[17]

The third of March saw the 475th ensconced at their old December 1944 target of Clark Field, outside Manila, Luzon. Gunfire could be heard from the war twenty miles west but the men and officers, now sporting very unofficial Filipino woven straw hats, looked a little dazed for a far different reason. To the north and west paved roads bordered the large complex, the first seen since Australia two years before. To the east Clark's myriad runways spread out. Two towns, Angeles and San Fernando, beckoned and also supplied laborers, craftsmen, and vendors, some selling eggs inflated to thirty cents each.

Hangar facilities, Clark Field, Luzon. (Anderson Collection)

Two views of wrecked Japanese craft recovered on Clark Field, 1945.

Nor were accommodations shabby. The group inherited an abandoned camp replete with some Japanese-built buildings and bomb shelters. For instance, the 432nd took over a large frame building eventually used as a mess-recreation hall for the enlisted men. A fifty by sixty foot, porched house, including a dignified mahogany bar, became the group officer's mess. And for the first time the group had reliable piped water for showers. The new camp's worst problem was noise — aircraft, road traffic, and a few hundred yards north, more "Long Toms" that fired support missions day and night. For

Lieutenant Raymond M. Giles' damaged P-38, the left engine shot up on one of the long distance raids to Formosa. (Raymond M. Giles photo)

A bomb dropped accidently at Clark Field, Luzon. A B-24 sits directly in front with a B-17 in profile to the right. (Anderson Collection)

all that disturbance every man hoped for a long stay at Clark; the only exception being personnel like Captain William J. H. Pruss, who gladly traded the luxury of Clark for a ticket home.[18]

The air war continued trends begun in February. Half of the March missions involved divebombing, strafing, and napalm attacks. Those missions were in close support of the troops who marked targets with shell fire or phosphorus grenades lobbed from spotting craft passes monitored by both airplane and ground controllers. The group expended 756 1,000 pound bombs, 54,625 .50 caliber rounds, and 8,047 20 millimeter shells on Luzon targets.[19]

March was also the last month of substantial air combat for the group. In that month Satan's Angels had to reach out for kills with very long missions to Formosa, Indochina, and Hong Kong. On the fifth Perry Dahl, recovered from his harrowing evasion and escape at Ormoc Bay, celebrated his new captaincy by shooting down a twin-engine "Sally" bomber for the 432nd. While strafing along the west coast of Formosa, Dahl spotted the bomber at 1,500 feet, followed it in a dive taking out the right engine with his first burst. Two more hits scored before the stricken craft crashlanded on a beach as number eight for young Dahl.

The twenty-eighth proved the most eventful day for the group. Squadrons drew an escort mission for a B-25 antishipping strike off Indochina. Major John Loisel led the Red Flight of the 433rd flying low cover and spotted approximately a dozen bogies scattered from 5,000 to 10,000 feet. In a climb that pulled them from 1,500 to 7,500 feet, the 433rd flight banked into a diving turn targeting two Franks. Topside, eight Lightnings of the 432nd Squadron clashed with twenty Japanese fighters about to pounce on Red Flight below. The enemy flew in a box-like gaggle composed of two-ship elements. Periodically a bandit duo would peel off and attempt to engage, trying to get Clover Squadron to commit itself. Captain Perry Dahl deftly parried the elements with short head-on passes that broke off attacks. Defended above, Loisel shot one of the Franks down in flames for his eleventh and final victory of the war.

Japanese pressure built against Dahl's blocking force. An aggressive Hamp swung in on Red Flight Four, Lieutenant Wesley J. Hulett, hit him in the engine, and pulled away. Dahl's Blue Flight, led by the diminutive Lieutenant Robert H. "Gremlin" Kimball, dove on the Hamp and then pulled off because of jammed guns. Kimball's wingman, Lieutenant George Wacker, drew into position firing a burst that forced the Japanese to roll violently right and then into a split S. Wacker followed, his mount accelerating in the dive until at 300 yards he fired, the lieutenant's armor-piercing incendiaries finding gas tanks that exploded into flames.

Continuing to shield the pilots below, Dahl's flight fought off the enemy. One Japanese fighter slanted across the captain's line of flight, his fire downing the Hamp from a sixty degree angle. Rallying his flights, Dahl turned from Indochina's coast, the violent combat costing far too much gas for a safe trip home.

Loisel chased one more hostile off Hulett but down on a wing, the lieutenant slid into the overcast and disappeared. Over the radio Hulett told Loisel to send out a PBY. Loisel complied but the lieutenant was never found. The 431st had scored seven kills in that same flight. Joined up again, the squadrons flew the long haul home.[20]

The determined Japanese response encouraged a reprise so the group returned to those distant shores the next day. The mixed flight was led by Lieutenant Harrold D. Owen, and consisted of Lieutenants Lawrence C. LeBaron and Lawrence A. Dowler, all from Clover Squadron, and the 431st's Lieutenant John R. O'Rourke. They spotted eleven Zeke 52s, two loose groups of four and five with two straggling in the rear, flying at the eleven o'clock position and on the flight's level. Unseen, the four P-38s made a flat, shallow turn to the right bringing them out on the tail of the two Japanese stragglers, quickly dispatched by LeBaron and Owen for one each. Sweeping to the next, larger formation, LeBaron got another Zeke as did O'Rourke of the 431st. Then the enemy broke wildly, the sky filled with dogfighting ships.

Owen's port supercharger failed so LeBaron led, pursuing and downing his third "52" near the China coast as Owen guarded his stern. Dowler took one Zeke on a dangerous head-on pass, the Japanese holing both his propellers before diving in flames. Dowler's second kill came from a meticulous deflection shot that left the enemy craft burning in the sky. Breaking away, the four Lightnings wheeled for home. Owen's left engine was out so he flew 850 miles on the other, landing eight hours and fifty minutes after takeoff. The four pilots got seven ships, the 475th's last aerial victories of World War II.[21]

The lack of air combat became apparent. In April the 475th flew its highest number of sorties in its twenty-month history, 1,589 of them, but 1,356 (or 85 percent) were bombing and strafing missions. Japanese air units had either died in place or had been withdrawn to defend the Home Islands, especially after the June invasion of Okinawa. The greatest service the Fifth could perform was directly supporting the battle front.

Satan's Angels bombed and strafed. Two areas drew much of their fire, Baguio Mountain Province and Santa Fe, Nueva Viscaya Province. In two weeks the group dropped 430 tons of high explosives and 51 napalm canisters in the Baguio area alone. Santa Fe was visited on twelve days feeling the brunt of 352 tons of bombs. With that practice, the 475th's bombing proficiency skyrocketed. Ground-air controllers rated the group "excellent" with about 88.4 percent of its hits on target. Ground attack missions cost the group two pilots, Lieutenants Reed L. Pietscher and Laverne P. Busch, the latter dying before learning of the birth of his first and only child.[22]

In April the 475th also began "train busting," strafing locomotives. On a sweep over Formosa the 431st got three on the sixth. Two days later the 433rd got one. On 30 April two squadrons found rolling stock, the 431st again getting three locomotives, the 433rd two. Now the enemy could not travel without watching the skies.[23]

The extensive gunnery and bombing in that month strained the maintenance sections to the extreme. Sergeant Richard J. "Jim" Bullivant obtained three extra Identification-Friend or Foe (IFF) sets for spare parts. An officer discovered the unauthorized sets and said that he would court-martial Bullivant if caught with them again. Wisely, the sergeant operated on the phrase "if caught," keeping the contraband IFFs. No firing ranges were available at Clark Field, so the Lightnings had gone since Dulag without boresighting and harmonization. The lack of equipment also showed in the loading of bombs. With only jury-rigged "A" frames on two and one-half ton trucks, the armament men loaded 1,406.3 tons of ordnance in April — 1,058 tons in a six-day period alone — the twelfth through the eighteenth. The new fighter-bomber role worked a hardship on all hands. At 1600 on 17 April, V Fighter Command issued new orders to the 475th. On the next day they would move north and trade fields with the P-51 Mustang-equipped 35th Fighter Group. Their destination — Lingayan.[24]

In six weeks the 475th had transformed their Clark Field camp, the effects doubled by the sheer luxury of their material-rich environs. Most tents had been raised clear of the ground and many of the officers quarters were screened. At headquarters an enlisted men's club would have opened in two days. The officers' club had scheduled a dance that Thursday, booking the best dance orchestra available, the 11th Special Service band. Word had it that a bevy of nurses and Red Cross ladies promised to attend and now nothing. The V Fighter Command hammered in the last nail, the camp was to be left intact, none of the Clark Field camp could go north.

The 475th "Line" in the Philippines. (Anderson Collection)

The 432nd area, Lingayan Gulf, 1945. (Anderson Collection)

Officer's Club, Lingayan, Philippine Islands. (Cortner Collection)

Lieutenant Chester C. "Chuck" Parshall at the Lingayan strip. The steel matting is seen to good effect. (C. C. Parshall photo)

Clearly the P-38's long-range potential did not dictate the decision to move the 475th, given the similar distances to Luzon targets from Clark and Lingayan. The 35th had damaged a number of Mustangs at Lingayan through poor flying, grumbled group malcontents. Actually the rough, wavy mat strip made landings difficult because P-51s settled down nose high on landing gear featuring a tail wheel. The tricycle configuration of the Lightning took Lingayan's runway better. But the real culprit centered on the location of the new strip which paralleled the sea, the 90 degree cross winds buffeting the lighter Mustangs. The heavier P-38s could hit and hold the runway better on takeoffs and landings. Explanations, however, guaranteed no happiness. On the morning of the eighteenth an unhappy 475th loaded up on trucks and jeeps for its first over-land move to the shores of Lingayan Gulf.[25]

The move took three days, transport traveling the twenty-five-mile trip back and forth moving the 475th to, and the 35th from, Lingayan. There the group with conditioned ease began to build-up its newest camp of the war. The stories of the winds proved true, often raising swirls of sand in the camp situated in a coconut grove flanking the sea. The strip was as bad as the rumors portrayed, undulating its whole length. Group pilots quickly adopted full stall landings which vir-

tually dumped their aircraft onto the runway, the Lightnings' 16,000-pound weight holding them down through the remainder of their run.[26]

Officers and men picked their way through the grove surveying homesteads with practiced eyes. Possum Squadron found shacks and tent frames already built on the beach and quickly claimed their territory. The 432nd inherited a simple bamboo frame and pragmatically designated it the officers' club. Hades Squadron found nothing but bare ground.

A freeze on all building materials at Clark Field hampered the camp's development but the group found a brisk trade in native materials that eased the problem. Official prices saw bamboo poles go for twenty to thirty centavos each and Nipa palm fronds for roofing selling at twenty pesos a thousand. In time showers were created amidst continued construction crowned by the one sure sign of permanence, the group's movie projector and screen settled in a theater. While not as

Typical living quarters, raised, airy, open. (Anderson Collection)

elaborate as the one at Clark, the officers' club neared completion, canvas-roofed with a "few colored parachutes draped around. . . ."

By the end of the month morale improved. The wind-driven sand subsided and the camp stayed cool in the coconut grove, fanned by the onshore breezes. With the PX in place amenities could be bought and there were plenty of cigarettes. The line could swim in the ocean as they waited for the return of missions. Lingayan was peace incarnate compared to Clark Field. Sometimes it was as if there was no war at all.[27]

Lingayan strip took the shock of 130 missions composed of 1,327 sorties in May, the group aiding ground efforts as the Luzon Campaign forged on. Divebombing continued with increasing sophistication and effect. The system became practiced ritual. The Lightnings ran in at between 7,000 and 8,000 feet, jinxing to evade flak. At sixty degrees to a sixty degree diving angle, the pilots dumped dive flaps and throttled back to about twenty-five inches of mercury to keep from overrunning the target. Lining it up between the top two .50 caliber guns, they nosed over to an angle of sixty to seventy degrees, making sure that the needle and ball were level to insure a straight drop. At 5,000 to 3,000 feet, 475th fliers pulled the nose of the ship through the target and the instant it disappeared, "pickled" bombs loose, simultaneously retracting the dive flaps, increasing speed, and clearing the area. In this manner, the group expended 500.2 tons of bombs in May.[28]

Later, Frenchy DuMontier remembered those missions. As the war wound down and replacement pilots grew in experience and numbers, new pilots began to receive increased training in ground support techniques. With air combat dwindling in the Philippines even veteran aces had to participate in those missions. This was an opportunity for the yardbirds to show the "old guys up." On one mission DuMontier took a flight out to pound a bridge that had resisted several raids. Grandly Frenchy announced he would get the target with the first pass. He missed but had the satisfaction of seeing others in the flight cover the bridge with bombs. Deadlier missions, however, lay in the future.[29]

The Japanese had retreated into the hills northeast of Manila and had taken refuge in the Ipo Dam complex twenty-five miles from the city. General Walter Krueger, head of the Sixth Army, was gravely concerned because Ipo supplied at least one-third of Manila's water. If the enemy could destroy the dam or poison its waters, the huge metropolis would be imperiled. The only other water source, Novaliches Reservoir, could supply but half of Manila's needs. Beginning on 20 February 1945 the Army began an offensive meant to clear the area of Japanese. Heavy casualties accompanied the slow push over mountains that limited maneuvering and channelized the Americans. In early May the 43rd Division, XI Corps, met fanatical resistance at Ipo. It was then decided to use massive airstrikes to "prep" the area for assault.[30]

On 14 May Kenney invited Whitehead to dinner at his home in Manila. Ruefully he explained that the pool was dry

Lieutenant Louis P. "Frenchie" DuMontier, June 1945, stands by **Madu IV.** *(Anderson Collection)*

because the Japanese capture of Ipo had forced water rationing. Kenney suggested Whitehead help Krueger's operations around Ipo so there could be water in the pool for a dip before dinner. Napalm, thought Kenney, might do the trick. The next day Whitehead called Krueger.

On the sixteenth the 475th was alerted to "bomb up" with napalm. The areas on either side of the dam had been divided up into squares and assigned to the 673 Lightnings, Thunderbolts, and Mustangs of the V Fighter Command. The sheer mass of aircraft demanded close coordination. Fighter group leaders took turns as daily air controllers who arrived early established contact with the ground observers, designated bombing runs, and then led the fighters in, marking the perimeters of the strike zone with white phosphorus bombs. Once the attacks began, the air controller circled the area directing subsequent strikes.

The 475th flew the first missions on the sixteenth. At 50 to 100 feet some attacked in standard formation, others in line abreast. At one time Lieutenant Harrold D. Owen led a combined group of seventy-five fighters on a single napalm attack. Initially both tanks on each fighter were dropped

The Ipo Dam fire raids seen through the lens of "Photo Joe," an F-5 photographic reconnaissance Lightning. The P-38s can be seen silhouetted against the left explosion. For the effect of the fire compare the charred landscape in the foreground with that of the background terrain.

"Coming home." Group Lightnings peel off to land. (Anderson Collection)

together but the unfinned containers sometimes collided, exploding in midair. On later attacks pilots toggled each drop tank separately with better results. As the 475th pulled off the targets, Mustangs swept through unburnt areas strafing Japanese flushed by the panic and flames. As the enemy fell back Satan's Angels and other groups followed their retreat with fire on the seventeenth and eighteenth. By the former date the group had delivered 187 napalm bombs to Japanese targets.

The 475th again flew to the Ipo area on 21-24 April. The air controller for the twenty-second was Group Operations Officer John S. Loisel. With a twenty-five-minute trip to the target, most men made half a dozen trips a day, the 475th expending 342 containers of jellied gas during that four-day period. The raids were not without incident. On one mission a 432nd pilot released his last bomb and felt it hang up. His wingman reported that the front shackle had released but the rear one had not, the canister left hanging nose down to the front. A series of violent maneuvers failed to shake it free so he had the wingman take another look to see if there was enough ground clearance to land. The reply was not reassuring; the wingman *thought* there was enough room. The 432nd man landed safely, later admitting that touch down was ". . . fairly tense."

On another mission Lieutenant Ralph Gutierrez, also of Clover Squadron, waited as his Lightning was loaded for another sortie. Taking off, fifteen minutes later he was over the target, a sea of flames for miles. Suddenly his engines sputtered and stopped — Gutierrez was out of gas. Going down onto the inferno, he spent five frantic seconds switching to his internal fuel supply. Engines whined, then caught, the sweating pilot easing out of the dive to complete the mission.

The 475th alone had made 331 sorties against Ipo dropping 661 napalm bombs. The 43rd Division captured the dam intact and secured the area with minor casualties. Air attacks alone killed 650 enemy but led to the death of 2,100 more. Ipo

had quite literally become hell on earth. After the last strikes Kenney was at headquarters when he remembered something; he had left the swimming pool valves on. He called home, only to be told by the sergeant there that the backyard was under a foot of water! Ipo Dam was in friendly hands again.[31]

Evidence that the war was winding down came to Satan's Angels through disparate mediums. Stories of the savage air battles over Okinawa and Japan contrasted painfully with the knowledge that May was the second consecutive month that saw no aerial victories. The war had moved north and the 475th knew it. On 8 May the capitulation of Nazi Germany brought restrained celebrations, but Japan kept fighting and so would the group. The first tangible evidence that an end beckoned arrived in an unexpected manner.

In the first week of the month Lieutenant Rudolph E. Palluck, Group Statistical Officer, announced the Redeployment Program. Based on accumulated points, the Army would discharge personnel deemed no longer necessary for the Pacific Theater of Operations or, now, European occupation duties. Points were awarded for:

1. Length of service after 16 September 1940;
2. Length of overseas service;
3. Combat decorations, including campaigns; and
4. Dependents.

Minimum points for eligibility, at the time of the announcement, was eighty-five.

The only controversial point revolved around dependents. The "non-parent" single officers and men did not dispute the category itself, but the relatively high number of points given for each dependent — twelve. Palluck, however, choked off debate by indicating that out of the 38 percent of the ground officers, 29 percent of the flying officers, and 18 percent of the enlisted men eligible for the program, the majority, 65 percent of the ground officers and 78 percent of the EMs, qualified without dependents. A film entitled "Two Down and One to Go" graphically explained the Redeployment Program although group cynics promptly renamed the movie "Two to One You Don't Go." The very existence of the program, however, provided evidence that momentous events were in the offing. On the fifteenth the 475th celebrated its second anniversary, a time for contemplating past accomplishments and future endeavors.[32]

From behind Japanese barbed wire Bill Hasty, captured the year before at Bobo drome, also saw the war progress. On 29 May General Curtis LeMay's XXI Bomber Command struck hard at Yokohama, and in its outskirts, the Brickyard Camp. An escorted, daylight raid of 517 B-29s droned overhead in huge formations. As the city reeled under the 2,570 tons of incendiaries, 150 Zeroes ripped through the Superfortresses despite their Mustang escorts. Hasty saw wounded B-29s spill out their crews, some men burning, some trailing ripped parachutes, some floating into the burning city below. But the XXIst exacted a terrible price for its dead, 8.9 square miles of Yokohama burnt to ash. The lieutenant was evacuated from

"Doc," Captain George R. Smith, 475th Flight Surgeon, and Lieutenant Colonel Claude M. Stubbs in 1945.

Lt. Col. John S. Loisel, last war-time group commander of Satan's Angels. (Anderson Collection)

the Brickyard Camp and crossed Honshu northwest to his last point of incarceration, Niigata.

Niigata Camp, hard on the sea of Japan, was relatively small, six officers and about seventy-four men. The tiny two-story buildings were badly built with the ocean wind whistling through the cracks. Worse, a small building at the

camp's entrance housed Sergeant Watanabe. The sergeant would sit before a small window looking down the camp street. Upon seeing the tiniest infraction (often none at all) Watanabe would rush out and beat the offender. For all that Hasty had witnessed, his war still continued, so he sat on a straw mattress and waited.[33]

For the 475th June followed much the same pattern as May, no air combat and much ground support of I Corps as it pushed the enemy deeper into the mountains of Luzon. In 124 missions the 475th dropped 503.6 tons of bombs and 898 napalm tanks. Strafing used up 47,032 20 millimeter rounds and 345,721 .50 caliber bullets. Five long trips swept Formosa, shooting up rolling stock and boats, but the raids were costly. On 18 June the 431st lost two pilots when Japanese ack-ack shattered the right wings of P-38s flown by Lieutenants Alvin C. Roth and Edward Carley, Jr. Both Lightnings exploded upon striking the sea five miles off Formosa.[34]

Aircraft numbers rose to eighty-four during the month, all of which were L-5 models, with the exception of three. A parts shortage plagued maintenance. The worst problem was a lack of hydraulic engine-driven pumps and fuel selector valve assemblies, an attempt to use hydraulic pumps from B-25s proving unsuccessful. In other areas things improved. Heavy duty "tugs" for towing aircraft finally arrived, as well as C-13 Portable Electric Power Plants needed to recharge batteries, a deviation from its original purpose of starting aircraft engines in cold weather.[35]

Lingayan took on the look of comfortable familiarity enhanced by supplies of almost embarrassing abundance. Three ice machines, each rated at 300 pounds per eight hours, produced chilled drinks only dreamt of a month before. More pedestrian but critically important was the arrival of water-proofing mixtures for the pyramid tents so favored by the group. A walk through the personnel equipment "stock-room" revealed plentiful items: sunglasses, watches, the new C-1 inflatable life vest with survival equipment, and sundry other goods not seen for some time. Happily the same cornucopia that produced equipment also issued food in heretofore unimaginable variety, including hot corn on the cob. The arrival of an Army-issue pastry chef convinced most of the group that the war had to be about over.[36]

The sixth month also marked the passing of familiar faces. *Satan's Angels Courier* reported one of the first home on the new rotation program was Claude M. Stubbs, now a lieutenant colonel. It was Stubbs who so ably supplied a new group designated the 475th on its drive across the Pacific. Major "Pappy" Cline also departed as C.O. of the 431st after two years in the field and two victories. Returned veteran, Major John H. Vogel, took command of Hades Squadron. Noncommissioned officers like Technical Sergeant Paul W. Joyner with the 433rd since Australia, were rotated home as well. The 27 June issue also ran the proud headlines: "Two Presidential Unit Citations Conferred Upon 475th Fighter Group." The two awards were for sweeps over Wewak, 18 and 21 August 1943, and the defense of Oro Bay, 15 and 17 October, the same year. In those two engagements, the article explained, the group destroyed fifty-six hostile craft with ight others "crippled." Rightly, the citation went to men and officers, all working towards a common goal. Both awards reflected ". . . great credit on the personnel of that organization and on the United States Army Air Force."

A newly-revamped *Satan's Angels Courier*, on the Fourth of July, 1945, ran an article on internal promotions within the group. The article announced, "Lt. Col. John S. Loisel Appointed Deputy Group Commander." At twenty-five, Loisel had accumulated 850 hours of combat air time and eleven kills. His promotion was applauded by the group. Captain Edwin R. Weaver, McGuire's wingman on his last mission, moved up to Group Operations Officer in a well-deserved move. Of no less pride, *Satan's Angels Courier* was distributed by V Fighter Command as a model combat zone newspaper. Thus the 475th moved into July, a month closer to the war's end.[37]

On the Fourth of July, 1945, MacArthur declared the Luzon Campaign closed and the Philippines a free and independent nation. Continued fighting in northern Luzon indicated the general's comments a bit premature but the struggle was carried out by small, unorganized groups of Japanese. The 475th's combat record for the month confirmed the slow wind-down on that island.

Only seventy-seven missions were flown in July, three of which went to the China coast, the rest directed against Luzon targets. Bombs, napalm, and strafing — the litany continued. Hardened targets diminished, replaced by attacks on enemy troops in mountainous terrain so the vast percentage of ordinance carried by the squadrons were 854 belly tanks of napalm directed by forward air controllers like the Sixth Army's "Bygone-1." The highlights of that month involved a 432nd aerial ambush of an escaping Japanese truck convoy that left eleven destroyed and the 433rd's destruction of two ammunition dumps. Two pilots were lost on operations.[38]

With an eye to the final invasion of Japan, the group's equipment continued to receive reinforcement. The last J-20 Lightning disappeared from the records, the group now flying the L-5 variant P-38, eighty-three of them by August. Serviceable aircraft increased as lessening combat gave the line a chance to work on craft all in anticipation of the climatic struggle ahead. Maintenance and "guns" also worked to modify the existing craft to new weapons. Christmas tree racks now held two-inch rockets. Following instructions for the new "Wingline" air-to-ground tactics, crews painted radiating lines from leading wing edges to act as guides in high altitude strafing, divebombing, and rocket attacks.[39]

The group also reformed its leadership under the rotation system. On the fourteenth, MacDonald received the second Distinguished Service Cross earned by a pilot flying with the 475th, the first going to Mac McGuire the day he died on Los Negros. The next day MacDonald, after leading the group so well for twenty months, stepped down and turned command over to Deputy Group Commander Loisel. During his tenure as Group Commander, his men destroyed 321 Japanese aircraft in aerial combat. He left the SWPA as its leading ace

with twenty-seven victories. Though missed by the men, they took solace in the fact that Loisel was a worthy replacement.

Captain Edwin R. Weaver, Group Operations Officer, took command of the 431st, Hades Squadron, replacing Major John H. Vogel. Like Loisel, a returning 475th pilot, Captain William F. Haning, Jr., became Group "Ops" Officer. Major Elliot Summer rotated stateside relinquishing command of the 432nd, Clover Squadron, to Major Dean W. Dutrack.[40]

The 475th received word to cease operations by 23 July. The long anticipated move to Okinawa was about to begin. Old hands at the moving business, supply sections had begged and borrowed, just short of theft, preparing for the day of departure. Of greatest importance was the twenty-two kegs of nails in all sizes and lumber. The supply personnel then sought out screening, olive drab paint, hinges, wire, and sewing-machine needles for the parachute repair section. Those, and hundreds of other items, were found and hoarded for the day of departure.

Other sections matched supply in quality if not quantity. Transportation had, for the first time since Amberly, all vehicles in first-class or new condition. The Group Historian tactfully attributed this phenomenon to ". . . resourcefulness and persistence." The line had consistently produced miracles from nothing during the arduous trek across the Southwest Pacific. On the eve of their last campaign they received the repair kits and equipment needed months before. Kitted out in full, the line felt confident they could "keep 'em flying" again.

Transportation became the biggest problem with confusion at the highest levels of command manifesting itself in a series of departure dates that rose and fell like the tide. Air echelons planned to leave for Okinawa first on 29 July, then 1 August, and finally 23 July. In the end, they were given an 8 August departure date . . . or perhaps later. The water echelon was scheduled to leave 29 July. LSTs arrived by the twenty-fifth but informed the group they had to pick up another contingent. At 0830 the next day the ships were reassigned to the 475th loading and departing by early afternoon. By 29 July they had moved into Subic Bay to pick up some miscellaneous personnel and then returned to Lingayan. The 475th departed there on the thirtieth heading north, encountering the the first temperate climate in years. On 6 August, with the group scattered from Ie Shima to Lingayan, the 475th first heard that the U.S. had exploded an atomic bomb over Japan.[41]

The group's reaction to the news was guarded. The sheer magnitude of the bomb simply eclipsed people's ability to grasp its military effect. If the nuclear weapon's very existence shocked Vice President Harry Truman when he learned of it after Roosevelt's death four months before, the 475th's reactions were understandable. The hopeful posited Japan's immediate surrender; the cynical pointed out the failure of Nazi Germany's "secret weapons" and guessed that America's would come to the same pass. The news did, however, enliven conversation for the remainder of the trip.[42]

That same day the convoy anchored off Yontan, Okinawa, awaiting disposition. On the eighth the U.S. dropped a

The end of the line, Ie Shima, and the end of the war. (Anderson Collection)

Lieutenants Robert K. Weary, pilot, and Robert A. "Heavy" Hall, group intelligence officer. (Anderson Collection)

The two "surrender" Bettys on their way to Ie Shima, Manila, and MacArthur. Painted white, they are escorted by two dark colored B-25s seen at the upper left and lower center, flanking the Japanese bombers. (Anderson Collection)

second atomic bomb on Nagasaki, Japan. On the ninth the water echelon left an Okinawa crowded with Fifth Air Force bombers and proceded four miles west to a coral isle called Ie Shima, noted only as the place where the G.I.'s correspondent, Ernie Pyle, had died from an enemy sniper bullet. Later that day word came down that Dick Bong, America's highest scoring pilot, had been killed when the experimental P-80 jet he was flying crashed. Offloading finished by 13 August and the camp arose in the center of the island.

The men were grateful for the careful scavenging done by Supply because building materials were scarce. Lumber that traveled with the group from the Philippines went into the standard, necessary buildings while the men again pitched tents on the coral ground. When completed the Ie Shima camp looked very military, a far cry from the idyllic bamboo and frond facilities at Lingayan.[43]

Beyond the coral dust of Ie Shima important events sped on. On 10 August the Soviet Union declared war on Japan forcing the enemy to turn north and west in defense. On that

same day the Japanese suggested conditional surrender terms. Negotiations continued. Fearing continued air attacks might sidetrack the peace process, President Truman ordered the American air arms to stand down from the eleventh through the thirteenth. When the Japanese did not respond to the unconditional demands of the Allies, orders went out for the resumption of air attacks on the Home Islands. On 15 August another message flashed announcing Japanese acceptence of the surrender terms. Whitehead passed the news to the troops, hands on hips, billed service cap set squarely on his head, eyes shaded by aviator sunglasses. Frantic moments were spent recalling raids already bound for enemy targets. Peace had come to the Pacific.[44]

While statesmen sparred the 475th had ceased attacks with the rest of the Fifth. After a restrained celebration, made so, one suspects, by the lack of alcohol on the tiny island, a strange "normalcy" ruled the day. The group had much new equipment and with no operations, maintenance slowed, then stopped. Further the cessation of hostilities meant occupation duty with Korea getting the nod. This meant another move and so no effort went into improving the camp. Instead, Satan's Angels relaxed for the first time since Amberly Field.

Baseball equipment came out and games were played on that coral atoll. For the sedate, endless poker and bridge games began and ended with the chuck of a card but always accompanied by conversation. Gone were the pessimists' "Golden Gate in '48." Talk now revolved around a nonmilitary future. Group Intelligence Officer Lieutenant Robert A. "Heavy" Hall, between bridge games avidly watched by Ormoc the monkey, planned to go home and help in his brother's bar, and maybe do more of the artwork begun in the Pacific. Some tentatively opted to stay in the Army Air Forces; still others enjoyed the luxury of no plans at all.

As the realization that the war was over sank in, men counted points for rotation home. Heated discussions arose

Dark colored Fifth Air Force B-25s escort the white Japanese Bettys into Ie Shima. (Ted Hanks Collection)

The Japanese peace delegation lands at Ie Shima. (Ted Hanks Collection)

over fine particulars of interpretation. Records were combed looking for one overlooked activity that could accrue more points. "Campaign Luzon was no longer a ribbon or star to be lightly dismissed. It was a down payment on that one way ticket home."[45]

On 15 August MacArthur ordered a Japanese delegation to his headquarters at Manila, ". . . empowered to receive in the name of the Emperor, the Japanese Government, and the Japanese General Headquarters, certain requirements for carry into effect the terms of surrender." Four days later, 19 August, a sixteen-man delegation headed up by Lieutenant

General Torashiro Kawabe, Vice-Chief of the Imperial General Staff, departed for the meeting that would create the surrender documents concluding World War II.

When the news broke of the Manila meeting the men sensed that the war, their war, had finally ended. MacArthur instructed the Japanese contingent to paint their Mitsubishi G4M Betty transports white with green crosses in place of the *hinamaru*, the red sun of Yamato. Their call letters were to be B-A-T-A-A-N, a fine historical twist commemorating a battle lost long ago. When the Japanese confirmed the instructions, they asked for call sign J-N-P. MacArthur firmly repeated his original demand, and so it was.

At noon, 19 August 1945, a crowd waited by Ie Shima's single western strip for the enemy's arrival. The Japanese were escorted in by "Squeeze" Wurtsmith's former group, sixteen silvery Lightnings of the 49th, flanked by B-25s and a single B-17. They allowed the two white transports to land first. A number of Satan's Angels watched the final act unfold. Clover Squadron pilot Lieutenant Ralph Gutierrez had mixed feelings about the whole affair. Happy the war was closing down, the enemy's fanatical resistence had made him wary; a surprise gas attack could do great damage and Ie Shima was a very small island. One of the 433rd's sheet metal specialists, Corporal Edward "Ed" Barski, watched as the Japanese airplane taxiied to the north end of the strip. Stopping, the emissaries deplaned and were escorted to a waiting American C-54 which flew them to Manila and the completion of their errand. Their transports were refueled, their crews under armed guard to protect them from the hostile crowd.[46]

And so the 475th ended like it began, with movement and purpose. The seers in the group predicted correctly, Satan's Angels headed north for occupation duty in Korea. By

The Japanese emissaries board a U.S. transport on the way to Manila — and MacArthur. (Ted Hanks Collection)

Americans, including 475th personnel, gaze at the specially-marked "surrender" Bettys on Ie Shima. (Anderson Collection)

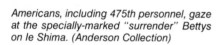

Another view of the Bettys. The enemy delegation transferred to American transports for the last leg to Manila. Note armed G.I.s in front of the Betty, protection for the Japanese air crews left behind. (Anderson Collection)

American and Japanese help push the "peace" bombers into position. (Ted Hanks Collection)

month's end sixty-seven enlisted men transferred to the 22nd Replacement Depot, the first move leading to America. The group was present and accounted for — all except one.

The first inkling the 433rd's Bill Hasty had that the war had ended came on 14 August. He awoke at Niigata Camp to discover no guards present. Major Fellows, former artilleryman and senior officer present, later told Hasty that the Japanese lieutenant commanding the camp said earlier that he "had urgent business in Tokyo," did not know when he would return, and left. The major, Hasty, and four other American officers took command of the camp. A while later dark and sea blue Navy airplanes, an F6F Hellcat and an SBD Douglas divebomber, hovered over the camp on the edge of a stall. Packages tumbled out of opened cockpits: food, candy, cigarettes, all eagerly gathered up by the men and taken back to camp. Hasty was hungry too; he had lost about sixty-five pounds in captivity, his last decent meal coming from half a Red Cross carton in February.

Neither was the Army Air Forces slow to aid POWs scattered throughout Asia. By 17 August Boeing B-29 Superfortresses of the 20th Air Force roared off strips bound for 300 prison camps identified by Allied intelligence and Japa-

nese authorities. Niigata Camp received some of the first flights. For three days one or two B-29s in trail came low over the camp dropping fifty-five-gallon drums, with easily removable tops, into a pine forest adjacent to the camp. Still the men awaited first contact with fellow Americans.

On 20 or 21 August, a U.S. Navy landing party arrived at the camp led by Lieutenant Commander Harold E. Stassen, former Governor of Minnesota (at that time, the youngest governor in U.S. history), and a prominent figure in postwar America's politics. He informed the assembled men that help would arrive soon. The POWs waited. On 2 September 1945 the Japanese surrendered to the Allies on board the *USS Missouri* anchored in Tokyo Bay. While that solemn proceeding closed the most savage war in modern memory, Fellows, Hasty, and two officers walked to Niigata, found the local yardmaster, and commandeered a train. Two days later, 4 September, Niigata Camp mustered for the last time. Forming up, they marched past the commandant's quarters, past the mean little window Sergeant Watanabe used to spy through, past the barbed wire and gun towers. As they swung out onto the road, Bill Hasty never looked back. The 475th was now and truly on its way home.[47]

FOOTNOTES

1. *Official History*, frames 1334, 1398; *Ibid.*, Annex D1-2, Movement Order, 7, 12 January 1945, frames 1416, 1419.

2. *Official History*, frames 1399-1400; Maurer, *USAF Credits*, pp. 119, 655-57.

3. Craven and Cate, *The Army Air Forces*, vol. V, pp. 393-97, 411; Hess, *Sweep*, p.

210; also see above, p. 83; Peter Young, ed., *Atlas of the Second World War* (NY: Berkley Publishing Co., 1972), p. 163.

4. Documentation on the death of McGuire was derived from Art Covello, ed., *The Major T.B. McGuire, Jr., Story* (NJ: Major Thomas B. McGuire, Jr., Memorial, 1981),

pp. 2-4, 16-17; Carroll R. Anderson, "McGuire's Last Mission," *Air Force* (January 1975), rpt. ed. in above, pp. 9-13, 14-15; Douglas S. Thropp, Jr., Files: "Individual Combat Report of 2nd Lieutenant Douglas S. Thropp, Jr., 9 January 1945," pp. 1-2; Captain Edwin R. Weaver, "Individual Combat Report of Captain Edwin R. Weaver, 9 January 1945," pp. 1-2; Letter: Douglas S. Thropp, Jr. to H.N. Madison, handdrawn maps of Mission 1-668, pp. 1-3; Letter: Carroll R. Anderson to H.N. Madison, 6 January 1981, p. 5; Anderson Papers: Norris J. Clark, "Mission Report," 7 January 1945, pp. 1-2; Jeffery L. Ethell, "Number Two Isn't Second Best," *Air Classics*, vol. 12, no. 11 (November 1976), *passim*; *Official History*, frames 1401-03; Interview: John S. Babel, October 1987; Tilley Interview; Letter: H.N. Madison to Author, July 1987; Toll, *Tropic Lightning*, pp. 15-17; Kenney, *Reports*, pp. 436, 498, 503; Hess, *Sweep*, pp. 211-12; Craven and Cate, *The Army Air Forces*, vol. V, bottom notes, pp. 396, 406; Brammeier, "Fighter Operations," pp. 45-47; Anderson Files: Letters, Christopher Herman to Sister, 24 October 1944-12 January 1945, pp. 1-4; Letter: Mizunori Fukuda to Carrol R. Anderson, 9 March 1974, p. 2; Letter: Osamu Tagaya to Anderson, N.D., pp. 1-2. Carroll R. Anderson indicates that McGuire was turning with Japanese fighters by mid-June 1944. Anderson, "Thomas McGuire," p. 8. As McGuire tightened his turn, gas compressing to the rear of his drop tanks might have also changed the Lightning's center of gravity causing the fighter to sink during the turn. See Bob Davidson's "Fork-Tailed Legend," *Airpower*, vol. 2, no. 6 (November 1972), pp. 24, 28-29.

5. Toll, *Tropic Lightning*, pp. 45-46; Toll Letter, June 1987, p. 11; *Official History*, frames 1401-02. A detailed sketch of Purdy's career, and his escape, can be seen in Carrol R. Anderson, "Jack Purdy," *Journal of the American Aviation Historical Society*, vol. 16, no. 1 (Spring 1971), pp. 50-56.

6. *Official History*, frames 1403-04. See note 2, frame 1404.

7. *Official History*, frame 1087; MacDonald Interview.

8. Green, *Famous Fighters*, pp. 76-77; Weber, "P-38J-M," p. 5.

9. DuMontier Interview, July 1987; *Official History*, frame 1087; Shelton Letter, p. 4.

10. *Official History*, frame 1406; Smith, *Triumph*, p. 73.

11. *Official History*, frames 1463-65, Annex D-2, frame 1482; Letter: Robert K. Weary to Author, July 1987, p. 1 (hereinafter, Weary Letter); Toll Letter, p. 6; Survey: Leo W. Blakely, Jr., May 1987; Survey: Gary Oskamp, May 1987.

12. *Official History*, frames 1468-69.

13. *Official History*, frame 1467.

14. Tilley Letter, pp. 5-6; *Official History*, frames 1468.

15. *Official History*, frames 1466-67; Toll Letter, p. 10.

16. *Official History*, frames 1470; *Ibid.*, frame 1501, Annex J-8, "Aircraft Accident Report;" Hanks Letter, pp. 11-12; Interview: John R. Neff with Author, 12 October 1987.

17. *Official History*, frames 1471-72; *Ibid.*, frame 1489, Annex H-1, "Radiogram," 27 February 1945; Lynch, et al., *Satan's Angels*, p. 68.

18. *Official History*, frames 1511-12, 1520; Tilley Letter, p. 6; Weary Letter, p. 1.

19. *Official History*, frame 1513.

20. *Official History*, frames 1513-16; Hess, *Sweep*, pp. 214-17; Maurer, *USAF Credits*, p. 657.

21. *Official History*, frames 1517-18; Hess, *Sweep*, p. 217; Maurer, *USAF Credits*, pp. 655-56.

22. *Official History*, frames 1574-76; Anderson Files, Annex G-1, February-July 1945.

23. *Official History*, frames 1578-79.

24. *Official History*, frames 1580-82; *Ibid.*, frames 1614-16, Annex J 1-3; *Ibid.*, frame 1617, Annex K; *Ibid.*, frames 1667-68, Annex D; Survey: Richard J. Bullivant, May 1987.

25. *Official History*, frames 1582-84; Tilley Letter, p. 6; Toll Letter, p. 7; Weary Letter, p. 2; DuMontier Letter, p. 1.

26. Toll Letter, p. 7; *Official History*, frame 1584.

27. *Official History*, frames 1585-87; Weary Letter, p. 2.

28. *Official History*, frames 1532, 1633.

29. DuMontier Interview, June 1987.

30. Smith, *Triumph*, pp. 367, 403-12.

31. *Official History*, frames 1654-56; *Ibid.*, frame 1655, Annex A; Craven and Cate, *The Army Air Forces*, vol. V, pp. 435-36; Smith, *Triumph*, p. 413; Kenney, *Reports*, pp. 545-46; Toll Letter, pp. 9-10; Survey: Harrold D. Owen, May 1987; Interview: Ralph Gutierrez, October 1987 (hereinafter, Gutierrez Interview).

32. *Official History*, frames 1644-45.

33. Hasty Interview, October 1987; Hasty Memoirs; Craven and Cate, *The Army Air Forces*, vol. V, pp. 639-40.

34. *Official History*, frames 1703-04, Annex C-D-5-6, frames 1722-23, 1728-29.

35. *Ibid.*, frames 1707-08.

36. *Ibid.*, frame 1709.

37. *Official History*, frames 1709, 1712; *Ibid.*, frames 1748-50, Annex J; *Satan's Angels Courier*, (Lingayan, Philippines), 27 June 1945, pp. 1-4; Survey: Paul W. Joyner, May 1987.

38. *Official History*, frames 1777-78, 1784; *Ibid.*, frames 1791, 1928, Annex A.

39. *Official History*, frames 1784-85; *Ibid.*, frames 1822-25, Annex H-1-3, "Wingline Instructions;" Brammeier, "Fighter Operations," p. 79.

40. *Official History*, frames 1784-86.

41. *Ibid.*, frames 1779, 1781-86; frames 1818-21, Annex G1-3; MacDonald Interview; Loisel Letter.

42. *Official History*, frame 10.

43. *Ibid.*, frames 10, 132; Kenney, *Reports*, pp. 568-69.

44. Kenney, *Reports*, p. 570-71; Willoughby and Chamberlain, *MacArthur*, pp. 290-93; Spector, *Eagle*, pp. 557-58; Craven and Cate, *The Army Air Forces*, vol. V, pp. 732-33; *Official History*, frame 133.

45. *Ibid.*, frames 11-13; Interview: Robert A. Hall, October 1987.

46. Letter: Edward Barski to Author, July 1987, pp. 1-2; Gutierrez Interview; Kenney, *Reports*, pp. 572-73; Willoughby and Chamberlain, *MacArthur*, p. 293; *Official History*, frames 134-35; Campese Letter.

47. *Official History*, frame 12; Craven and Cate, *The Army Air Forces*, vol. V, pp. 734-35; Hasty Interview, October 1987; Hasty Memoirs; *Current Biography: 1948* (NY: H.W. Wilson Co., 1949), pp. 597-600, especially p. 599.

"In Proelio Gaudete": An Epilogue

The wartime 475th Fighter Group symbolically came to an end in April 1946. Lieutenant Colonel John S. Loisel finally rotated home, the last of those who had formed the veteran cadre around which the group had coalesced back at Amberly Field in May 1943. The 475th's C.O. since July 1945, Loisel had flown 301 combat missions for a total of 852 hours of flying time. The colonel had shot down eleven enemy craft, earned the Silver Star and the Distinguished Flying Cross with three Oak Leaf Clusters. He had led the 475th from war to uneasy peace.[1]

Occupation duty in Korea had not been easy. America's turning from war saw drastic reductions in personnel starting in September 1945 and not bottoming out until February 1946. At its nadir on 31 January 1946, the group's entire compliment numbered 97 officers and 63 enlisted men. Hardest hit was Clover Squadron, the 432nd, with a mere 49 officers and 15 "other ranks." Major Dean W. Dutrack, the 432nd's last wartime commander, held seven different command positions until his return to the states in September 1947 in the constant shifting produced by the manpower shortage.

But many men had looked forward to the personnel reductions. Mechanics Corporal Kermit O. Dakken of the 431st and Sergeant Milton R. Pancoast of the 433rd concluded their long tour of duty with the group in October and November of

Kimpo Airfield, home to the 475th after leaving Yung Dong Po, their first base. Photograph was probably taken in early 1946. (James Dawson photo)

1945. Also in those months, two Sergeants — 432nd Sergeant John H. DuPlika and 431st Staff Sergeant Roy F. Raines — left Korea after serving with the group since shortly after its inception in May of 1943. These men were among the many war-weary veterans who had rejoiced in battle, and now rejoiced as they headed home.[2]

The effect on the group's operational abilities was disasterous. A wartime engine change had taken eight hours; in January 1946 that same task took eight days. Oil dilution equipment, discarded in the tropics, was needed for flying in Korea. No warm clothing was forthcoming as the men bundled up in Japanese cold weather suits. They existed on canned food until spring of 1946. Only forty-eight of the group's sixty-nine Lightnings could fly and only eight to ten could be checked "in" to fly each day. Only through the 475th's most easily maintainable aircraft, an AT-6 Courier and five L-4Js, could the pilots log enough monthly flying time for flight pay. Still the group doggedly tried to carry out its training, reconnaissance, and security patrol missions. Loisel brought the 475th through all that and things began to improve by the time he went home.[3]

No member of Satan's Angels had to look back in shame. In two years of war the 475th helped spearhead MacArthur's drive across the Pacific's Southwest with 3,042 missions, composed of 21,701 individual sorties. Eighty-six percent of those sorties were offensive in nature.[4]

Sergeant James Dawson in front of a typical quonset hut living-quarters at Kimpe. Due to a lack of American camera film, Dawson used aerial mapping film, cut to fit, to produce the pictures in this chapter. (James Dawson photo)

*The end of **Putt Putt Maru**. In April 1946 the line ran a full-power check on MacDonald's former Lightning. It jumped the chocks, slewed 180 degrees to the right, and struck an unoccupied tug. Damage: a bent prop, wrecked nose gear, and a wrinkled nose just forward of the cockpit. The stalwart Lightning was written off and became a source of parts. (James Dawson photo)*

The 475th shot down 547 Japanese aircraft in aerial combat. This was balanced against the total loss of eighty-seven Lightnings, an overall kill ratio of 6.3:1. Those numbers, however, were deceiving. Losses attributable directly to enemy action numbered thirty-four, thus a ratio based on pure air combat would be 16:1! By all calculations, Satan's Angels had performed admirably in its air superiority role.[5]

The human cost was high — eighty-seven pilots lost in the war, men who never went home. Weather was the biggest killer, accounting for thirty-three of the group's pilots. Air-to-air combat came in second with twenty-seven, while anti-aircraft fire shot down seven fliers. The remainder fell to the vagaries of war: empty fuel tanks, accidents, and plain bad luck. The enlisted men, NCOs, and nonflying headquarters staff suffered less casualties, losing six men during the war.

The squadrons — Hades, Clover, and Possum — had done their share. Officers and men wore eight campaign ribbons with one squadron receiving an additional ribbon: the China Defensive; New Guinea; Bismarck Archipeligo; Western Pacific; Leyte; Luzon; Southern Philippines; the China Offensive; and Air Combat, Asiatic Pacific Theater. The group received a third Presidential Unit Citation at war's end for the Philippine operations of 1944, which concluded with the "Christmas Day Battle" over the Clark Field complex. Additionally, a grateful Filipino people awarded Satan's Angels the Philippine Presidential Unit Citation. By then, however, most of the group's personnel had returned to the forty-seven states they left years before. For them, the peace they had fought so hard to secure was reward enough.[6]

FOOTNOTES

1. *Official History*, frames 535-36.
2. Survey: Kermit O. Dakken; Survey: Milton R. Pancoast; Survey: John H. DuPlika; Survey: Roy F. Raines.
3. *Official History*, frames 408-09, 412-13; Dean W. Dutrack to Author, 23 September 1987, p. 1; Survey: Walter L. Mapes, June 1987; Survey: James P. Dawson, Jr., May 1987.
4. *Official History*, frames 36, 64-70; Annexes F1-4, G1-2.
5. John R. Neff, compiler, "Appendices": 475th Fighter Group Victories, 475th Fighter Group Roster.
6. Maurer, *Combat Squadrons of the Air Force*, pp. 532-35.

A Bibliographic Overview

This work chronicled a social organization created for combat; its documentation reflects the complexity of that effort. Primary sources included a survey sent to all 613 surviving members of the 475th Fighter Group, of which 90 responded, approximately 15 percent. Eventually the collection will be deposited at the 475th Fighter Group Museum, Planes of Fame complex, Chino Airport, Chino, California. Collateral information came from interviews, both telephone and tape recorded, as well as miscellaneous documents such as journals, diaries, photographs, and official papers.

The *Official History of the 475th Fighter Group*, Maxwell AFB, United States Air Force Historical Research Center (formerly the Albert F. Simpson Historical Research Center), record group 4-4710-99, provided a wealth of descriptive narrative as well as data that traced the group's day-to-day existence. Statistical summaries ended each month's report. While the complete series could not be located, issues of *Satan's Angels Courier*, the 475th's newspaper, provided both broad coverage of the war as well as homey reportage of group life. An invaluable aid to any research on the group was the "Bluebook," written by early 475th Historian Louis E. Lynch, et al., *Satan's Angels, 475th Fighter Group, 14th May 43 — 31st Dec. 44* (1946). A privately printed history of the group, it carried Satan's Angels through December 1944. Of special value was its roster of officers and men, plus lists of air victories and decorations.

Important secondary sources began with Wesley Frank Craven and James Lea Cate, eds., *The United States Army Air Forces in World War II*, the official history of America's wartime Army air arm. Of particular interest were chapters in volumes IV, V, and VI that cover the later Pacific air campaigns. The official U.S. Army in World War II series, edited by Kent R. Greenfield, also contributed to the work; Samuel Miller, *Victory in Papua* (1957), John Miller, Jr., *Cartwheel: The Reduction of Rabaul* (1959), M. Hamlin Cannon, *Letye: The Return to the Philippines* (1954), and Robert Ross Smith, *Triumph in the Philippines* (1963) provided insight to land actions and, surprisingly, considerable detail on air activities, both Allied and Japanese. Quality Army maps also fleshed out and explained the movements of the 475th through the SWPA. The officially informed USAAF, *Army Air Force Guidebook* (1944) produced the "Big Picture" of the Army Air Forces at war's end. A generally informative book, it covered organizational topics as well as providing a combat narrative of the war.

Published autobiographies, biographies, and journals also formed portions of the 475th's story. Douglas MacArthur, *Reminiscences* (1964) and Charles A. Willoughby and John Chamberlain, *MacArthur, 1941-1951* (1954) lent insight into the command decisions that sent the 475th into battle. Invaluable in understanding the Fifth Air Force's actions was George Churchill Kenney's *General Kenny Reports . . .* (1949), while his superior, General H. H. "Hap" Arnold, placed the Pacific War within the broader context of a *Global Mission* (1949). Charles A. Lindbergh's *The Wartime Journals of Charles A. Lindbergh* (1970) provided detailed information on his tour in the SWPA.

Surveys of the war against Japan are well served by Ronald H. Spector's *Eagle Against the Sun: The American War Against Japan* (1959) which mixes fact with judicious interpretation. A good supplemental text is John Costello's *The Pacific War, 1941-1945* (1981). The early retreat of the United States Army Air Forces in the Pacific is examined in detail by Walter P. Edmonds in his *They Fought With What They Had* (1951). Southwest Pacific fighter campaigns are examined in William N. Hess, *Pacific Sweep* (1974), while Edward L. Maloney's edition of *Fighter Tactics of the Ace's [sic] — S.W.P.A.* (1978) was essential in understanding winged warfare in the tropics. Japanese aerial experience in the New Guinea and Guadalcanal period are seen through the eyes of ace Saburo Sakai in *Samurai!* (1957), with corrections and clarifications in Henry Sakaida's *Winged Samurai* (1985). Confirmed air kills were checked in Maurer Maurer, ed., *USAF Credits for the Destruction of Enemy Aircraft, World War II* (1978).

Specialized information was gleaned from a number of sources. Periodicals included *Aerospace* (formerly *Airpower*) *Historian*, *Air Classics*, *Airpower*, and the *Journal of the American Aviation Historical Society*. Unofficial 475th Fighter Group historian Carroll R. "Andy" Anderson's articles, found in the above periodicals, provided intimate glimpses of Satan's Angels' wartime activities. The problems of the pre-war Air Corps' fighter doctrine can be seen in Ronald W. Yoshino's "A Doctrine Destroyed: The American Fighter Offensive, 1917-1939" (Unpublished Ph.D. dissertation, Claremont Graduate School, 1985). An able summary of the 475th was written by Charles L. Brammeier, "USAAF Operations in the Southwest Pacific: Role of the 475th Fighter Group" (Student Report #87-0320, Air Command and Staff College, 1987).

Appendix 1

475th Fighter Group Victories

The Victory list was compiled from two main sources, the *Official History of the 475th Fighter Group*, August 1945 War End Totals, frames 42-49, and Maurer Maurer, ed., *USAF Credits for the Destruction of Enemy Aircraft*. Any differences between the two tallies can, for the most part, be attributed to the stringency of the USAF Accredidation process. Although certainty of a particular victory may seem incontrovertible at the time, later examination of the evidence may invalidate the record. Poor quality of gun camera footage or lack of eye witnesses typify reasons which may cause a victory to be disallowed. Conversely, later examination could add to a pilot's score, affirming kills that were only considered probable. Correlation of combat reports from Allied as well as Japanese sources have also yielded previously unknown conformation for victories.

A listing of overall totals follows:

	USAF	*Official History*
Total Victories by 475th personnel	583	594
Victories earned by personnel before or after duty with the 475th	- 36	- 42
475th FG Total	547	552

It should be noted that two pilot's totals are missing from the 475th Group listings. Richard I. Bong, America's leading ace of World War II, flew briefly with the group and scored five victories during that time. However, those scores are attributed by the USAF to the official group of assignment, the V Fighter Command, and not Satan's Angels. Likewise, Charles A. Lindbergh's sole victory is not recognized by either the USAF or the *Official History*. His civilian status denied him a combat kill recognized under USAF Accredidation Rules and is listed here as a matter of record.

Even though the two tallies would both equal 547 if Major Bong's five victories claimed by the group were subtracted, other factors involving several other pilots enter into the final calculations, making that comparasion merely coincidental.

The pilots are listed, in descending order, according to their USAF accredited score. The score claimed by the group is to the right, in parenthesis.

NAME	USAF	475th FG
McGuire, Thomas B., Jr.	38	(38)
MacDonald, Charles H.	27	(27)
Roberts, Daniel T., Jr.	14	(15)
Lent, Francis J.	11	(11)
Loisel, John S.	11	(11)
Summer, Elliot	10	(10)
Dahl, Perry J.	9	(9)
Forster, Joseph M.	9	(9)
Hart, Kenneth F.	9	(8)
Smith, Meryl M.	9	(9)
Allen, Davis W.	8	(8)
Harris, Frederick A.	8	(8)
Champlin, Frederic F.	7	(9)
Dean, Zach W.	7	(7)
Elliot, Vincent T.	7	(7)
Fisk, Jack A.	7	(7)
Jett, Verle E.	7	(7)
Lewis, Warren R.	7	(7)
Purdy, John E.	7	(7)
Wire, Calvin C.	7	(7)
Brown, Harry W.	6	(7)
Czarnecki, Edward J.	6	(6)
Gresham, Billy M.	6	(6)
Ince, James C.	6	(6)
Lucas, Paul W.	6	(6)
McKeon, Joseph T.	6	(5)
Pietz, John, Jr.	6	(6)
Reeves, Horace B.	6	(6)
Smith, John C.	6	(6)
Wenige, Arthur E.	6	(6)
Cloud, Vivian A.	5	(5)
Condon, Henry L., II	5	(5)
Gholson, Grover D.	5	(5)
Kirby, Marion F.	5	(5)
Lutton, Lowell C.	5	(5)
Mankin, Jack C.	5	(5)
Monk, Franklin H.	5	(5)
Morriss, Paul V.	5	(5)
Nichols, Franklin A.	5	(5)
Tilley, John A.	5	(5)
Fulkerson, Floyd H.	4	(4)
Grady, William J.	4	(4)
Grice, Charles A.	4	(4)

NAME	USAF	475th FG	NAME	USAF	475th FG
Gronemeyer, William C.	4	(4)	Houseworth, Carl H.	2	(2)
Hedrick, Howard A.	4	(4)	Hulett, Wesley J.	2	(2)
King, Donald Y.	4	(4)	Hunt, Robert E.	2	(2)
LeBaron, Lawrence C.	4	(4)	Kiick, Richard D.	2	(2)
Mayo, Leo N.	4	(4)	Koeck, Robert A.	2	(2)
O'Brien, William S.	4	(4)	Meyer, Dale O.	2	(2)
Owen, Harrold D.	4	(4)	Neal, Alvin R.	2	(2)
Ratajski, Charles J.	4	(4)	Peregoy, Arthur L.	2	(2)
Rittmayer, Jack B.	4	(4)	Peters, Paul R.	2	(2)
Schinz, Albert W.	4	(4)	Provencio, Enrique	2	(2)
Tomkins, Frank D.	4	(4)	Redding, Carl R.	2	(2)
Wilson, Campbell P. M.	4	(3)	Rieman, Clarence J.	2	(2)
Zehring, Herman W.	4	(4)	Roberts, Ethelbert B.	2	(2)
Babel, John S.	3	(3)	Tomberg, Robert M.	2	(2)
Beatty, George R.	3	(3)	Ballard, John R.	1	(1)
Brenizer, Chase, Jr.	3	(3)	Bartlett, Christopher O.	1	(1)
Bryan, Leroy C.	3	(3)	Benevent, Foch J.	1	(1)
Dowler, Laurence A.	3	(3)	Blakely, Leo W.	1	(1)
DuMontier, Louis D.	3	(3)	Clodfelter, Wood D.	1	(1)
Farris, James R.	3	(3)	Crosswait, Robert L.	1	(1)
Hadley, Robert L.	3	(3)	Dewey, George G.	1	(1)
Hood, John J.	3	(5)	Dunlap, Ronald E.	1	(1)
Ivey, William H.	3	(3)	Edesberg, Edward B.	1	(1)
Jeakle, William G.	3	(3)	Ettien, Clifford L., Jr.	1	(1)
Jordan, Herbert H.	3	(1)	Fogarty, John E.	1	(1)
Kimball, Richard D.	3	(3)	Gray, Harold W.	1	(1)
Kimball, Robert H.	3	(3)	Hagan, Virgil A.	1	(1)
Lundy, Noel R.	3	(4)	Hammond, Jerome R.	1	(1)
Malloy, James M.	3	(3)	Herman, Christopher J.	1	(1)
Martin, Thomas E.	3	(3)	Herman, Robert L.	1	(1)
Moreing, James A.	3	(3)	Howard, John H.	1	(1)
Morrison, Samuel M.	3	(3)	Hudnell, W. T., Jr.	1	(1)
Oxford, Thomas M.	3	(3)	Kidd, Alvin R.	1	(1)
Prentice, George W.	3	(4)	Kirschner, Kenneth D.	1	(1)
Ritter, William T.	3	(3)	Mann, Clifford J.	1	(1)
Roberts, Lawrence D.	3	(3)	Maxwell, Glenn K.	1	(1)
Ross, LeRoy H.	3	(3)	McKenzie, Albert A.	1	(1)
Rundell, John T., Jr.	3	(3)	Michener, John E.	1	(1)
Toll, Henry C.	3	(3)	Miller, Joseph E., Jr.	1	(1)
Wilmarth, Clarence M.	3	(3)	Morris, Austin P.	1	(1)
Anderson, Calvin O.	2	(2)	Noblitt, Lewey J.	1	(1)
Barnes, James H.	2	(2)	Northrup, Stanley C.	1	(1)
Bellows, Donno C.	2	(2)	O'Rourke, John R.	1	(1)
Berry, John A.	2	(2)	Olson, Dean W.	1	(1)
Cleage, Ralph T.	2	(2)	Olster, Mortimer	1	(1)
Cline, Robert F.	2	(2)	Parkansky, John K.	1	(1)
Coburn, Albert L.	2	(2)	Parlett, Lakin L.	1	(1)
Cochran, Herbert W.	2	(2)	Parshall, Chester C.	1	(1)
Cohn, John A.	2	(2)	Powell, Ormond E.	1	(1)
Ekdahl, Wilson F.	2	(2)	Price, Joseph P., Jr.	1	(1)
Gabik, George J.	2	(2)	Revenaugh, Donald D.	1	(2)
Haning, William F., Jr.	2	(2)	Richmond, W. L., Jr.	1	(1)
Hannan, John L.	2	(2)	Ryerson, Morton B.	1	(1)
Holze, Harold E.	2	(2)	Schoener, Pierre C.	1	(1)

NAME	USAF	475th FG
Schuh, Robert B.	1	(1)
Sieber, William G.	1	(1)
Simms, Thomas J.	1	(1)
Smith, Paul	1	(1)
Sperling, Joseph E.	1	(1)
Stiles, Howard V.	1	(1)
Temple, John W.	1	(1)
Thropp, Douglas S., Jr.	1	(1)
Veit, George M.	1	(1)
Wacker, George	1	(1)
Waldman, William M.	1	(1)

NAME	USAF	475th FG
Willis, Charles B.	1	(2)
Willis, Donald D.	1	(1)
Fostckowski, Theodore	0	(1)

ENEMY AIRCRAFT VICTORIES
BY ASSOCIATED PERSONNEL

NAME	USAF	475th FG
Bong, Richard I.	40	(5)
Lindbergh, Charles A.	—	(1)

Appendix 2

475th Fighter Group Roster

The listings of personnel who, at one time or another, were associated in an official capacity with the 475th are certainly incomplete. The primary sources for these rosters are Louis Lynch, et al., *Satan's Angels, 475th Fighter Group, 14th May 43-31st Dec. 44*, and *The Official History of the 475th Fighter Group*. The rosters presented here are based upon those compiled by Lynch, while the *Official History* was gleaned for personnel information for the period of January 1945 through August 1945. Unfortunately the *Official History* mentions few personnel as a matter of course, excepting commanding officers, due to its practice of chronicling the group as a whole. Therefore personnel, particularly enlisted personnel, have inevitably been overlooked in those months when the *Official History* served as the sole source of personnel information.

The spellings of names used are primarily from *Satan's Angels*, unless reliable evidence for correction was obtained.

The symbols following some of the names indicate that the individual died during the course of the war; the symbol (*) indicates Killed In Action, (♦) indicates Missing In Action, and (★) denotes Deceased, death caused by disease or accident not directly related to enemy action.

Personnel are separated into rosters for Headquarters and Squadrons, and are listed alphabetically within ranks. The rank listed is the highest found before separation from the 475th.

Because of the complexity of this task and the relative paucity of resources, errors or inconsistencies exist with our apologies.

HEADQUARTERS

COMMANDING OFFICERS
PRENTICE, George W., Lt. Col.
MacDONALD, Charles H., Colonel
SMITH, Meryl M., *
   Lt. Col.(Temporary C.O.)
LOISEL, John S., Lt. Col.

MAJORS
CHENEY, Thomas W.
DEWEY, George G.
FERNANDEZ, Arsenio R.
HAWLEY, Reginald G.
LINEHAM, Thomas U.
McAFEE, Oliver S.
NICHOLS, Franklin A.
RICHARDSON, LeRoy H. ♦
SCHINZ, Albert W.
SMITH, George R.
STUBBS, Claude M.
WEXLER, Nathan E.

CAPTAINS
BELDING, Robert V.
BRAKE, Harry A.
BUTLER, Burnell C., Sr.
COOPER, Dennis G.

DAVIS, Francis J.
DELASHAW, Fred A.
DOSSETT, Elbert
HANING, William F., Jr.
IVEY, William H.
JOHNSTON, Rudolph W.
KATZKY, Albert L.
LeBARON, Lawrence C.
LENT, Francis J. ♦
LYNCH, Louis E.
MILLER, Danforth P., Jr.
OLIVER, Bennett
PALLUCK, Rudolph E.
POTTS, Morgan
PRUSS, William J. H.
RICHARDSON, Wm. W.
SMITH, Clyde E.
SMITH, William H.
SPAULDING, Thorne E.
WAINER, Amos S.
WALDO, Cornelius J.
WILLY, Norman B.

FIRST LIEUTENANTS
CALHOUN, George F.
CARR, Walter W.
LANGDON, Garrett W.
MacCLENDON, William M.

McGREGOR, Alexander
MILLER, Martin L.
PHILLIPS, Joseph G.
REYNOLDS, Frederic D.

SECOND LIEUTENANTS
CONSIDINE, Thomas A.
REINHARDT, Walter C.
SAUNDERS, Thomas A.
SIMPSON, Rolan G.
WADE, Jean D.

MASTER SERGEANTS
BASTIAN, Richard G.
COCKERILL, Clay U.
DE LUCA, Frank A.
GREENE, Kenneth C.
JOSEPH, Orville
LEWIS, Carlton
McGILVARY, Ernest A.
ONEY, Richard S.
SHANKLIN, Carter A.
STAPP, Otto
WEIKEL, Clarence H.

TECHNICAL SERGEANTS
BARTOSH, William F.
BLACKBURN, Ralph D.

BRUHN, Jack F.
BRYANT, Clarence A.
CHAPMAN, Homer C.
DREW, Edward F.
DURANT, Robert S.
DWYER, Michael W.
ELGIN, Neil E.
LALLI, Anthony
LEAHY, James J.
LUCIA, Herman L.
McROBERTS, Wallace
SMITH, Donald V.
SOUTH, Wilfred J.
SPARKS, Clifford H.
WHEELER, Kermit W.
WILSON, Roger R.
YOCKEY, Verne S.

STAFF SERGEANTS
CIPRESSEY, Vittorio A.
CLIME, Vincent R.
DUNLAP, Lloyd A.
ELMORE, Fernando
KING, Robert C.
POE, Thomas M.
SEREY, Paul R.
TAYLOR, Allan C.
TEMPLE, Raymond S.
WELCH, William W.

SERGEANTS
AXNESS, Arthur J.
BEGH, Carl E., Jr.
BLAZ, Thomas V.
BURTON, Willard E.
CHORBA, William N.
DOYLE, John J.
EDE, Frederick N.
FOWLER, John T.
GIBSON, Luther W.
HEMING, Leo L.
LAMBERT, B.L.
LEVESQUE, George L.
MELTZ, Jerome
MORGAN, James P.
MURPHY, James J.
OAK, Clarence W.
POOLE, Joseph S.
SHIELDS, John F., Jr.
SISSLER, Dean P.
SPRINGER, Robert W.
WILLIS, Berthel W.
ZAMORA, Manuel

CORPORALS
BALM, William N.
CHERNOFF, Alan

COYNE, Joseph M.
DAVIS, Robert W.
EMERY, Ralph C.
EVERITT, Lewis E.
GORDON, Wilbert M.
HOWARD, George P.
RISKE, R.
ROACH, Charles R.
SANDERBACK, Edward C.
SCHROEDER, Corwin E.
SHANKWEILER, Paul W.
SPLETTER, Norman J.
STEELE, Maury E.
TRACAS, Pete C.
UTTERBACK, Paul W.
WARGA, Charles A.
WICKMAN, Harold K.
WILLIAMS, Thadis A.

PRIVATES, FIRST CLASS
ARZOLA, Robert G.
AUSTIN, Charles E.
BLAZOCK, Leo G.
DEEGAN, Joseph C.
DUNLAP, Norman R.
ESTES, James L.
EVANS, Robert O.
FASS, Arnold E.
LAMB, Sherman E.
REMIOR, Leland F.
SKRZYPCZYNSKI, Norbert J
SMITH, Viston R.
SNYDER, Manford V.
STRONG, Glen N.
WARREN, Charles L.

PRIVATES
BENNEWITZ, Ralph R.

431st SQUADRON

COMMANDING OFFICERS
NICHOLS, Franklin A., Major
JETT, Verle E., Major
McGUIRE, Thomas B., Jr.*, Major
CLINE, Robert F., Capt.
VOGEL, John H., Major
WEAVER, Edwin R., Capt.

MAJORS
RITTMAYER, Jack B. *

CAPTAINS
ALLEN, David W.
BELLOWS, Donno C.

BROWN, Harry W.
CIOLEK, Eugene S.
CHAMPLIN, Frederic F.
CLARK, Norris J.
GRONEMEYER, William C. ◆
HART, Kenneth F.
HERMAN, Robert L.
HOOD, John L.
HOUSEWORTH, Carl H.
KIRBY, Marion F.
MANKIN, Jack C.
MARTIN, Thomas E.
MONK, Franklin H.
MORRISS, Paul V.
O'BRIEN, William S. ◆
PIETZ, John, Jr.
REEVES, Horace B.
SETZER, Harry A.
SWITNER, Malcolm E.

FIRST LIEUTENANTS
BALLARD, John R.
BARTER, Cyprus C.
BENEVENT, Foch J.
BENJAMIN, Sanford H.
BOX, James F.
CASEY, Robert G.
COHN, John A.
CROSSWAIT, Robert L. ◆
CZARNECKI, Edward J.
DALLAS, William W.
DAWSON, Dulphus R.
DuMONTIER, Louis D.
EKDAHL, Franklin W.
ELLIOT, Vincent T.
ERICKSON, Arthur L.
FINNEY, Herbert S. *
FOSSACECA, Samuel A.
FULKERSON, Floyd H., Jr ◆
GIERTSON, Owen N.
HALL, Robert A.
HERMAN, Christopher J.
HOLZE, Harold E.
HUTCHINS, David B.
JACKSON, Edwin B.
KIDD, Alvin R.
LUTTON, Lowell C. ◆
MARKS, Stanley R.
MAX, Howard N.
MAYER, Allen C.
NEAL, Alvin R.
O'ROURKE, John R.
OLSON, Jack F.
OXFORD, Thomas M.
PALMER, Edward C., Jr.
PARSHALL, Chester C.
PEARSON, Merle D.

PHILLIPS, Chester D. ◆
PROVENCIO, Enrique ◆
RIEGLE, Robert R.
ROARK, Richard E.
SAMMS, Charles R.
SCOTT, Walter N.
SMITH, George W., Jr. *
SMITH, Paul ◆
STEPHENS, George F.
STERN, Robert W.
THROPP, Douglas S., Jr.
TILLEY, John A.
VARLAND, Erling J. *
VEIT, George M.
WEARY, Robert K.
WENIGE, Arthur E.
WERNER, Robert A.
WERTZBAUGHER, L. W.
WOODRUFF, Frank N.
ZEHRING, Herman W.

SECOND LIEUTENANTS
BARNES, James H.
BLYTHE, Orville
CARLEY, Edward N. *
CLODFELTER, Wood D. *
CORTNER, Warren J.
DONALD, Robert P. *
DUKE, Andrew K. *
DUNLAP, Ronald P.
DURKIN, John J.
GRAY, Harold W.
HAWTHORNE, Martin P. *
HEDRICK, Edward J. ◆
HOOD, James E.
HUNT, Robert E.
JONES, Bascom S.
JONES, MacLeod ◆
KNOX, John B. ◆
KOECK, Robert A. *
LANDEN, Nathaniel V. *
LEIDENBERG, Edward J.
LENTZ, Lloyd C.
LOE, Claude M., Jr.
LONG, Frank F.
MacDONALD, Milton A. ◆
MADISON, Harold N.
MAVITY, Robert A.
McBREEN, Donald F.
MOREING, James A.
O'NEILL, Edward J.
OLSTER, Mortimer
PARE, Roger A.
PATTERSON, Robert B. *
POWELL, Ormond E. ◆
RICHARDSON, Kenneth M. ◆
ROBERTSON, Joseph A. *

ROTH, Alvin C. *
SCHMIDT, Ralph E. ◆
SCHMITT, Arthur J. ◆
SMITH, Robert J. ◆
SMITH, William C.
TEDFORD, Joseph E.
WELDON, John R. ◆

FLIGHT OFFICERS
TURNER, Thomas W.

FIRST SERGEANTS
ASTON, Harlan M.
DIXON, Harry A.

MASTER SERGEANTS
AKIN, George M.
CLEVELAND, Glen H.
FITZGERALD, Alfred G.
FORD, Charley P.
GENARLSKY, Bruno M., Jr
GILLUM, Edwin F.
HOFFSTATTER, Robert J.
HOWERTON, Leland F.
HUDSON, Howell A.
KMIEC, Joseph
LACKIE, Raymond J.
LEWICKI, Clemens
LUN, A. H.
MALIN, Joseph R.
MITCHELL, Fred B., Jr.
PISZKIN, Stanley
ROCK, Roland C.
ROGERS, Preston W.
STANICH, Steve
STRAUS, Vincent F.
VENTERS, Claude
WHEELER, Claud E.
WHITE, Gwynne W.
WILKE, Herman O.
WILSON, William G.

TECHNICAL SERGEANTS
ALLAN, Melvin J.
ANDERSON, Woodrow F.
APPLEWHITE, Robert H.
BACK, Milton B.
BAIRD, Raymond
BALL, William C.
BARROW, J. D.
BELL, James C.
BINDER, Richard M.
BISHOP, Burton L.
BISTRONISH, John
BRICE, James C.
BROCK, John E.
BROWN, James F.

CAMPBELL, Michael P.
CHILDS, Edgar H.
CLARK, Edward P.
COLLINS, George D.
COLLINS, Walter
COLSON, Lawrence E.
CORBIN, Charles W.
CRAM, Spencer F.
CRUMPLER, Tom W.
DI ROCCO, Anthony
EDGLEY, Charles E.
EVANS, Kiah
FITZWATER, Charles R.
FRANCIS, Harry H.
GALLANT, Joseph A.
GRAY, Everett W.
HAAS, George J.
HALL, Edward R.
HALL, William H.
HAZEL, Nevin H.
HENSON, Eddie
HOBBS, Curtis H.
HOLLAND, Lawrence W.
HRAMIKA, George, Jr.
JACKSON, James L.
JESCHKE, George E.
JOHNSON, Victor C.
KEMPTER, William D.
KING, Carl A.
KISH, Frank Z.
KROPP, Joseph M.
LEMANSKI, Thaddeus J.
LOWRY, Earl R.
LOWRY, William V.
MAGILL, James
MORTON, Knight H.
MOSES, Samuel T.
MOTT, Hugh F.
NASH, Douglas W.
NAUGHTON, James C.
O'NEIL, Robert R.
POSEPHNEY, John J.
POWELL, Luke W.
ROBERTSON, Jeffrey R.
RUSSELL, Marshall B.
SKAGGS, James E.
SPITLER, James W.
STANLEY, John L.
STEPHENS, Yancy Q.
STROUD, Henry G.
VAN METER, Hallie
WAGNER, Daniel H.
WEST, George E.
WILDING, Jack E.

STAFF SERGEANTS
ALSUP, Hugh

ANDERSON, Malcolm E.
ARTHUR, Harry E.
ASHER, John R.
BALCHIK, John J.
BATTLE, Walter F., Jr.
BAUMAN, Michael
BAYLEY, Arthur F., Jr.
BEAN, William D.
BOAL, James C.
BRUMFIELD, Charles H.
CALOYERN, Anthony T.
CAMPESE, Nicholas H.
CASTELLANO, Sam A.
CHERRO, Thomas J.
COET, Noel
COONS, George W.
DESOCIO, Dominic L.
DOWNARD, Homer H.
DUDZIEC, Henry J.
EDHOLM, Arthur W.
FAREWELL, Edwin R.
FENSTERMACHER, Robert
FERBER, Bernard J.
FORESEE, Roy R.
GARDNER, Curtis D.
GEROT, Darrell G.
GILBERT, Orph J.
GORDON, Charles E.
GREEN, Max E.
GRODER, Arthur
GUTTRY, James C.
HALKO, George
HANNA, Homer H.
HARRELL, George F.
HARTMANN, Eugene
HARVEY, Fred P.
HAYES, Robert E.
HIMM, Thomas F.
HINES, Elmer T.
HOLMES, Clyde L.
HUGHES, Noel E.
IRVINE, Henry G.
IRVINE, Roger D.
KELLY, Leo C.
LEARY, Daniel F.
LELAND, John C.
LEUNING, Raymond C.
LONG, William C.
LOWNSDALE, Edward V.
MATES, Stanley D.
McKELVEY, Clarence W.
MILES, John L.
MOCK, Charles H.
NEAL, Alvin M.
NIELSON, Frederick S.
O'NEILL, Earl J.
PHILLIPS, Baxter M.

PRELL, Seymour V.
REINHARDT, Roy E.
ROBERTS, DeWitt
ROSEN, Marvin O.
ROTTMUND, Joseph R.
RUDD, Thomas W.
RUSKIN, Bernard
RYSKAMP, Frederick R.
SABER, William E.
SCHLOTTERBECK, William L
SIEBERT, Donald J.
SMITH, James A.
SMITH, Marvin E.
SPAHR, Von D., Jr.
SWARTZ, Harry R.
TAFF, William H.
THORNTON, Joe B.
TOCNERI, William J.
WACHHOLTZ, Gustav
WALKER, Newton E.
WITTSCHACK, Edward H.
WRIGHT, Walter C., Jr.
YOUNG, Charles W.

SERGEANTS

ANTROPIK, Patrick
ARMENTROUT, Roy R.
AYE, Francis P.
AYERS, James O.
BACON, Richard N.
BAILEY, Calvert I.
BASSETT, Robert E.
BENJAMIN, William, Jr.
BLACK, Melvin S.
BOHLMAN, Vincent H.
BOULTON, Edward
BOURNE, Bayse B.
BRAYTON, Kenneth L.
BRODY, Jacob
BROWN, Charlie A.
BUNCHER, James J.
BUNGO, Wasco
CAMPBELL, Wallace W.
CAPASSO, Carl J.
CERNESE, Frank B.
CONWAY, Patrick T.
COOK, Harold R.
COSBIE, Robert M.
DANIELL, Jesse F.
DAVIDS, Ray H.
DAVIS, Noel D.
DEAN, Walter H.
DEMEO, Alfred
DODGE, Russell C., Jr.
DULIN, Frank B.
EMERSON, Gerald W.
ERWIN, Leroy E.

ESTES, Charles L.
FORBIS, Elwood W.
FRAMARIN, Primo A.
GRAY, Hanley
HARBOUR, Don J.
HARRIS, John F.
HIGH, Oliver C.
HINTON, Robert L.
HOUK, Joe A.
JOHNSON, Floyd W.
JOHNSON, Marion A.
JONES, Joe M.
JUSKO, Joseph
KEES, Ray A.
KENNISON, Frank
LEATHAM, Louis N.
LEWIS, Leroy C.
LIEBIG, George H.
LINARD, James C.
LUBIAK, Stanley J.
MARTIN, George W.
MARTIN, Ira H.
McKAGUE, Wilbur J.
MEYER, William H.
MEYER, William H.
MORAN, Francis B.
MORAVEC, Edward O.
MORAWSKI, Frank W.
MORTIMER, Gladstone B.
O'CONNELL, Thomas A.
OTT, James C.
OVLASUK, John
PAIANCA, Joseph A.
PEAK, Thomas R.
PELEKOUDAS, Cerls G.
PETROSKI, Nicklos
PHILLIPS, James B.
POST, Milton
PRINCE, Pershing J.
RAINES, Roy F.
RAWDIN, Robert W.
RAY, James D.
REVERUZZI, Joseph
RIALS, Carlos
ROBINSON, Jack
SAUNDERS, Charles W.
SCARDILLI, Frank
SCHIAKE, Vernon M.
SCHMIDT, Walter J.
SEAMANS, Cecil O.
SNELLGROVE, Milo
SNIPES, Eugene A.
SNYDER, Robert C.
SOBAIA, John F.
SPOONER, Ralph E.
STAPLES, Houston A.
STRECKER, Henry

STRUBLE, Robert L.
UGGS, Charles A.
THOMPSON, Rodney V.
TRAPP, Charles A.
VANDERGEEST, Richard F.
WALKUP, Richard A.
WHITELEY, Arthur L.
WHITNEY, Roland F.
WILSON, James L.
WONDERLY, John B.
WOODS, Howard R.

CORPORALS
ALIARD, Romeo J.
BARGMAN, Allen D.
BEAKE, William H., Jr.
BINNING, Robert E.
BRAYFIELD, Billy N.
BREAULT, Alfred L.
CAMPBELL, Charles R.
CAREFENO, Marco A.
CLARK, George F.
COLBERG, Stanley R.
COLVIN, Urban A.
COOPER, William B.
DAKKEN, Kermit O.
DUGGIN, Calvin H.
DULANEY, Paul L.
EVANS, Clyde W.
FOULK, Carl L.
FURRA, Hyman
HENDERSON, Albert E., Jr
HENDRICK, Smead E.
HICKS, Gerald B.
JOHNSON, Edward J.
JOHNSON, Robert F.
JORDAN, Richard J.
KNOTT, Jack D.
LEES, Ralph C., Jr.
LIBBERTON, William S.
MASTERFRANCISCO, Tony
MEEK, J.
MILTON, Zane B.
MOORE, John B.
NELSON, Erle W.
PANEPINTO, Ignatius J.
PARSONS, Richard K.
PIERSON, Edward H.
POSTMA, Menze
QUARLES, Waldo M.
REGAN, William J.
RICKS, Billy J.
RITCHIE, Alexander
ROBINSON, Francis J.
ROSE, Herbert M.
SELLMER, Thomas J.
SHEEHAN, John J.

SNYDER, Ambrose W.
SOPTELEAN, Samuel, Jr.
STEGER, Elbert W.
STOKES, Guy J.
SULLIVAN, Harry A.
TAYLOR, Alfred
TODD, Ira P.
VICTOR, Herbert A.
WALDEN, Jack B.
WALDHELM, Jack M.
WHALEY, Christopher, Jr.
WOFFORD, Allen O.
WRIGHT, Elmer E., Jr.
YENNIE, Fred, Jr.

PRIVATES, FIRST CLASS
CALVERT, Warner E.
CLANCY, Daniell F.
COMPTON, Alvin E.
CRONK, Robert L.
FINK, Gerald G.
GORMLEY, James J.
HERRING, William C.
KEELING, Troy L.
LOK, Walter L.
MEHARG, James
MEYERS, Joseph J.
NEWLOVE, George F.
OFFNER, Charles J.
PAPAS, William
PRZYBYSISKI, Stanley P.
RICE, Joseph R.
ROGINSKI, Albin J.
SEXTON, Thomas E.
SIMONE, John A.
SOWERS, Lyle S.
STAMLER, Harold
STERN, David
STUART, James F.
THYNE, James J.
VAN ETTEN, Richard C.
WAUSMAN, B.
WIEGAND, Charles E.
WILLETT, Melvin J.
WINSLOW, Kenelm K.
ZAHN, Lee Roy

PRIVATES
ALTMAN, Albert H.
BATTEER, Joseph F.
BUCKE, William F., Jr.
DAPORE, Wilbur V.
DAVIS, John D.
DE CROCE, Frank
GARRED, Francis G.
HICKEY, James J.
KURTZE, Robert L.

MILLER, Eddie M.
MOHLER, Joseph C.
NELSON, Jess W.
REYES, Roberto
ROSENCRANS, Robert W.
SAUERSTROM, Stanley
SHAFARA, John S.
SULLIVAN, William H., Jr

432nd SQUADRON

COMMANDING OFFICER
TOMKINS, Frank D., Major
LOISEL, John S., Lt. Col
CONDON, Henry L., II *, Capt.
DUTRACK, Dean W., Major
SUMMER, Elliot E., Major

CAPTAINS
ANDERSON, Elder J.
BLAKELY, Leo W., Jr.
BYARS, Donald N.
DEAN, Zach W.
GHOLSON, Grover D.
GRESHAM, Billy M. *
HARRIS, Frederick A. *
HEDRICK, Howard A.
INCE, James C.
KIICK, Richard D.
KIMBALL, Robert H.
LUCAS, Paul W. ♦
McGUIRE, Eugene I.
MALLOCH, Ronald C.
OWEN, Harrold D.
PEREGOY, Arthur L.
PHILLIPS, Alexander K.
RICHARDS, Rowland
RUNDELL, John J.
SETZER, Harry A.
WALDMAN, William M.

FIRST LIEUTENANTS
ALLEN, Paul T.
BARLERO, Walter A.
BEATTY, George R.
BURGESS, Dale E.
CLOUD, Vivian A.
DAHL, Perry J.
DICKEY, Edward G.
FARRIS, James R.
FIDLAY, John D.
FORSTER, Joseph M.
FOX, Sam
FRAZEE, Merle W.
FREEMAN, Walter H.

FRINK, Emory B.
GEARHART, Howard C.
GOODWIN, Arthur
GUTIERREZ, Ralph
HADLEY, Robert L.
HANNAN, John L.
HANSON, Ferdinand C.
ILNICIKI, Alexander N.
KAY, Robert E.
LAWHEAD, Stuart M.
LUNDY, Noel R. *
MANN, Clifford J.
MAYO, Leo M. ◆
MEYER, Walter H.
MICHENER, John E.
MORAN, Darrell W.
MORGAN, Wayne E.
MURPHY, John A.
NELSON, Roger C.
NOBLITT, Lewey J.
OLSON, Dean W.
PEAVYHOUSE, Dallas G.
RATAJSKI, Charles J.
RENFRO, Lawrence D.
RITTER, William T. ◆
SAVALE, William F.
SHELTON, Jack M.
SIMMS, Thomas J. ◆
TEMPLE, John W.
THISTED, Lewis F.
TOLL, Henry C.
WEBER, John F.
WILLIS, Charles B.

SECOND LIEUTENANTS
ANDERSON, Calvin O.
BARROW, Edward E.
BARTLETT, Christopher O ◆
BRYAN, Leroy C.
CAMP, Allan *
CHRISTIAN, Edwin A.
COLLINS, C. J., Jr.
DUNN, Raymond J.
ELLIOT, William A. ◆
FOGARTY, John E. *
FOSTAKOWSKI, Theodore *
GARRISON, Donald H. ◆
GILES, Raymond M.
GRIFFITH, Owen C.
HIRSCH, Lee J., Jr.
HOWARD, Harold R. *
HUBNER, Robert L. ◆
KOLES, Robert L.
KRALL, Daniel R.
KRANTZ, Raymond J.
LAMB, John M.
LARSEN, Arnold W.

LASETER, Grady M. ◆
LUDDINGTON, Jack F. ◆
MARTIN, Troy L. *
McKENZIE, Albert A.
MORRIS, Austin P.
PALMER, Roger C.
PARLETT, Lakin L.
PIETSCHER, Reed L. *
ROBERTS, Lawrence D.
RYRHOLM, Richard S. *
SCHUH, Robert B.
SCHWALIER, Charles D.
SULLIVAN, Charles J.
WACKER, George
WEISFUS, Walter W. ◆
WILLIAMS, Edgar W.
WILLIS, Donald D.

FLIGHT OFFICERS
BARTON, Joe B. *
DE WESSE, Charles R. ◆
DOWLER, Lawrence A.
NACKE, Charles C. ◆

CHIEF WARRANT OFFICERS
KOWALSKI, Gregory L.

FIRST SERGEANTS
STROTHER, Charles G.

MASTER SERGEANTS
BARNES, Ernest A.
BISHOP, Carl S.
BROWN, Stephen L.
DYGAS, Stanley C.
EILER, George A.
FAZZI, James A.
GLASSER, Earl L.
HARVEY, Paul A.
KENDY, Joseph
KOBALY, John
KUPNIEWSKI, Anthony J.
MAGANN, John S.
MORRISON, Billy
MUNDORFF, Harry M.
PRICE, Robert G.
SULLIVAN, Crawford F.
WILSON, Allen E.

TECHNICAL SERGEANTS
ATKIN, Dillon D.
AXT, Cecil E.
BANAS, George
BALL, Hulon C.
BIBLOWITZ, Nathan S.
BIGELOW, Charles E.
BLYTHE, Carl H.

BOOKER, Carroll P. ★
BRUBAKER, Joseph W.
BURK, Donald L.
CARROLL, Timothy F.
CAMPBELL, Milton L.
CARTER, Henry C.
CLASBY, Sam H.
CLATWORTHY, Paul
COLE, Jasper H.
CONNERS, James T.
CORTESE, Donald L.
CROCKETT, Andy C.
CUDZIL, Stanley A.
DANKO, Anthony V.
DAUTEL, Harvey O.
DERTING, Homer L.
DITMORE, George
DOTY, Howard W.
DOWELL, Doyle A.
EGY, Phillip J,
FITHIAN, Carroll H.
GAGE, Ransom B.
GRAHAM, Everette M.
HALL, Douglas W.
HARRELL, Robert G.
HENDLEY, Charles, Jr.
HOFFEND, Donald E.
HOPPER, Donald
HOWES, Wilson A. S.
INGOLD, Melvin F.
KANYUCK, George E.
KAPLAN, Leonard
KENNEDY, Douglas F.
KENNINGTON, Harold E.
KIEMAN, Henry N.
KINCH, Charles M.
KOFILE, Joseph
LAWRENCE, Kenneth E.
MARTIN, Able G.
MAY, Michael
MEYER, Victor E.
MILLER, Alden W.
MONTGOMERY, Frederick D.
NASLUND, Grover T., Jr.
NOTZ, Matt F.
NUSS, J. R.
OAKS, Harry L.
PAGE, Francis J.
PARSELLS, Elmer V.
PINKERTON, A. J.
PITCHFORD, Cormin M.
POLZIN, Ervin R.
RANDAZZO, Joseph G.
REITMAN, Harry
REZMIERSKI, Leonard E.
RICHARDSON, Elmore S.
SACCA, Matthew

SCHULTE, Martin H.
SMITH, Ralph M.
SLANINA, Joseph A.
SPENCER, Frederick H.
SPEZZANO, Richard J.
STARK, Edwin M.
STIDD, Rozell A.
THARP, Harry M.
THOMAS, David V.
TURNER, Charles W.
WATSON, Elton
WEISS, Samuel
ZARENSKY, Joseph

STAFF SERGEANTS

BAYLESS, Alden L.
BEANE, George T.
BERMAN, Samuel
BOCH, Joseph A.
BRENNAN, Bernard J.
BULINO, Andrew, Jr.
CADGER, Kenneth G.
CHRISTOPHER, John W.
CONLEY, Norgal L.
CONWAY, John R.
DALBEC, Valentine L.
ELMORE, Fernando, Jr.
ELMORE, John R.
EMERY, George H.
EVARELLI, Ugo V.
FACCONE, Ralph
FINKLESTEIN, Edwin W.
FLANAGAN, Loren D.
FONCK, John H.
FONTENOT, James
FREUND, Theodore R.
FRIEZE, Lawrence A.
GARRIGAN, Henry W.
GIMBLE, Edward J.
GODDARD, Kenneth L.
GOLDMAN, Maury
GRICE, Ernest L.
GRIFFITH, Charles H.
GROSS, Frank E.
HARDING, Albert H., Jr.
HEAP, George H., Jr.
HENDRICK, Richard M.
HILL, Harold E.
HOLDER, Enos M.
HOTCHKISS, Joseph H.
HUTCHINSON, Robert D.
JESIONLOWSKI, Stephen V.
JOHNSON, Alfred H.
JOYCE, Nolan
KELLER, Kendall N.
KASHINSKY, Jack
KUNZ, Melvin F.

LAGASSE, Horace W.
LAMELZA, George
LASDIN, Benjamin S.
LASHO, Peter
LUBITZ, John F.
MALONEY, John E.
MALUSKEY, Joseph J.
MAYNARD, George A.
MEREDITH, Aubrey C.
MEYER, William C.
MILLIKIN, Thomas L.
MILLS, Leonard C.
MONGI, John J.
MORROW, Joseph R.
MURPHY, Leslie N.
NATHAN, Joseph F.
NICHOLSON, Mack H.
NOBLE, Daniel E.
OSTOPOWITZ, Joseph B.
OWEN, Robert M.
PEMMA, Henry A.
PLECKER, Carl E.
PREISS, Harvey G.
QUARANTA, Edward P.
RANALI, Philip L.
REECE, Lewis L.
REEVES, Charles F.
ROSEN, Melvin R.
SACKS, Ralph R.
SCHENCK, Robert H.
SCHULTZ, Donald G.
SCHWARTZ, Edward
SHELOR, Roy E.
SMITH, Douglas R.
SONSTERUD, Edgar T.
STEIN, Jack W.
TEAGUE, Provis A.
VOGT, Joseph B.
WESALA, Theodore W.

SERGEANTS

ALBERTER, Michael E.
ALBRIGHT, Lyle P.
ASH, Ralph H., Jr.
AVRECH, Herman
BABCOCK, Phillip S.
BAFFO, Sebastian C.
BARBARIO, Orlando D.
BEITZEL, Roland P.
BEN, Boleslaus
BENOSIUS, Algird B.
BORT, Andrew C.
BROOKS, George F.
BULLIVANT, Richard J.
CAIOLA, Anthony J.
CANTOR, Alfred
CARLSON, Frank L.

CLARK, Melvin
CLEMENTS, William C.
CONTINO, Christopher
CORCORAN, Vincent J.
CUMMINS, Roscoe L.
DALY, George D.
DAMSCHRODER, Charles A.
DAUB, Frank E.
DEA, William F.
DELP, John A.
DEMPSEY, Kenneth E.
DEWSNAP, Arthur F., Jr.
DI STEFFANO, Michael
DUPLIKA, John H.
DUPUIS, Earl J.
ERICKSON, Clarence W.
FARLEY, Louis J.
FARMER, Gus C.
FOURNIER, Thomas J.
GALLAGHER, William D.
GALVIN, John T., Jr.
GDOWSKI, Anthony
GIRAUD, Ralph E.
GRAZIANO, James J.
GREENBURG, Irving
GUELDNER, John F. ★
HAIR, Melville M.
HARLESS, Lawrence L.
HARMON, Leo E.
HARRIS, Harry N.
HASTINGS, Frank W.
HAVILL, Charles D.
HAYS, Robert
HINZMAN, Okey G.
HODEL, Vernon A.
HOLLIDAY, William F.
HOXIE, Gordon D.
HUGHES, James R.
HULLIGER, Leroy J.
JIMENEZ, Joseph C.
JOHNSON, Alton
JOHNSON, Robert W.
JONES, Thomas E.
KEBERSKI, Stanley
KECK, Harley F.
KEHOE, Thomas W.
KENNY, James P.
KINGSTON, Arthur K.
LEE, Richard J.
LEE, Young C.
LEITZES, Martin H.
LIBBY, Donbury K.
LUCINSKI, Joseph W.
MALANDRAKIS, Manuel
MANSON, William I.
MERRICK, William R.
McDONALD, Cyril V.

McLAUGHLIN, Ralph E.
MINER, Carl V.
MOODIE, Harry G.
MURPHY, Raymond W.
NECKE, Louis C.
NOSUL, Alfred
OLSON, Carl E., Jr.
PATTERSON, Willie B.
PATTON, James W., Jr.
PAUL, Raymond F.
PETERS, George L.
PIECZONKA, Leo K.
PINAULT, Joseph R.
RESNICOFF, Sam
RISH, James B.
ROTUNNO, Aldino
RUTHERFORD, Stanley C.
SANDVIG, Robert A.
SAWYER, James E.
SELDE, Eugene V.
SHALOFSKY, David H.
SHEASLEY, Clair D.
SHOPE, James D.
SIRES, Manford H.
SMITH, Robert F.
SOLLY, Henry G.
STROSCHEIN, Walter L.
TAYLOR, John F.
TERRYBERRY, Stanley J.
THOMPSON, Lorry R.
TURCOTTE, Ralph N.
VARIEUR, Leo R.
WALKER, Thomas W.
WAPEN, Francis A.
WARD, Glen P.
WARD, Russel A.
WEIDNER, Archie, Jr.
WEISS, Robert D.
WHITE, Roy C.
WILLIAMS, Roy K.
YATES, George E.

CORPORALS

BEAUCHAMP, Dick S.
BOLES, Robert E. L.
BRADFORD, Dewain H.
CABE, Gerald D.
CHASTAIN, Joseph F., Jr.
CIRAFESI, Charles
COLLINS, Bion W.
CONWAY, Daniel J.
CRANDALL, Alfred
CROFFORD, Raymond D.
DEPP, Robert C.
DOWDEN, William F.
DUCOTE, Alvin J.
GLEASON, Francis E. ★

GOUDEAU, Denis J.
HAMERICK, Earl K.
HOLDEN, Arthur L.
JEFFREYS, Everett L.
JOHNSON, Tip
JONES, K. C.
KAMINSKI, Walter
KRUEGER, Robert B.
LANDSRUD, John W.
LAROCHE, Arthur
LOSSON, Charles J.
MARTINEZ, Joseph M.
MARTYNA, Joseph T.
MAZZARO, Angelo A.
McGRAY, Herbert D.
METZ, Donald M.
MINER, William A.
MORAN, William A.
OBERHOLTZER, Roy H.
PAULSON, Wayne D.
PILLER, Robert S.
POMETTO, Anthony L., Jr.
PORTER, Thomas B.
PRESCOTT, Thomas
ROCHON, Chester
ROSEN, Daniel
ROSENBAUM, Martin L.
SCHALL, Milfred K.
SHAFFER, David
SHEA, William A.
SIMPSON, Richard D.
SORENSON, Robert J.
STEFFNEY, Joseph T.
TRUHN, Russell
TIENKEN, Thaddeus M.
TSIHNAHJINNIE, Andrew V.
TWEEDLE, Alden B.
VELARDE, Fred
WATSON, Charles W.
WHITE, Allen D.
YAMKA, Walter F.

PRIVATES, FIRST CLASS

BRAUER, Stanley W.
CLARDY, Jimmie H.
COKE, Loyd D.
DESORMIER, Arthur L.
HOLLAND, Fred T.
JOHNSTON, Ernest F.
LAYNE, Leroy
LENGLING, Kenneth
LIVINGSTON, William
OSTGARDEN, Ernest O.
PETTY, James A.
RODGERS, Charlie M.
ROUSE, George E.
SHIELDS, Martin J.

SMITH, Lavern
SPRAGUE, Lewis K.
STEINER, William J.
SUMMA, Frank
SUSKI, Stanley J., Jr.
SYLVER, Lyle W.
THOMAS, Raymond P.
TIGHE, William F.
TINKER, Curtis F., Jr.
TROXELL, Kenneth A.
VANCOVER, Grayson
WALLIS, Irvin L.
WEISS, Norman H.
WILSON, Roger L.

PRIVATES

CLIFTON, Garland F.
COUSINO, Leo R.
CONTRERAS, Diego F.
ECKEL, Donald W.
JONES, Harold S.
LARGE, James V.
LOWRY, Maloy T.
MARDIS, Jack H.
RENO, Philip E.
RHORER, Ralph R.
SCHNABEL, John P.
SIBRIAN, William E.
SKOLASINSKI, Richard G.
VERA, Arthur
VOLBRECHT, Steven A.
WAGNER, Richard C.
WULF, Jackey C.
YAW, Kenneth D.

433rd SQUADRON

COMMANDING OFFICERS

LOW, Martin L., Major
ROBERTS, Daniel T., Jr.,* Captain
LEWIS, Warren R., Major
WILSON, Campbell P. M., Captain

MAJOR

WILSON, James R.

CAPTAINS

BABEL, John S.
BEST, George J.
BOSSE, Frank K.
BRENIZER, Chase, Jr.
COCHRAN, Herbert W.
EHLINGER, John L.
FARLEY, Thomas J.
FISK, Jack A.

GRADY, William J.
GRICE, Charles A.
HOWE, Charles E.
EAKLE, William G.
KIMBALL, Richard D.
KNECHT, John F.
MAXWELL, Glenn M.
McKEON, Joseph T.
MURRAY, Richard A.
PALMER, James M.
PARKANSKY, John K.
PETERS, Paul R.
RALPH, Kenneth W.
RICHMOND, William L., Jr
ROBERTS, Ethelbert B.
ROSS, LeRoy H.
SIMPSON, Robert H.
THOMPSON, Herbert M.
TILLAPAUGH, C. H.
TOMBERG, Robert M.
WILMARTH, Clarence M.

FIRST LIEUTENANTS
ANDERSON, Carroll R.
BERRY, John A.
BURCHETTE, John B.
CHARLES, Conrad E. A.
COBURN, Albert L.
DUPRE, Webster H.
EDESBERG, Edward D.
FORBES, George J.
GABIK, George J.
GADD, Parker C.
GALLAGHER, Lawrence R.
GRIFFIN, Henry M.
GUNN, F. H.
HAMMOND, Jerome R.
HERSH, Robert
HORTON, William D.
HOWARD, John H.
JORDON, Herbert H.
KALIEZOWSKI, J. J.
KALISH, Harry A.
KUNTZ, William H.
LAMPERT, Francis G.
LONGMAN, Louis L. ◆
LOWMAN, Irving D.
LUCIER, Phillip H.
McDERMOTT, John R.
MICKELNAIR, M. P.
MILLER, Joseph E., Jr.
MOLLOY, James N.
MORRELL, Robert G.
MORSE, Alan D.
NEELY, Austin K. ◆
NELSON, John A.
NORTHRUP, Stanley C.

O'NEIL, Joseph, Jr.
ORR, Marion P.
OWEN, Raymond O.
OWENS, William T., Jr.
PRICE, Joe P.
PURDY, John E.
REVENAUGH, Donald G. ◆
RIEMAN, Clarence J.
RYERSON, Morton B. *
RYSSELBURGHE, Oliver J.
SCHAFFER, Ralph M.
SCHICK, Robert W.
SHEETZ, Maurice S.
SIDNAM, Alan N.
SMITH, John C. *
SMITH, Tristian P.
SPERLING, Joseph E.
THOMPSON, Thomas H.
WIEMER, Donald G.
WILEY, Coy D.
WIRE, Calvin C.
YARBROUGH, Lewis M. ◆
YEWELL, Robert J.
ZARLING, Charles G. *

SECOND LIEUTENANTS
ATWOOD, Edwin O.
BADGETTE, Dale A. ◆
BLAISDELL, Arthur A.
BUSCH, Laverne P. *
CLARKE, Richard G.
CLEAGE, Ralph T.
CORRIGAN, Raymond P. *
DALY, Jack J.
DANFORTH, Carl A. ◆
ETTIEN, Clifford L., Jr*
GETTLER, Jerome A.
HAGAN, Virgil A. ◆
HANCOCK, Richard L. ◆
HASTY, William L.
HULETT, Wesley J. ◆
JOSEPH, Charles H. *
KING, Donald Y. ◆
LIKINS, Walter N.
McDONALD, Charles W.
MEYERS, Dale O. *
MORRISON, Samuel M.
O'NEILL, John J.
PEPPER, John H.
POMPLUN, Albert E.
REDDING, Carl L.
REINHARDT, Walter C., Jr
SCHOENER, Pierre C.
SCHULTZ, La Vern
SEXTON, Francis M.
SIMONS, Clarence B.
STILES, Howard D. *

WONG, Herbert M.
YORK, John K.

FLIGHT OFFICERS
COHEN, Joseph
KIRSCHNER, Kenneth D. ◆
RICHARDS, William L.
YEARSLY, Robert W.

WARRANT OFFICERS
WAGNER, Donald E.

FIRST SERGEANTS
REED, Grady H.

MASTER SERGEANTS
BALOGH, Alexander, Jr.
BEDWELL, L. P.
BROWN, Virgil W.
CONLEY, Donald A.
DANIEL, John W.
DU RUSSELL, Roy D.
FAIRBANK, William W.
HANKS, Theodore W.
INGRAM, Cecil B.
JUNG, Robert H.
LEONELLI, Ben
LEVINSON, Benjamin
MARTIN, William E., Jr.
MILLER, Donald F.
PAAR, Charles E.
SMITH, Dwight M.
STRINGER, Herman A.

TECHNICAL SERGEANTS
ALBERTS, Herman D.
ALFSON, Joseph A.
ALTUS, Robert W.
ANDERSON, Kenneth W.
ANDERSON, Raymond A.
ASHWORTH, Paul E.
BARNEY, Berkley
BARTOW, Joseph F.
BLOOM, James R.
BRACKELSBERG, Clyde R.
BROSKI, Richard E.
BROWN, George A.
CIRILLO, Peter H.
COTTRELL, Joe W.
DAINELASKAS, George F.
DE BECK, Edward P.
DE FRANCE, Fred F.
DEITZ, Ralph K.
DI PIETRO, Nicholas A.
DOUGLAS, Oscar H.
DRINKHARD, James M.
EICHELBERGER, Richard C.

EVERETT, William L.
GANS, Frank A.
GARRETT, Lewis D.
GITHENS, George F.
GUERRE, Robert A.
GUINN, James E.
HALL, Edwin E.
HAMILTON, James M.
HASTIE, Thomas E.
HEATH, Glenn W.
HERNANDEZ, Phillip F.
JOHNSON, Orville L.
JOYNER, Paul W.
KIMLIN, Howard F.
KLINE, George J.
KULKA, Edward A.
LEDEIER, Frank P.
LENARD, Leon R.
MASSENGALE, Denzile L.
MAXWELL, Wright A.
McARTHUR, William M.
McCONNELL, Walter F.
McGINNIS, Raymond L.
McGOVERN, John F.
MIDKIFF, Leonard E.
NEAD, Paul E.
NELSON, George H.
NEUMANN, Otto E.
PORTZLINE, Alan E.
PRESCIUTTI, Nazzareno C.
PULLIN, Thomas W.
RASMUSSEN, Robert M.
REESE, William J.
RHODES, James P.
ROSHOLT, Clinton E.
RYAN, Richard J.
SANDERS, Edwin
SANFORD, Grady
SCHOTT, James A.
SHARP, Robert H.
SHIVE, Steward S.
SMITH, Edward D.
STANLEY, Rayford C.
STIGLICH, Edward F.
STOUT, George F.
STRADER, Charles E.
STRATION, John C.
SULLIVAN, Morris L.
TOTH, Joseph
UTTER, Jack H.
WINKLER, Claude W.
YOUNTS, Clare E.
ZACK, Joseph P.

STAFF SERGEANTS

ALLISON, Gail J.
ASHKENAZI, Joseph E.

ASHLOCK, Donald C.
AUERBACH, Louis
BARRON, Henry
BAUN, Clifford J.
BEVILL, Nathaniel
BRODERICK, Earl W.
BRYANT, Gerald F.
BURDETTE, Carey E.
CAMMISO, Donato
CLARK, Aubrey H.
COADY, John W.
CROWE, Fred C.
CULPEPPER, Benjamin L.
DE HOLLANDER, Robert A.
DEYO, Frederich J.
DOLE, Malcolm E.
EDELL, Irwin
FARTELY, Charles K., Jr.
FRANKEL, Robert E.
FRIEDRICH, Carl D.
GAUNTLETT, Harold G.
GOLLA, Clemens B.
GRAVES, Howard W.
GREEN, Harold B.
GREVIS, Stanley T.
GROSS, Albert
HAASE, Herbert W.
HARDEN, Skelton
HLICHNIK, Stephen J.
HOWARD, Roscoe T.
HOWE, John E.
HOWELL, William R.
HUFF, Charles C. ★
INMAN, Charles W., Jr.
JOHNSON, Albert S.
KELLEY, Robert P.
KOZAK, Lewis J.
LAIRD, Harry L.
LANDWEHR, Bruno B.
LEFEVER, William A.
LEONE, John J.
LILLY, Winfred
LONG, Overton W.
LUKE, Paul H.
MAIERS, Emmett M.
MANSFIELD, William O.
MASSEY, Milton P.
MEYERS, Henry J.
MILLER, Emory S.
MITCHELL, George C.
MOON, William B.
MOREHOUSE, Robert F.
NICHOLSON, Donald A.
NORKUS, Edward A.
NOSEK, Henry X.
O'DRISCOLL, Thomas B.
OWEN, Douglas H.

PUTZKER, George R.
RATH, George W.
RAUB, David H.
RETZLEFF, Walter R.
RITTER, George W. H.
RUIZ, Thomas
SAUER, Elmer C.
SCOTT, Robert W.
SENKLER, Arthur F.
SERBES, Spiro
SHOWALTER, Willie O.
SMEATON, Donald M.
SMITH, Russel H.
SOLAK, Louis H.
SORRELLS, Paul J.
STOBER, Edgar D.
TAYLOR, Walter D.
THOMPSON, Kermit L.
THOMPSON, Ray D. ★
TRASKO, Raymond J.
VAN HORN, John H.
VICTORY, Rex E.
WEAVER, George E.
WICHTER, Morris
WOODS, Ross A.

SERGEANTS

ADAMS, Arthur G.
ALLEN, Henry J.
ALTWEGG, Wilfred J.
AMESCUA, Amador V.
ANDREWS, Harold A.
BACHTOLD, Robert F.
BARROW, Jessie M.
BEAUCHAMP, Lloyd
CAPRETTA, Alfred G.
CATOE, Nick A.
CAZIN, Frank A.
CHAMBERLAIN, Lawrence C.
CHUBOY, Steve, Jr.
COGER, Reagan W.
COLEMAN, Carl J.
DAVIS, Donald B.
DAVIS, Meredith R.
DI CARLO, James W.
DOWNEY, William E.
DURRAND, Dawson D.
FINKE, Lester J.
FLEISCHHACKER, Anthony W
FRANK, James D.
GARDNER, William C.
GEIST, John J., Jr.
GIRAFFA, Domenie A.
GRIFFITH, Clarence L.
GROSSMAN, Fred
GRUNKE, William H.
HALE, Charles S.

HALL, Maxwell F., Jr.
HAMILTON, Edward J.
HARGIS, Leon C.
HARRIS, James O.
HEIDRICK, Raymond S.
HENNEBERRY, Richard F.
HESS, Howard L.
HUNT, Ladd F.
JOSS, Harold J.
JURA, Peter
KALKSTEIN, Aloysius G.
KINCANNON, J. T.
KOVELESKY, Joseph P.
KREVOKUCH, Emil
KROHN, Severin
LAHTI, Viljo H.
LAHUTA, Joseph
LIVINGSTEN, George R.
LYONS, Jerome P.
MADIA, Mario P.
McMURCHIE, Angus R.
MORGAN, Harold A.
NIDER, Robert L.
O'CONNELL, Jerome R.
PAARLBERG, Kenneth P.
PARKS, Charles J.
PASSOA, Benjamin
PERKINS, William L.
PERRY, Kenneth H.
POPE, Lucius D.
POPLOWSKI, Joseph
RISLEY, Chester, Jr.
RITTER, Edward F., Jr.
ROWLETIE, Percy E.
RUSSO, Gabriel
RUSSO, John
RYAN, Verne T.
SARGENT, Julius S.
SARTEN, Leo E.
SCARPA, Gondolfo L.
SEGAL, Dave A.
SEIP, Edward R.
SHERMAN, Donald R.
SKILLMAN, Franklin A.
SKURKA, Stephen J.
SMITH, Noble S.
SMITH, Ralph S.
SMITH, Robert F.
SNYDER, Lilburn T.
SPANO, Vincent
STANDAFER, Glenn L.
STUBBLEBINE, Richard A.
TAYLOR, Lonnie, Jr.
TERNES, Myron N.

VEITCH, James H.
WATERS, Thomas E.
WEISS, Armen F.
WEST, Kenneth E.
WILLIAMS, Roman P.
WILSON, Robert G.
WOOD, George H.

CORPORALS

ANDERSON, Maurice F.
BARON, Henry R.
BARSKI, Edward
BOYER, Russel E.
CAMPBELL, Ralph H.
COLLINS, Delton C.
CURTIS, Clarence F.
DANIELSON, Robert H.
DECKER, Bernard T.
DURAKO, John A.
EMERSON, Alfred M.
FRAZIER, Irving L.
GOMEZ, Marco A.
GOUGH, David M.
GRAY, Albert A., Jr.
HARTWICK, Norman
HAWLEY, Reed F.
HERSHEY, Dale R.
HJERRALD, George W.
IVERSON, Robert N.
KOLLE, Earl M.
KROLL, Robert W.
LAWSON, William B.
LITOW, Harold
MADDOCK, William R., Jr.
MAUSER, John T.
McMILLIN, John F.
MILLIS, Benjamin R.
MOONAN, John J.
MURPHY, Edward P.
NELSON, Robert S.
NIELSON, Soren P.
PACI, Rinaldo A.
PARROTT, James R.
QUIGG, Elmer E.
RACOOSIN, Henry L.
RICHARDSON, Sam A.
RODEFELD, Edward A.
ROPER, Roy H.
SANDERBECK, Edward C.
SCHREPFER, Robert A.
SHELDON, Charles R.
SNYDER, Jack R.
SORREL, Colan B.
SPRING, Elmer E.

STARK, Donald H.
STREIBICH, Dole E.
SWANBURG, Robert I.
VAN DYKE, Alfred J.
WATSON, James A.
WAY, Donald E.
WEBB, Everett R.
WERNER, Ernest
WINKS, Robert E.
WILSON, Ardmore C.

PRIVATES, FIRST CLASS

ANDERSON, Archie N.
BEALER, Harold J.
DE PAUL, Anthony V.
DICKINSON, Frank A.
DINAN, Richard J.
GRESHAM, Harry B.
HIGGINBOTHAM, Buster A.
MALICKE, William T.
MATTSON, Marshall R.
POLITO, Marco J.
POPPENDICK, William
ROBIDAS, Roger O.
RUDE, Karl K.
SAEGAR, John E.
SCHULE, Arnold H.
SELLER, Richard W.
SOUZA, Arthur B.
STONE, Albert
STROKO, Edward P.
SULLIVAN, Leslie A.
SWERTINSKI, Stanley F.
TEEVAN, Robert A.
THORNE, Charles A.
TRUDEAU, Maurice P.
WARREN, Richard F.
WCZNICK, Marvin J.

PRIVATES

CONNER, Paul J.
DAVIS, Roy D.
GRESHAM, Paul H.
HARRINGTON, Robert J.
RIGGS, George S.
SNOW, William F.
STOECKIG, Allen M.
SWACHAMMER, Merlyn L.
VLNA, Vincent A., Jr.
WEIDEMANN, Frank H.
WEISHAAR, Darryll G.

Index

By Susan L. Barton

Ronald W. Yoshino culminated his education with a Ph.D. in American history, specializing in combat air power, granted by the Claremont Graduate School, Claremont, CA, in 1985. Presently Dr. Yoshino is on the faculty of Riverside Community College, Riverside, CA, and resides in Claremont with his wife and two daughters. This is his first history book.